D0077039

RETURNING WARS' WOUNDED, INJURED, AND ILL

RETURNING WARS' WOUNDED, INJURED, AND ILL

A Reference Handbook

Edited by Nathan D. Ainspan and Walter E. Penk
Foreword by Daniel K. Inouye

Contemporary Military, Strategic, and Security Issues

PRAEGER SECURITY INTERNATIONAL
Westport, Connecticut • London

Library of Congress Cataloging-in-Publication Data

Returning wars' wounded, injured, and ill : a reference handbook / edited by Nathan D. Ainspan and Walter E. Penk ; foreword by Daniel K. Inouye.
    p.   cm. — (Contemporary military, strategic, and security issues, ISSN 1932–295X)
    Includes bibliographical references and index.
    ISBN 978–0–313–34729–0 (alk. paper)
    1. Disabled veterans—Services for—United States—Handbooks, manuals, etc.
2. Veterans—Services for—United States—Handbooks, manuals, etc.   3. Disabled veterans—Rehabilitation—United States.   4. Veterans—United States—Handbooks, manuals, etc.   5. Veterans' families—United States—Handbooks, manuals, etc. [proposed]   I. Ainspan, Nathan D. (Nathan David), 1966–   II. Penk, Walter.
    UB363.R49   2008
    362.1086'970973—dc22   2008019910

British Library Cataloguing in Publication Data is available.

Library of Congress Catalog Card Number: 2008019910
ISBN-13: 978–0–313–34729–0
ISSN: 1932–295X

First published in 2008

Praeger Security International, 88 Post Road West, Westport, CT 06881
An imprint of Greenwood Publishing Group, Inc.
www.praeger.com

Printed in the United States of America

The paper used in this book complies with the Permanent Paper Standard issued by the National Information Standards Organization (Z39.48–1984).

10 9 8 7 6 5 4 3 2 1

For my wife, Dolores Krajicek Little, Ph.D., who devotes her living to the lives of veterans. Walter E. Penk

For my wife, Debbie Ann Doyle, Ph.D., who was always there with her support during the preparation of this book—and every other time in everything else I have done. With all my love, Nathan D. Ainspan

Contents

Foreword

On April 21, 1945, my life changed forever on Colle Musatello, a blood-stained ridge near San Terenzo, Italy. I led my platoon up the heavily defended ridge. Our mission: to take Colle Musatello, and thereby control an important junction and cut off the enemy's line of retreat. During the fighting, I was first hit by a sniper's bullet in the gut. Still, I managed to take out two machine-gun nests. Then a German soldier, whose face I don't remember, fired a rifle grenade from close range that smashed into my right elbow, exploded, and all but tore my arm off. Another German, just before he died, squeezed off a final burst from his machine gun, and a bullet caught me in the right leg, throwing me to the ground, causing me to roll over and over down the hill.

Somehow, I managed to get back on my feet, and continued to direct my platoon until enemy resistance ceased and defensive positions were established.

Our mission was accomplished, but I knew I would lose my right arm. It was literally in shreds and was useless. It had to be amputated, and I had stopped thinking of it as belonging to me.

For the next twenty months, I was in rehabilitation. One of my most valuable lessons while recuperating came from an Army nurse from Texas who told me: "You can't depend on other people. Now you have only one hand with which to do all the things that you used to do with two hands. And you have to learn how."

Since I was right-handed, I had to learn to do everything with my left hand, from writing to tying my shoelaces, to using chopsticks—all with my left hand. Moreover, the Army therapists taught me things that I never knew how to do before, like carpentry, plumbing, and electrical work. They also taught me how to drive a car.

We were required to play two sports, so I swam and played basketball. We also had to learn how to play a musical instrument, so I learned to play the piano. Prior to my injury, I played the clarinet and the saxophone. I often carried my mouthpiece with me so I could jam if the opportunity arose. During my rehabilitation, the individual who taught me how to play the piano was a one-armed former jazz man who could play with the best of them. He must have been a good teacher because at one of my recitals some said I played the best one-handed "Danny Boy" they had ever heard.

The Army therapists weren't trying to train us for any particular trade or occupation. They gave us the feel of many different skills, some of which we might consider as our future livelihood, by allowing our recuperation to proceed without pressure and at a relaxed pace. The training was only intended to demonstrate to us that an amputee could do many different things. It was a way of giving us confidence and hope. I also learned that with motivation and perseverance, anything can be achieved.

Each year, I celebrate the anniversary of my injury because I believe I might not be where I am today if it had not happened. On April 21, 1945, I lost my right arm in combat. But I never lost hope.

Aloha,
Daniel K. Inouye
Washington, DC

Daniel K. Inouye, a recipient of the Medal of Honor, served with the legendary 442nd Regimental Combat Team during World War II, and was discharged with the rank of Captain. Since 1963, he has represented the state of Hawaii in the U.S. Senate and achieved prominence as one of the chamber's most effective members.

Preface

This book is for the hundreds of thousands of active duty service members, Reserve and National Guard members, and veterans returning from the recent conflicts with wounds and injuries—visible and invisible, physical and psychological. For anyone who served our nation in uniform and left a part of themselves behind on the battlefield, this book is a guide for you. This book is also for the friends, family members, physicians, counselors, chaplains, and others who know, love, and care about our returning service members. The chapters in this book will offer you practical advice, guidance, and answers to some of the new questions that you may be asking yourself or about the veteran in your life, including possibly these:

- What is happening to me?
- Why do I always feel tired?
- Why does my husband speed and swerve when he drives?
- Why does my wife not want to hold the kids?
- How can I make my way through recovery?
- How do I navigate the government bureaucracies to get treatment?
- Where can I find a job as veteran with a disability?
- Can I still get an education with this disability?
- Is continued service in the military an option?
- Where can I turn to for help?
- And how can my family understand what is happening to me?

We wrote this book to help you answer these questions. Although many of these answers can be found by conducting research online, looking through brochures, consulting doctors, reading academic journals, looking through piles of publications, or asking people at the Department of Veterans Affairs (VA), we know it can be a difficult, cumbersome, and time-consuming process to find this information. And if you need this information to help you with the recovery process, you probably do not have the time or resources to visit libraries and dig around, or patiently make your way through layers of bureaucracy to find your answers.

That is why we created this book. Your two editors assembled a knowledge-able group of contributors who have been working with military veterans for many years (some have been involved with veterans for decades) and asked them to gather this information and present it so that you can quickly assimilate and immediately act on it. To provide you with even more up-to-date informa-tion as things change, we have created a Web site to accompany this book at http://www.warswounded.com. The Web site contains more resources including helpful organizations, useful materials, Web sites, and information about recent developments that can impact your life. There is also a space for you to add your own suggestions and share other information with your fellow wounded warriors and their families and friends.

The theme throughout every chapter in this book is return, reintegration, and resiliency. As you *return* from military service, we provide you with information to help you through this process, to let you (or your veteran) know what is happen-ing to you physically and psychologically, explain what you are going through, and how to persevere through the different bureaucracies. To help with *reintegra-tion*, we provide recommendations and suggestions on how you can again become a part of your community, whether you want to continue to serve our nation in the military or find a job in the civilian realm and/or advance your education. And by *resiliency*, we hope that the material in this book can provide you a new perspective, a new way of thinking, and present you with resources that you and your supporters can draw upon to help counter the feelings of helplessness, hope-lessness, and frustration that tend to accompany the wounds of war.

The nineteenth-century writer Ralph Waldo Emerson wrote "you are the book's book" to demonstrate that the core of the American character is self-reliance. No one can solve your problems for you. No one can give you any-thing, not even happiness: you can only take it. You can only rely upon yourself. Therefore, we created this book to compile the means and resources so that you can use them to overcome the risks brought about by your experiences in war. As a veteran, no one but you knows what you experienced and what you think about your experiences. And no one but you can learn from other war fighters who found the answers for problems they discovered as the fighting stopped and the search for peace at home had started. For the family members and friends reading this book, no one but you can know what you are experiencing as you cope with the wounds of war in your family, and no one but you can take the ac-tion to preserve yourself and help your veteran and yourself through the recovery process.

This book should not be read passively, but rather we wrote it so that it should be marked up to remember the sections that are important to you and actions that you want to take, and passed around to share information with those around you. If you borrowed this book from a library, however, we ask that you not do this and that you take notes on what is important to you. This book is supposed to be a portable collection of resources, so use it that way. Use this book as a starting point to make connections, find answers, and build your resilience as you proceed through the recovery and reintegration process. The Web sites mentioned in this book (along with other important information and critical resources) are all included on the Web site we have designed to accompany this volume at http://www.warswounded.com.

We do offer one caveat about the resources available to veterans. Lately, there have been reports and even congressional hearings about some organizations that were supposed to be providing services to veterans but appeared to be more involved with raising money for the group's leaders. All of the contributors to this book have worked to insure that the places we list are legitimate and exist to help veterans. However, the old Latin phrase *"caveat emptor"*—"Let the buyer beware"—should be kept in mind. While the majority of organizations and service providers out there are looking out for your interests, some people may use the current positive sentiment in favor of veterans with disabilities to try to enrich themselves. As you proceed through your reintegration, be careful and if something seems to good too be true, it probably is.

Finally, we reiterate that while this book provides a source of resources for you to begin to understand your disability and to begin conversations with medical providers and counselors, it is no substitute for face-to-face meetings with these professionals. If your injuries are affecting you to the degree that you are considering ending your life or you are harming yourself or others, please seek assistance immediately. Though you may be frightened or ashamed of these thoughts, remember that you are not alone, and people out there want to help you. If you are worried that you may act immediately on these thoughts, call 911, a local crisis hotline, or the national crisis hotline 1-800-SUICIDE (1-800-784-2433) or 1-800-273-TALK (1-800-273-8255) and let them know what is happening to you.

As your two editors were finalizing this book for our publisher we were in a quandary about what we would say in this introduction. As the deadline was approaching, we did not know how we could tie the following chapters together and how we could explain what we wanted to do with this book. But three days before our deadline, three stories appeared in major newspapers that connected the dots for us and showed us what we needed to say. In the first story, *The New York Times* reported on a study from *The New England Journal of Medicine* suggesting that one in six service members in Iraq had suffered at least one concussion and that these types of concussions has put each member at a greater risk for traumatic brain injury (TBI) and post-traumatic stress disorder (PTSD). The report went on to say that far more people than we thought—potentially thousands more—will be susceptible to these illnesses and will need the types of treatment and the advice and resources that we have assembled in these pages. The impetus for our book could not have been more clearly highlighted: Thousands more of our fellow citizens are going to have to learn how to cope with these potentially life-altering disabilities and the need for this book as a way to help them help themselves with these injuries became even more apparent.

On the same day, *The Washington Post* reported on a report released by the Army demonstrating an escalating number of suicide attempts and successful suicides among active duty Army soldiers. In 2002, the Army reported 350 suicide attempts, but in 2007 the number jumped to over 2,000 (with 121 soldiers taking their own lives) with the report suggesting that the numbers will continue to grow throughout 2008. The number one reason for these suicide attempts was relationship problems (mostly marriage issues but also problems with children and parents), but close behind relationships as the cause for suicides were legal, financial, and occupational problems—exactly the types of problems that are addressed in the book. These data haunted us and motivated us further by hoping that this book could get the right information, the right type of guidance, or even just a helpful word from someone who has been there to a veteran who might have lost hope and could be contemplating suicide. Maybe, we hoped, just maybe, we could provide some form of hope or self-resilience that could change that veteran's mind and possibly save someone's life.

A sergeant interviewed in the *Washington Post* article said about the help she gets from the Army for her psychological problems, "They gave me an 800 number to call if I needed help. When I come to feeling overwhelmed, I don't care about the 800 number. I want a one-on-one talk with a trained psychiatrist who's either been to war or understands war." While our printed material cannot substitute for face-to-face session, many of our writers have been to war, and all of them understand the effects of war. We knew that the pages of this book could provide the next best way to letting veterans learn this information and exploring it in private.

Finally, the story that really affected us was a front-page story in *The Washington Post* about a twenty-five-year-old Army lieutenant in the Reserves who was receiving care at Walter Reed Army Medical Center. Up to and during her service overseas, she had a stellar record. But she developed psychological issues after serving as a guard at a prison in Iraq, where she was repeatedly harassed by one of her commanders. At Walter Reed she was studying to be a nurse, so that she could help other soldiers with their recovery. But one night, she asked her father to take her back to her room, so that she could study. Instead, she took an overdose of dozens of antidepressants with other pills. Before she took the pills, she wrote a suicide note asking her family to take care of her dog. And another note she left ended with the wish that "hopefully this will help other soldiers." Fortunately, another soldier came by her room and noticed that she was groggy. The lieutenant survived and is now receiving psychiatric care. This story greatly impacted us and nearly brought us to tears. Knowing that thousands of other service members may feel hopeless and could be contemplating suicide, we knew that we had to get them information that might help and we hope that this book can do what she wanted to do. Through this book, we hope that we can help other soldiers who might be feeling the way she felt.

So to all of you who bravely served our nation in uniform, faced the challenge over there, and returned with injuries, we thank you with our profound admiration and gratitude. We offer the materials in this book to provide you and those around you with advice, recommendations, and suggestions to help expedite your recovery, improve your reintegration, and help you build resiliency. We are in your debt and we hope that these chapters will in some small way provide you with the answers and information that you need to move on with your life.

For the families and friends who selflessly gave up so much so that their service member could serve to protect the rest of us, and for the counselors, therapists, religious leaders, and others who work tirelessly to understand our service members and veterans, we offer to you our appreciation and our thanks and hope that you too will find this book helpful in your services you provide.

On behalf of all the contributors to this book, we thank you and hope that our words and advice may be of some assistance to you. We wish you all of the best in all of your endeavors.

> With our wishes for your own successful recovery,
> resiliency, and reintegration,
>
> Nathan D. Ainspan
> Arlington, Virignia
>
> Walter E. Penk
> New Braunfels, Texas

Chapter Contents

The following is a brief overview of the chapters in this book:

Chapter 1: Benefits for Veterans: A Historical Context and Overview of the Current Situation

This chapter places the current situation of veterans and disabilities in its historical context. It is included in the hope that it can help you place your experiences in a new context and let you see how what you are going through has been experienced by thousands of others down through the centuries. It also provides a brief overview of how society has conceptualized disabled warriors so that you can see how today's thinking is affecting you.

Chapter 2: Current Veteran Demographics and Implications for Veterans' Health Care

The chapter describes the demographics of how veterans from the current conflicts differ from those from previous wars, and the potential costs (social, cultural, and economic) to this country for treating them. It then projects these costs into the foreseeable future to show how these changes will impact the services provided to you and how these economic changes will affect your life.

Chapter 3: Injuries and Symptoms

The amount of medical information available to you can seem overwhelming, so in order to provide you with the critical information you need to quickly answer your important questions, we present tables of the information you will need to know in order to understand and immediately address the symptoms of PTSD (post-traumatic stress disorder), depression, traumatic brain injury (TBI), and the physical wounds of war inculding loss of limbs, burns, pain, and paralysis. Also included is a table of different examples of accommodations for many types of disabilities.

Chapter 4: The Physical and Psychological Impact of Your Injury and Disability

Every war-related injury—or the injury of your friend or family member—is going to impact the entire family and the veteran's network of friends and supporters. This chapter describes some of the most common injuries of the war and the psychological impact of these injuries. Each type of injury is examined, with specific attention directed to the ways that the injuries have multiplicative effects so that they can intensify the pain, such that psychological injuries can increase physical pain and physical injuries can create psychological issues.

Chapter 5: Fitness for Duty, Recovery, and Return to Service

After a combat injury, it can be a difficult process to transition from being an active soldier to being a patient recovering in a medical hospital. This chapter takes you through every step of the process from a description of how different types of injuries impact veterans and their family members to staying organized during treatment to how you can return to service in the armed forces. Because each branch of the armed services has its own vocabulary and procedures, each branch's processes and terminology is described in detail.

Chapter 6: Finding Employment as a Veteran with a Disability

This chapter takes you through all of the steps in the process of looking for a job from determining what you want to do and which skills you want to use to finding a job that appreciates you and is not afraid of your military service and your disability. It also highlights the benefits that military service and disability can bring to a potential employer, and how you can address issues that might come up during interviews. Information about starting your own business is also included.

Chapter 7: Education Options

Written by a Vietnam War disabled veteran who completed his law degree after his time in the military, this chapter provides the answers to the questions about how you can access the G.I. Bill and other programs to help you pay for your education—and your family members' education as well. Information about how to accommodate your disability in the classroom is also included.

Chapter 8: Disabilities and Injuries among Members of the National Guard and Reserve Units

National Guard and Reserve members are fighting alongside active duty members in record numbers in virtually all capacities and are thus receiving the same types of injuries and wounds but do not have the same resources and facilities available to them when they return home. This chapter presents some of the issues faced by returning members of the Reserve and Guard and their families and friends and offers advice and resources that can help you cope in these situations.

Chapter 9: Impact on Family and Friends

As service members protect our country, their family and friends are also affected by their call to duty. And the injuries of the service member create additional stress and hardships for the family members and friends. This chapter provides advice and recommendations for family members and friends on how to communicate and interact with disabled veterans and what can be done to care for and protect themselves during these difficult times.

Chapter 10: Peer Support Services

Many of the the services and answers that you need cannot be provided by medical and mental health personnel. So to fill this gap, many veterans and their supporters have organized themselves into peer support groups to help each other and to lend support and provide guidance to each other. In the process of assisting others, many veterans and family members gain strength and knowledge to assist in their own recovery process. This chapter describes the types of groups created by one area in Texas with suggestions on how to find and create such groups in your own community.

Chapter 11: The Psychological Impact of Disabilities

The last chapter focuses upon the psychosocial impacts of war and how to overcome them through some of the newest treatments and self-help programs available. The chapter is structured around three themes: (1) the new goals that warriors must develop for themselves as they transition home; (2) the maladies, particularly personal, social, and functional, with which most warriors struggle in their transitions from the battle field to their home life; and (3) the means to overcome these maladies. Some of the most recent techniques that have been developed to help veterans overcome these maladies are summarized to help the wounded warrior's transition from warzones to home.

Chronology

We have included a chronology in this book that charts the history of the treatment of veterans over time, and the way we think about and treat disabilities. The list complies the social factors, people's attitudes, legislative decisions, changes in the government's leadership, reevaluations of the definition of disability, and even actions and lobbying by veterans themselves that have all contributed to the changes in the way that our nation addresses and provides services to returning service members. As with the first two chapters of our book, it is included in the hope that it may provide you with some perspective on your own situation. It can also demonstrate how veterans and individuals with disabilities can organize themselves, protest the system, and influence the way that the nation's leaders make decisions to provide for the treatment that the nation owes those who have served.

About the Cover Photo

LT Melissa Stockwell of the U.S. Army receives physical therapy from Bob Bahr for injuries she received in Iraq at the Walter Reed Medical Center in Washington, DC in February 2005.

This woman's remarkable life and determination since her injury is illustrative of this book's themes: return, reintegration, and resiliency. LT Stockwell was a member of the Transportation Corps stationed as a platoon leader with the 1st Calvary Division in Fort Hood, Texas. She was in Iraq for only three weeks on a routine convoy patrol when a roadside bomb struck her convoy on April 13, 2004. The blast from the bomb resulted in the loss of her left leg from the knee down. It was her husband (who was also serving with the Army in Iraq) who informed her of the loss of her leg. She was first evacuated to Landstuhl, Germany for initial treatment and then transported to Walter Reed for rehabilitation. After 15 surgeries, further amputation to remove more of the leg above her knee because of infections, and more than a year of rehab, she was released from treatment and medically retired from the Army.

Since her retirement from the service, she has pursued new dreams and goals. Both she and her husband went back to school where she graduated with a degree from the prosthetics program at Century College in Chicago in 2007. After completing her residency and her board exams, she will be a certified prosthetist and looks forward to helping other wounded veterans. She also helps other veterans as a member of the board of directors for the Wounded Warrior Project.

Thanks to the help and support of organizations like the Challenged Athletes Foundation, Disabled Sports USA, and the Wounded Warrior Project, Mrs. Stockwell has pursued her interest in athletics—and pursues it in with a passion. She regularly competes in triathlons and completed the New York City Marathon on a hand crank bike. She has also learned to ski with adaptive equipment and become a competitive swimmer. After training full-time at the Colorado Springs Olympic Training Center she qualified for the Paralympics and represented the United States in the 2008 Beijing games. She describes this experience as "a dream come true—I feel as though I am the luckiest girl in the world."

CHAPTER 1

Benefits for Veterans: A Historical Context and Overview of the Current Situation

Rodney R. Baker

Editors' Comment

The first chapter of this book is a summary history of the way that veterans (and especially American veterans) have been treated over time. The author of this chapter, Rodney R. Baker, Ph.D., has been more than just a reporter of this history—he has been a part of it for forty years. Dr. Baker began his career with the VA in 1964 as a trainee in Tucson, Arizona, became chief of psychology at the VA Medical Center in San Antonio, Texas, and later became director of the mental health service line at that center. He retired in 2004 but continues to remain involved with the VA through leadership training and in consultation roles. He has written extensively on the history of the treatment of veterans and about the history of the VA.

The rest of this book is filled with resources and recommendations to help you directly address issues that veterans are encountering. This chapter and the next one are included to help you see that the ways that veterans have been treated have changed over time. And over time, things have improved as society's reactions to specific wars and thoughts about veterans have changed. In this country the needs of veterans were acknowledged (sometimes because veterans themselves took action and forced changes), and the nation altered its policies and programs. It is our hope that Dr. Baker's historical review will provide you with a sense of context for what you may be experiencing: knowing that other people have gone through these problems—namely millions of veterans in this country alone (not to mention all the veterans throughout recorded history) can hopefully take away some of the feelings of isolation or feelings of being overwhelmed and can give you a sense of resiliency and courage to successfully continue the rehabilitation and reintegration process.

Introduction

This chapter begins with a historical description of how different societies have viewed and met their obligation to provide benefits for those who have served their country in battle. It continues with a brief description of how the United States has met those obligations, and concludes with an overview of the nation's challenges in meeting those obligations today.

Why would you be interested in this history? There are two answers. First, the way our current society views and treats veterans is, in fact, based on over thirty-six centuries of care of veterans by different societies which has established the obligation that society has toward its veterans.

The second reason why an understanding of history is important may perhaps be of more personal relevance to the veteran and the family. With the end of war, the veteran seeks a return to a satisfactory life with family and friends. In many cases, that return involves adjusting to the visible and invisible scars of battle and the risk of being in harm's way. The adjustment may be accompanied by a sense of being alone, perhaps feeling overwhelmed and helpless, and not knowing where to turn for help. But the veteran is never alone. Millions of U.S. veterans have returned at war's end to cope with career, health, and other life adjustment issues. Many have needed help and an understanding that others have been through this experience and also needed to reach out for this help. Knowing this may help you with your feelings of being overwhelmed and helpless. Veterans in the past were never alone and neither are you. In addition, a review of history will reveal that our country's opinions of and reactions to veterans and their disabilities changed over time and knowing this may help you with understanding how others react to your disability—and realizing that these opinions may change over time as well.

The Historical Context for Care of Veterans[1]

Early History

The special treatment given to disabled veterans in the American Colonies and subsequent periods in U.S. history has its roots in ancient Greece around 1600 BC. The benefits given to early Greek soldiers marked one of the first recorded instances in which society recognized the special needs of veterans and its obligation to those veterans. Disabled veterans in Greece were given pensions, and public land was given to the children of Greek soldiers who had died in battles. The Roman Empire similarly granted land to surviving veterans, a benefit adopted in the nineteenth-century land grant program for U.S. veterans. In addition, the Roman Empire established the first military hospitals in the first century AD.

Subsequent modern societies continued to recognize the need to care for its veterans. During the crusades, France founded one of the first homes for poor and sick veterans and later established a home for soldiers. In 1670, King Louis XIV established the now famous *Hotel des Invalides* in Paris to care for aged and disabled veterans of the French army.

By the fifteenth century, the standing armies of Europe and the treatment needs of their disabled veterans led to the now generally recognized obligation of society to care for its soldiers. In what was considered a foundation document for the care of veterans, the English Parliament passed "An Acte for the Reliefe of Souldiours" in their 1592–1593 session to provide benefits for soldiers and sailors who had served in the British defeat of the Spanish Armada. Of historical note is the fact that the statute provided payments to disabled veterans based on the degree of disability, a feature still used in determining payments made to U.S. veterans today (Veterans Administration, 1967, p. 2).

Pre-1930 Care and Benefits for U.S. Veterans

In 1636, the Pilgrims of Plymouth Colony passed what is considered one of the first American veterans' benefit laws while they were at war with the Pequot Indians. The law provided that "If any man shalbee sent forth as a souldier and shall return maimed, hee shalbee maintained competently by the collonie during his life" (Veterans Administration, 1977). Other colonies passed similar benefit legislations. In 1749 a hospital for sick sailors was founded in Charlestown, SC, and the Pennsylvania Hospital was established in Philadelphia in 1752 for all veterans. The College of Philadelphia (later the University of Pennsylvania) became the first colonial medical school and, from its beginning, was affiliated with the Pennsylvania Hospital.

Following the Revolutionary War, benefit programs for veterans expanded. Service pensions were established in 1789 for disabled veterans with different payments according to the veteran's disability. In 1798, President John Adams additionally signed an act for the relief of sick and disabled seaman which led to the formation of the marine hospital system which later developed into the U.S. Public Health System. In 1811, the federal government established the first domiciliary and medical facility for veterans. The same year Congress designated the U.S. Naval Home in Philadelphia as a permanent home for disabled Navy officers, seamen, and Marines.

With the War of 1812, the Indian Wars, and the Mexican War, benefits for disabled veterans continued to expand, including hospital care of veterans. The Bureau of Pensions was established in 1833, assuming responsibility for pension laws first passed in 1789, and the U.S. Soldiers' Home was established in 1851. St. Elizabeth's Hospital opened in Washington, DC, in 1855 and provided the first major medical care system for the veterans with mental disorders. At the end of the Civil War, Congress established the National Asylum (later called Homes) for Disabled Volunteer Soldiers in 1865 with the first home opening in Togus, Maine, followed by the homes in Milwaukee, WI; Dayton, OH; Kecoughtan, VA; and Leavenworth, KS. These homes provided domiciliary and medical care to veterans. In addition, many states created similar homes for veterans after the Civil War.

The beginning of the twentieth century and the end of the Spanish-American War saw the emergence of veterans' organizations with interest in the welfare

Table 1.1 Participant Numbers and Battle Deaths From the
Revolutionary War Through World War I[a]

War	Participant Numbers	Deaths in Service
Revolutionary War	217,000	4,435
War of 1812	287,730	2,260
Indian Wars	106,000	1,000 (estimated)
Mexican War	78,718	13,283
Civil War[b]	3,713,363	498,332
Spanish-American War	306,760	2,446
World War I	4,734,991	116,516
Totals	9,444,562	638,272

[a] From data reported by the VA Office of Public Affairs, November 2006. Deaths in service include both battle deaths and deaths from other causes.
[b] Statistics for Confederate Forces for the Civil War are not authoritative. Participants for the Union Forces are listed at 2,213,363 (with 364,511 deaths in service) and participants for the Confederate Forces are estimated as 1,500,000 (with 133,821 deaths in service).

of veterans and their dependents. The United Spanish War Veterans founded in 1898 and the Veterans of Foreign Wars founded in 1913 vigorously supported pension legislation to assist veterans and their dependents. The first pension law for dependents of veterans passed in 1918 provided monthly payments to widows and children of veterans. Disabled veterans were given a new monthly pension in a law passed in 1920. In 1922, the War Risk Insurance Act of 1914 was amended to provide hospital care to veterans suffering from psychiatric and tuberculosis diseases. In 1924, this provision was further amended to provide hospital care to veterans without battle-caused illness or injury "provided a bed was available and the veteran was unable to pay for this care" (Veterans Administration, 1967, p. 82).

With the end of World War I, over 9 million Americans had served in its wars with 638,272 deaths (Department of Veterans Affairs, 2006a). Table 1.1 provides the numbers of participants and service deaths in each war. Benefits for surviving veterans and their families, however, were administered by separate departments and agencies and, in 1921, Congress created the United States Veterans' Bureau to consolidate the functions of the Bureau of War Risk Insurance and the Public Health Service. This consolidation still left three agencies administering veterans' benefits: the Veterans' Bureau, the Bureau of Pensions, and the National Homes for Disabled Volunteer Soldiers.

Post–World War I Crises Regarding Veterans Benefits

As World War I veterans struggled to return to civilian life, the nation entered a contentious period regarding its obligation to veterans. As early as 1919, a national discussion emerged with the question of whether or not veterans were due a bonus for serving during the war, with low pay, while non-veterans had stayed at home and benefited from the war-time industry (Veterans Administration, 1967). The American Legion and Veterans of Foreign Wars strongly favored passage of such legislation but, although the legislation was introduced multiple times, it was never passed.

In 1924, Congress passed the World War Adjusted Act which provided a bonus based on days served in the military. The provisions of this bonus, however, delayed payment for most veterans for twenty years.

With the depression and increased problems with unemployment, veterans renewed their demands for a bonus that would be paid immediately. In 1932, a group of veterans from Oregon began a march to Washington to raise support for the bonus. The "bonus march" attracted other jobless veterans along the way and by June thousands of marching veterans began arriving in Washington where they camped in primitive shacks and tents on the outskirts of Washington.

Proposed bonus bill legislation was again considered and, once more, was defeated. Many of the marchers remained in Washington and clashes surfaced between the police and veterans, including an unsuccessful attempt by Treasury Department agents and police to evict them. The District of Columbia police finally convinced President Hoover to order federal troops to assist in the evacuation. The area was cleared but not before resisting veterans set fire to their shacks and tents.

Congress authorized the Veterans Administration (VA) to pay for the transportation expenses of marchers back to their homes. Over 5,000 marchers took advantage of this opportunity, ending the bonus march of 1932.

Problems for veterans were not over, however, as the depression worsened. With President Franklin D. Roosevelt's election, he was faced with demands to balance the federal budget and reduce expenditures. Resulting legislation, commonly called the Economy Act, effectively revoked all benefits for veterans since the Spanish-American War, only the second time in U.S. history that the country had taken such a step.[2]

A new system of benefits was created for veterans but with much lower benefits. The change in benefits produced massive angry protests in Washington and, in March of 1934, Congress restored veteran benefits to the level they had been before the Economy Act.

Early VA History

As noted earlier, three agencies administered veterans' benefits prior to 1930: the Veterans' Bureau, the Bureau of Pensions, and the National Homes for Disabled Volunteer Soldiers. The desirability of having all veteran benefits administered by a single agency led Congress in 1930 to authorize President Herbert Hoover to establish the Veterans Administration (VA) to consolidate and coordinate all government activities affecting veterans. For the first time in U.S. history, the veteran could contact any office or hospital of the VA to seek benefits provided in legislation. With the executive order that established the VA, fifty-four VA hospitals were created from preexisting Veterans Bureau Homes and National Homes for Disabled Volunteer Soldiers. Many of these new VA hospitals were designated as facilities for the treatment of tuberculosis (TB) or had large TB treatment services. (TB was a major veteran illness at the time.)

With over 16 million military participants in World War II, the veteran beneficiary population would soon increase by that number. With the war's ending, passage of the GI Bill of Rights legislation in 1944 authorized new training and pension benefits for veterans, and the VA was given the responsibility for providing these benefits which by now included home loans and educational assistance. In identifying the GI Bill of Rights as one of the top fifty events or products that revolutionized the lives of consumers and the marketplace, Consumers Union noted that the bill not only created millions of new homeowners but that a college education was now available to those unlikely to have had the financial means to attend college prior to the war (Consumers Union, 1986). Their book also characterized the bill as standing for a soldier's right to fair treatment from a grateful nation.

It soon became apparent, however, that the VA as it was currently organized could not meet the new responsibilities emerging with the World War II veteran population. Many of the VA's physicians were on loan from the military and would soon be discharged from the military and leave the VA. Medical care was also poorly structured.

As newly appointed administrator of the VA, General Omar A. Bradley led the effort to reorganize the VA and improve the medical care given veterans. He pushed for legislation which would establish a Department of Medicine and Surgery as a separate department within the VA to be given the responsibility for improvement and oversight of medical care in VA hospitals. That legislation and General Bradley's proposal for special recruitment authority to hire physicians and nurses in the VA was eventually signed into law in January 1946 after Bradley threatened to resign as administrator if the legislation was not passed (Bradley and Blair, 1983). The legislation also established a system of affiliations with medical schools and universities to train the professionals needed to work in VA hospitals. Although the VA underwent a number of reorganizations and additions in mission in subsequent years, the basis for the organization of the modern VA was established with this 1946 legislation.

Soon after the end of World War II, the VA found itself unable to provide for the demands for hospital care for veterans because of the long-term hospital stays of many veterans and because of insufficient staffing for hospital beds. To reduce the need for hospitalization, especially for veterans with mental disorders, the VA started providing health care on an outpatient basis in mental health clinics that markedly reduced the need for hospitalization (Baker and Pickren, 2007). With the concept of work as therapy, the VA also initiated work rehabilitation and counseling psychology programs in VA hospitals which returned many veterans to a productive life outside of the hospital (Peffer, 1955; Waldrop, 2007).

The Korean and Vietnam Wars

Advances in military medicine and care of the wounded in the battlefield in the Korean and Vietnam wars paradoxically produced new problems for veterans and their care in the VA. More soldiers were surviving their wounds in battle and required follow-up care for their injuries. With almost 6 million military participants in service during the Korean War and almost 9 million military participants during the Vietnam War, the total number of participants virtually equaled the 16 million military participants in War War II. The number of deaths in service in War War II, however, totaled over 400,000 with only about one-fourth of that number of deaths in service recorded for both Korea and Vietnam (Department of Veterans Affairs, 2006a). During the Vietnam War, five out of every eight seriously injured soldiers survived their wounds.

The Vietnam War, however, introduced another problem for its veterans. The war was unpopular with the public, and dissatisfaction with the war was transferred to those who served in combat. These veterans not only did not receive the accolades given those who served in World War II, but they were often rejected and scorned by the public for doing their duty.

The VA itself was also slow to see the problems and health care needs of Vietnam veterans. Vietnam veterans dissatisfied with care in the VA assigned the same disgust they had of the public's response to their service for their country to a distrust of the VA, and many decided not to seek the treatment in the VA even though they were entitled to this treatment. A series of conferences held around the country in 1971 to alert senior VA medical center staff in the VA to the problems of Vietnam veterans helped VA medical centers start to recognize the special needs of Vietnam veterans and to improve their care (Baker and Pickren, 2007). Legislation in 1979 also created the Vietnam Veteran Readjustment Counseling Program in the VA which established what were called Vet Centers in the community which led many Vietnam veterans to first seek help for their readjustment problems. By 1985, there were 189 Vet Centers treating 371,000 Vietnam veterans and 80,000 family members (Cranston, 1986). In spite of these changes in the VA, Vietnam veterans were often reluctant (and some still are) to seek help from the VA.

The Post-Vietnam Era

The 1980s and 1990s were marked by several changes in the VA affecting care of veterans. In 1989 the VA was designated a cabinet-level department and renamed the Department of Veterans Affairs. This elevation of status to the President's Cabinet gave veterans and their care a special voice in the federal government.

This time period saw attention given to treating the ex–prisoners of war (POWs) whose treatment needs had been previously largely ignored (Baker and Pickren, 2007). New legislation provided ex-POWs with an elevated priority of care for treatment in the VA.

Care for veterans exposed to Agent Orange in the Vietnam War was also expanded in the post Vietnam era as was funding for outpatient treatment programs for veterans with substance abuse problems. Psychosocial rehabilitation (a combination of pharmacologic treatment, independent living and social skills training, psychological support, housing, social support and network enhancement, and access to leisure activities) and vocational work programs regained the popularity they had after World War II and helped many veterans resume productive work lives. Toward the end of this period, the VA was also providing care to increased numbers of female veterans, reflecting the increased role of women in the military. Special outpatient women's health clinics were also funded for both general medical as well as mental health care.

Finally, the post Vietnam era also saw the VA making significant improvements in the quality of care provided in such areas as primary care, the continuity of that care, and the tracking of and use of health care guidelines in directing care. These improvements were recognized and applauded by the rest of the country's health care systems. In addition, the system of computerized medical records developed by the VA became the envy of other health care systems and provided both an improved continuity of care for patients as well as easy transfer of care as veterans moved to other parts of the country.

The post Vietnam era, however, was not without problems for the treatment of veterans. The 1980s found the country faced with competing economic concerns and demands for reducing the federal budget. In the VA, the focus of care was turning away from expensive hospitalization and almost half of its hospital beds were closed. Fortunately, a renewed attention to outpatient care accompanied this change in focus and helped give impetus to the new outpatient programs noted earlier, including increased emphasis on community-based care and recovery-oriented services.

It can be noted that for the first decades following World War II, virtually all those in Congress were veterans themselves. They recognized the needs of veterans and were eager to provide help and benefits for their fellow veterans such as the assistance contained in the GI Bill of Rights. During the post-Vietnam era, the number of veterans in Congress dropped significantly and, with the increased economic concerns facing the United States in the 1980s, attention to veterans' issues was not given the priority they had following World War II. It is only recently with the wars in Iraq and Afghanistan that attention given veterans has resurfaced as a political priority.

The Current Situation for Veterans Benefits and Care at the VA

The VA today is faced with the need to treat two distinctly different veteran populations. The first is the aging World War II, Korean, and Vietnam veterans. That population currently represents about three-fourths of the health care workload of the VA. The average age of the Vietnam veteran is now 65 and, together with smaller numbers of World War II and Korean veterans, these older veterans

Table 1.2 Numbers Receiving Pension and Compensation by the VA By War Periods (as of September 30, 2006)[a]

War	Pension and Compensation Rolls Veterans	Children, Parents, and Surviving Spouses
World War I	9	11,427
World War II	429,518	248,608
Korean War	226,467	65,265
Vietnam War	1,103,561	164,930
First Gulf War	700,560	26,063
Totals	2,460,115	516,293

[a] From data reported by the VA Office of Public Affairs, November 2006 (Department of Veterans Affairs, 2006a). For compensation and pension purposes, the Persian Gulf War period has not been terminated and includes veterans of Operation Iraqi and Enduring Freedom.

need more extensive care for the health problems generally associated with the elderly. Needed treatment programs range from nursing home to hospice care.

The second population needing attention by the VA includes the veterans of the Iraq and Afghanistan wars. They already comprise over 700,000 veterans (or 28 percent) on the VA's compensation and pension rolls (see Table 1.2), and this population will continue to grow with more individuals retiring from the military.

The health care needs of the veterans of our most recent wars once more present special problems for the VA. Health care on the battlefield continued to improve and increased the numbers of severely wounded veterans with severe, multiple, and complex traumas. The statistic reported earlier that five out of every eight seriously injured soldiers in the Vietnam War survived their injuries rose to seven out of eight in the Iraq and Afghanistan wars.

In 2005, legislation enabled the VA to create four regional polytrauma centers to coordinate medical rehabilitation services for these veterans. Included in the rehabilitation services for these veterans are the counseling and support needed for their wives, husbands, children, and parents. Traumatic brain injury and other rehabilitation services are also provided in VA treatment sites closer to the veterans' homes after discharge from the regional polytrauma centers. Their need for psychiatric and psychological care is also considered to be equal to that of veterans of the Vietnam War.

The extensive and prolonged use of National Guard and Reserve units in the second Iraq war (Operation Iraqi Freedom) created still another need for new medical care and rehabilitation services from the VA. The disruption of their careers and family life and the prolonged exposure to danger and stress not only results in significant stress treatment issues similar to those of their enlisted military colleagues, but reentry into community life after deployment raises adjustment issues of a magnitude not seen since World War II. As noted below, almost 90,000 reservists and National Guardsmen received education and training benefits from the VA in fiscal year 2005. Although they are also currently eligible for health care in the VA for two years after deployment, this benefit is not well known. Some have difficulty accessing this care, in part because of acknowledged resource limitations of the VA and delays in addressing their care needs as well as those of the enlisted military veteran population.

The range and type of benefits and number of veterans receiving those benefits today can be best appreciated by an overview of the care and benefits provided to all veterans in the VA's 2005 fiscal year (Department of Veterans Affairs, 2006b):

- More than 5.3 million veterans received care in VA health care facilities, and 78 percent of disabled and low-income veterans had enrolled for health care;
- 587,000 patients received inpatient care, and nearly 57.5 million outpatient visits were provided to veterans;
- The VA's total budget was $71.2 billion with $31.5 billion spent on health care and $37.1 billion spent on other benefits;
- Disability compensation, death compensation, and pension payments were paid to 3 million veterans and almost 600,000 spouses, children, and parents of deceased veterans;
- The VA helped pay for the education and training of 336,347 veterans and active-duty personnel, 87,589 reservists and National Guardsmen, and 74,360 survivors of veterans; and
- $1.1 trillion in life insurance coverage was provided to 4.5 million veterans, active-duty members, reservists and Guardsmen, plus 3 million spouses and children, and $2.1 billion was paid in death claims and other insurance disbursements.

From the same report, it was noted that 24.3 million veterans are currently alive. Approximately 63 million Americans are potentially eligible for VA benefits and services because they are veterans, family members, or survivors of veterans. A summary of federal benefits for veterans and their dependents, including benefits for deployed reserve and National Guard participants, can be obtained at any VA office (Department of Veterans Affairs, 2007).

With media and public attention of the problems our nation's returning veterans have recently had in obtaining needed care, a President's Commission on Care for America's Returning Wounded Warriors was appointed (their Web site is at http://www.pccww.gov/) and was headed by Senator Bob Dole and former Secretary of Health and Human Services Donna Shalala. The commission released their report in July 2007 (http://www.pccww.gov/docs/Kit/Main_Book_CC%5BJULY26%5D.pdf). Although the report acknowledged the high quality of care in military battlefields and care received in the military and VA health care systems, the report faulted a number of areas of care, especially in the coordination of care between the Department of Defense (DoD) and VA health care and disability systems.

Among its specific recommendations, the report called for DoD and the VA to more aggressively prevent and treat the two primary health consequences of combat: post-traumatic stress disorder (PTSD) and traumatic brain injury. Of special note were estimates that up to 20 percent of returnees from Iraq and up to

11 percent of returnees from Afghanistan were affected by PTSD. The report further noted that many service members believed it a sign of weakness to acknowledge symptoms of psychological stress and called for both DoD and the VA to work more aggressively to reduce the stigma of PTSD and other psychological consequences of combat.

Still another major recommendation of the commission was the need to significantly strengthen support for families of veterans seriously wounded in combat and requiring long lengths of hospitalization. Especially acknowledged were the problems encountered when family members relocated for extended periods of time to be with the returnee in the hospital and that many of these family members gave up a job to be with the returnee and serve important caregiver roles.

Congress has yet to respond to these and other recommendations in the report. The following months will be critical in determining the resolve of our nation to respond to the needs of our veterans and their families.

In concluding this brief overview of benefits available to veterans in the VA today and remaining concerns, it is also important to note that the VA is the largest but not the only source of help for veterans. The Department of Labor provides vocational programs for veterans, and most states have programs for veterans ranging from state homes to financial assistance. Veteran service organizations also provide help and guidance to veterans.

As noted in the introduction to this chapter, you need not feel alone in the need for assistance in adjusting to your discharge from military service to our country. This overview and the following chapters are intended to provide an understanding of and guidance on obtaining available benefits so richly earned.

Notes

1. Unless otherwise noted, much of the material in the history sections comes primarily from the Veterans Administration (VA) 1967 report on *Medical Care of Veterans* prepared for the House Committee on Veterans Affairs. Readers interested in a more detailed history of these benefit programs and the social forces and legislative actions leading to the creation of the VA are invited to read this report (Veterans Administration, 1967). This report is limited in availability but can be found in the VA Central Office Library in Washington, DC, and the Library of Congress. It can also be found in the VA psychology archive collection in the Archives of the History of American Psychology at the University of Akron.

2. The first time was in 1829 when many Revolutionary War pensioners were dropped from the rolls because of lack of funds to pay them (Veterans Administration, 1967).

Bibliography

Baker, R. R., and Pickren, W. E. (2007). *Psychology and the Department of Veterans Affairs: A Historical Analysis of Training, Research, Practice, and Advocacy.* Washington, DC: American Psychological Association.

Bradley, O. N., and Blair, C. (1983). *A General's Life: An Autobiography of the Army, Omar N. Bradley.* New York: Simon & Schuster.

Consumers Union (1986). *I'll Buy That!* Mount Vernon, New York: Consumer Reports Books.

Cranston, A. (1986). Psychology in the Veterans Administration: A Storied History, a Vital Future. *American Psychologist,* 41, 990–995.

Department of Veterans Affairs (2006a). *America's Wars.* Washington, DC: Department of Veterans Affairs.

——— (2006b). *Facts about the Department of Veterans Affairs.* Washington, DC: Department of Veterans Affairs.

——— (2007). *Federal Benefits for Veterans and Dependents.* Washington, DC: Department of Veterans Affairs.

Peffer, P. A. (1955). The member-employee program. *Department of Medicine and Surgery Program Guide for Psychiatric and Neurology Service, G-1, M-2, Part X, March 1955.* Washington, D.C.: Veterans Administration.

Veterans Administration (1967). *Medical Care of Veterans.* Washington, DC: U.S. Government Printing Office.

——— (1977). *VA History in Brief,* VA Pamphlet 06-77-1, May 1977. Washington, DC: Veterans Administration.

Waldrop, R. S. (2007). The Beginning of Counseling Psychology in VA Hospitals. In R. R. Baker (ed.) *Stories from VA Psychology* (pp. 127–133). Bloomington, Indiana: AuthorHouse.

CHAPTER 2

Current Veteran Demographics and Implications for Veterans' Health Care

Ann M. Hendricks and Jomana H. Amara

Editors' Comment

As with the first chapter in this book (on the historical treatment of veterans), we include this chapter on the demographic composition of veterans and economic projections of the VA to provide you with a sense of perspective of some of the issues you may be currently facing. The authors of this chapter are two economists: Ann M. Hendricks, Ph.D., is the Director of Health Care Financing and Economics (a research center at the VA Boston Healthcare System) and Associate Professor of Health Policy & Management at Boston University's School of Public Health; Jomana H. Amara, Ph.D., P.E., is Professor of Economics at the Defense Resources Management Institute at the Naval Postgraduate School in Monterey, CA. Both have conducted research on the economics of health care and are currently working together to study the ways that the current conflicts in Iraq and Afghanistan are financially impacting the VA.

This chapter describes recent trends in the demography of veterans requesting services from the VA, including the numbers, age, and make-up of the veteran population, what types of illnesses they have, and how these changes are impacting the agency and the care that it provides. The impact of the large number of veterans returning with post-traumatic stress disorder (PTSD) and traumatic brain injury (TBI) is also discussed. Drs. Hendricks and Amara conclude with projections about how these continuing trends will impact the VA—and the social, cultural, and economic impacts that will emerge from these trends—into the near future. These changes in the VA may impact you directly, and knowing these trends, you may be able to anticipate them and adapt—rather than react—to them.

Introduction

This chapter describes the disabled U.S. veteran population today, the costs in-volved in treating this population, and discusses implications for future health care needs. It relies on publicly available data and information. It does not ex-plore the ramifications of veterans' disabilities for education, insurance, loans, burial, compensation, or pensions. It first presents information about overall trends in the total numbers of U.S. veterans and compares demographic char-acteristics of veterans with VA disability ratings and the overall veteran popu-lation. The discussion then moves to information about the health care needs of disabled veterans and makes simple projections for the Veterans Health Ad-ministration (VHA) services and budgets over the next forty years. The Depart-ment of Veterans Affairs (The VA) has two major administrations: the Veter-ans Benefits Administration (VBA) and Veterans Health Administration (VHA). This discussion focuses on the VHA. Relatively little detailed information ex-ists for veterans of the most recent conflicts in Iraq and Afghanistan since we are still in the process of collecting the data and learning the full im-pact of these wars on veterans. But where it is available, it is included in this analysis.

The terms "disabled" and "disability" have both common and official mean-ings. Individual patients may think of themselves as disabled, but their condition may not meet an official definition that would qualify them for a program of care. Alternatively, many veterans officially rated as partially disabled may not appear to have any disability. This chapter will try to distinguish only between the every-day meaning of disabled and the official VA designation. The disability systems of the Medicare or Medicaid programs, the Social Security Administration, or the military will not be referenced here, but veterans should be aware that the VA is not the only agency concerned with—and defining the term—"disabled Americans."

The U.S. veteran population was estimated at 23.5 million in 2007. Of these veterans, 30 percent reportedly have a disabling physical, mental, or emo-tional condition, primarily from causes unconnected to their military service (National Center for Veterans, 2003). This proportion appears much higher than the rate reported for other working-age and older adults, even given the higher average age of veterans. For example, national health statistics show that about 14 percent of Americans eighteen years and older have a disabil-ity (defined as a limitation in their ability to perform usual activities because of a physical, mental, or emotional problem) but this lower rate reflects the fact that American adults are younger, on average, than American veterans. When the rates across age groups are re-weighted to reflect the age distri-bution of veterans, about 20 percent of U.S. adults would have such limita-tions, a rate that is still two-thirds the rate of self-reported disabling limitations among veterans. This difference has implications for the health care needs of veterans.

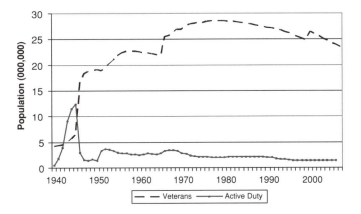

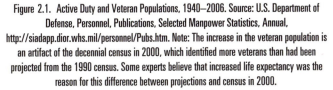

Figure 2.1. Active Duty and Veteran Populations, 1940–2006. Source: U.S. Department of Defense, Personnel, Publications, Selected Manpower Statistics, Annual, http://siadapp.dior.whs.mil/personnel/Pubs.htm. Note: The increase in the veteran population is an artifact of the decennial census in 2000, which identified more veterans than had been projected from the 1990 census. Some experts believe that increased life expectancy was the reason for this difference between projections and census in 2000.

The U.S. Veteran Population

Over the past seventy years, the number of veterans has grown following the nation's involvement in World War II, the Korean conflict, and Vietnam, all of which used drafts to enlist military personnel (Figure 2.1). The total number of veterans peaked in the early 1980s. Since then it has generally declined as many older veterans died and the military downsized at the end of the Cold War. However, the large cohorts from World War II, the Korean conflict and the Vietnam War still make up the majority of today's veterans. In 2007, most of the 23.5 million U.S. veterans were age 60 or older.

Military conscription ended in 1973 and today's members of the armed forces join voluntarily. Across all services, there are about 1.4 million active military personnel today. Only a small increase in the number of total active military personnel is currently planned. The stable numbers of active military projected for the next few decades imply that the total number of veterans will continue to decline through 2030 to about 14 million (Figure 2.2). By that time, the number of veterans over age 75 will be greater than the number under the age of 40.

Women make up 7.4 percent of all living veterans, about 1.7 million individuals. They are younger than male veterans; about half of women veterans are currently younger than 50 while only about a quarter of the men are that young. This difference in age reflects increased military opportunities for women after the Vietnam War. Women have been a much larger proportion of active military from the 1980s onward. Given these changes in the active military, projections

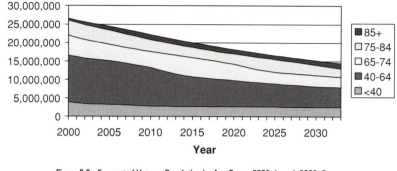

Figure 2.2. Forecast of Veteran Population by Age Group, 2000 through 2033. Source:
http://www1.va.gov/vetdata/docs/1l.xls, accessed July 17, 2007.

for the next twenty-five years show small increases in the total number of women veterans, to about 2 million or one out of every seven veterans.

The racial make-up of the veteran population is also changing. In the early 1990s, non-Hispanic white Americans were 85 percent of all veterans; today, the proportion has fallen to 80 percent. Another 11 percent are non-Hispanic African Americans. Hispanic Americans make up 5.6 percent and the remaining 3 to 4 percent are Native Americans, Asian Americans, those of Pacific Island descent, or people who identify as having mixed racial heritage. Based on current active military enrollments, the racial composition of veterans in 2033 is projected to become more diverse, but non-Hispanic white Americans will still be the majority (over 70 percent) with the other groups proportionately larger than they are today.

The largest cohort of current veterans, over 7 million, is from the Vietnam War (National Center for Veterans, 2003). Another 6 million or so are counted as "peacetime" veterans with service between major conflicts. There are more than 5 million living veterans from World War II and the Korean War combined, while the period since the first Gulf War period accounts for 4.5 million. In another twenty-five years, there will be virtually no veterans still alive from World War II or the Korean War. About 2.5 million Vietnam veterans will still be alive, but the rest of the veteran population will have served from 1980 onward.

What is the impact of the current actions in Iraq and Afghanistan on the number of U.S. veterans? The number of veterans discharged since 2002 that served in Operation Enduring Freedom and Operation Iraqi Freedom (OEF/OIF) is about 700,000 as of April 2007, 54 percent of whom were reservists or members of the National Guard and may have already had veteran status. During those same years, the total number of veterans discharged is estimated at about 1.6 million, approximately 6.8 percent of all living veterans. This total number includes the OEF/OIF veterans, but many more who served elsewhere around the globe or in the Gulf during the first Gulf War.

The OEF/OIF veterans are much younger than the average veteran; more than half are younger than 30. More than half were in the Army and 89 percent were enlisted rather than officers. Women are only about 11 percent of this cohort (about 70,000 as of August 2006) and white Americans comprise 70 percent. These characteristics are directly attributable to the fact that these veterans have only recently been on active duty.

Disabled U.S. Veterans

Service-Connected Disability

In 2001, almost a third of all veterans (over 8 million out of about 25 million at that time) reported having a disabling condition, but only 43 percent of these (about 3.5 million veterans) reported that the disability was related to their military service (National Center for Veterans 2003). This number is greater than the number reported in the early 1990s, when 10 percent or about 2.7 million veterans reported having a disability related to their military service National Center for Veterans 1995). The increase in the number of disabled veterans between the surveys of 1992 and 2001 was due primarily to the large proportion of veterans from the first Gulf War (24 percent of the total, or about 800,000 people) with VA disability ratings as well as to the fact that conditions can become more disabling as the veterans age, leading them to apply for and to be granted disability ratings.

"Service-connected" is the term applied by VA to disabilities connected to military service. It can mean that the disabling condition stemmed from a combat casualty, but it also includes injuries and illnesses from veterans' peacetime service or their basic training. These conditions can be physical, emotional, or mental in nature.

As mentioned in other chapters in this book, physical casualties in recent wars are far more numerous than deaths. Table 2.1 details the U.S. military deaths and casualties from the Civil War to OEF/OIF. The table indicates an increasing ratio of casualties to deaths over time starting at about one casualty per death during the Civil War and ending at about nine casualties per death for OEF/OIF. This change can be attributed to the improvement in medical services, particularly those located close to hostilities, over the years. Battlefield medicine, evacuation procedures, and battlefield medical support services have evolved tremendously leading to greater survival rates for troops. In addition, the very high ratio of casualties to deaths for OEF/OIF is a result of the use of body armor and helmets. This protective gear shields the user from bullets and shrapnel, improving overall survival rates.

Despite the high ratios of casualties to deaths, the number of physical casualties in OEF/OIF is small compared to the number of disabled veterans from earlier actions. For example, veterans from the Vietnam War era still comprise over 40 percent of today's disabled veterans, in large part because the largest number of veterans who are still alive served during those years. In addition, several

Table 2.1 U.S. Military Deaths and Casualties from Principal Wars[a]

Conflict	Number Serving Worldwide	Death	Casualty	Ratio Casualty: Death
Civil War (1861–1865)	2,213,363	364,511	281,881	1:1
Spanish-American War	306,760	2,446	1,662	1:2
World War I	4,734,991	116,516	204,002	2:1
World War II	16,112,566	405,399	671,846	2:1
Korea (1950–1953)	5,720,000	36,574	103,284	3:1
Vietnam (1964–1973)	8,744,000	58,209	153,303	3:1
Persian Gulf War (1990–1991)	2,225,000	382	467	1:1
OEF/OIF[b] (2001 to present)	1,400,000	2,714	24,795	9:1

[a] Data as of February 17, 2007, Department of Defense, http://siadapp.dior.whs.mil/.
[b] Number from Analysis of VA Health Care Utilization Among U.S. Southwest Asian War Veterans, VHA Office of Public Health and Environmental Hazards

important conditions were recognized as service-connected only after the Vietnam War. The primary one is post-traumatic stress disorder (PTSD), which the American Psychiatric Association added as an official diagnosis only in 1980. Because this condition may not be recognized as disabling until years after a service member has become a veteran, the number of Vietnam veterans with disabling mental or emotional conditions far exceeds the 153,000 recognized by the military at the end of the war.

The impact of PTSD on the numbers of disabled veterans from OEF/OIF is not yet known, but preliminary information on those filing for benefits suggests that it will be substantial. Estimates that one in six OIF veterans and one in nine OEF veterans displayed symptoms of PTSD support this conclusion. Of OEF/OIF veterans using VA health services, however, only 40,000 meet this condition to date (VHA Office of Public Health and Environmental Hazards 2007).

Demographics of Disabled Veterans

The service-connected disabled veteran population mirrors the overall veteran population. For example, like the general veteran population, disabled veterans range in age from 20 to at least 90 and the majority are 60 or older (National Center for Veterans 2003). This distribution is due in part to the impact of the Vietnam War in the late 1960s and in part to decreases in veterans' health as they age. One study conducted for the Veterans' Disability Benefits Commission (created by the National Defense Authorization Act of 2004) found that between the years 2000 and 2005, the peak ages for disability enrollment are when the veterans are in their 50s rather than closer in time to military service or later in the work life, near more traditional ages for retirement (Buddin and Kapur, 2005).

In this commission report, the impact of OEF/OIF is only somewhat noticeable: the numbers of disabled veterans aged 20 to 25 have increased slightly since

2000. The nation's experience with veterans from other conflicts, however, suggests that more veterans from OEF/OIF will be identified over time as having disabling conditions tied to their military service.

Historically, the risk of a service-connected disability has varied across the services. The Navy (excluding the Marines) has seen the lowest proportion of veterans qualify as service-connected disabled (10.7 percent), especially compared to the Air Force and Marines, which have had 16 percent and 16.4 percent, respectively (National Center for Veterans, 2003). The proportion for the Army is 14.8 percent. The majority of veterans with service-connected disabilities (53.8 percent), however, served in the Army. This large proportion mirrors the fact that more than half of living veterans were in that branch of service. Another 40 percent of all service-connected disabled veterans served in the Navy (again, excluding the Marines) or in the Air Force, with somewhat more having been in the latter branch. Marines constitute about 12 percent of all disabled veterans. For the Coast Guard, 12.3 percent of their veterans have had service-connected disabilities, but they make up only 1 percent of all disabled veterans.

In proportion to their numbers in the service, women veterans are almost as likely as men to have service-connected disabilities. Among women veterans, 13.5 percent report service-connected disability ratings compared to 13.8 percent of men. As with the women veteran population overall, disabled women veterans tend to be younger than men with disabilities. This difference in age contributes to differences in commonly reported diagnoses. For example, twice the proportion of male veterans report high blood pressure: 35.5 percent compared to 18.6 percent for women. More than three times as many men require a hearing aid: 9.7 percent compared to only 3.1 percent of women. While roughly the same percentages of men and women report diagnoses of PTSD (3.8 percent and 3.9 percent, respectively), more than twice the proportion of women report other mental or emotional problems (e.g., major depression): 14.3 percent compared to 5.7 percent of men.

Within the OEF/OIF veteran cohort, the reported cases of PTSD are within one or two percentage points of each other by gender (15 percent for men, 14 percent for women), race (15 percent for both white and non-whites), and age (16 percent for those under age 30 and 14 percent for those 30 or more) (National Center for Veterans, 2003). The marked differences are by branch of service (18 percent for those in the Army or Marines but only 5 percent for the Air Force and other Navy personnel) and rank (21 percent for enlisted personnel compared to 7 percent for officers).

Other diagnoses exhibit different patterns across service branches, ranks, and demographics than the PTSD diagnosis. For example, older OEF/OIF veterans (30 and older) were more than twice as likely to be treated for circulatory disorders as younger ones. Men were more likely than women to have circulatory disorders (14 percent compared to 10 percent) as were nonwhite veterans compared to whites (16 percent and 12 percent, respectively). The proportions were virtually identical by service branch, however, and more nearly equal by rank than was the case for PTSD (19 percent for enlisted versus 14 percent of officers). These comparisons do not capture care for those veterans who were not seen within the VA, which might be greater for officers than enlisted personnel.t

VA and Health Care for OEF/OIF Veterans

As described in the previous chapter, the nation's first attempt to compensate veterans' for their military service was a pension law enacted by Congress in 1789. As successive wars increased the number of veterans, the variety of benefits evolved with provisions for disability compensation, education benefits, life insurance, heath services, housing loans, burial benefits, and pension benefits available to older or disabled low-income veterans. Many of these benefits were also extended to veterans' dependents and survivors. For information on the benefits available to veterans through the VA, download the VA's "Federal Benefits for Veterans and Dependents Guide" at http://www.va.gov/opa/vadocs/fedben.pdf or call the VA benefits hotline at (800) 827 1000.

Both the Department of Defense (DoD) and the VA are responsible for the wellbeing and welfare of veterans, especially those who were injured or disabled while on active military duty. As described in the previous chapter on the history of the VA, the VA was established in 1930 when Congress authorized the President to consolidate the activities of all government activities affecting war veterans. World War II resulted in a massive increase in the number of veterans. Congress enacted a large number of new benefits for veterans, most significantly the World War II GI bill of 1944. Further acts were passed for the benefit of veterans of the Korean conflict, the Vietnam conflict, and the All-Volunteer force. In 1989, the Department of Veterans Affairs was established as a cabinet-level position.

The Veterans Benefits Administration provides compensation for veterans with a service-connected disability. Eligibility for benefits requires serving on active duty and being released under honorable conditions. Compensation for disability is based on the degree of disability, rated from 0 to 100 percent disabling. An example of a 0 percent service-connected disability is a diagnosis of tuberculosis contracted during World War II, but subsequently cured. The veteran might not consider himself disabled by this past condition, but if it ever recurred, his medical care would be covered by his veteran's benefit.

All veterans with a service-connected disability rating can be treated at VA medical centers, but care is prioritized by the degree of the disability. Veterans with ratings of 50 percent or higher have priority 1; those with ratings of 30 percent or 40 percent have priority 2; all others with service-connected disability ratings are classified as priority 3. Table 2.2 summarizes all eight priority groups. In 2001, there were about 2.7 million veterans with ratings, 11 percent of all living veterans. Only 2.3 million of these received compensation benefits that year, however, because of the number with a 0 percent rating. VA estimates that

Table 2.2 Priority Groups and Their Eligibility

Priority Group	Definition
1	• Veterans with service-connected disabilities rated 50% or more disabling • Veterans determined by VA to be unemployable due to service-connected conditions
2	• Veterans with service-connected disabilities rated 30% or 40% disabling
3	• Veterans who are former POWs • Veterans awarded the Purple Heart • Veterans whose discharge was for a disability that was incurred or aggravated in the line of duty • Veterans with service-connected disabilities rated 10% or 20% disabling • Veterans awarded special eligibility classification under Title 38, U.S.C., Section 1151, "benefits for individuals disabled by treatment or vocational rehabilitation"
4	• Veterans who are receiving VA aid and attendance or housebound benefits • Veterans who have been determined by VA to be catastrophically disabled
5	• Nonservice-connected veterans and noncompensable service-connected veterans rated 0% disabled whose annual income and net worth are below the established VA Means Test thresholds • Veterans receiving VA pension benefits • Veterans eligible for Medicaid benefits
6	• Compensable 0% service-connected veterans • World War I veterans • Mexican Border War veterans • Veterans seeking care solely for disorders associated with: – exposure to herbicides while service in Vietnam; or – exposure to ionizing radiation during atmospheric testing or during the occupation of Hiroshima and Nagasaki; or – service in the Gulf War; or – service in a theater of combat operations during a period of war after the Gulf War or during a period of hostility after November 11, 1998; or – illnesses possibly related to participation in Project 112/Project SHAD.
7	Veterans who agree to pay specified copays with income and/or net worth ABOVE the VA means Test threshold and income BELOW the geographically based threshold for their locality • Subpriority a: Noncompensable 0% service-connected veterans who were enrolled in the VA health care system on a specified date and who have remained enrolled since that date • Subpriority c: Nonservice-connected veterans who were enrolled in the VA health care system on a specified date and who have remained enrolled since that date • Subpriority e: Noncompensable 0% service-connected veterans not included in Subpriority a above • Subpriority g: Nonservice-connected veterans not included in Subpriority c above

(Continued)

Table 2.2 (*Continued*)

Priority Group	Definition
8	Veterans who agree to pay specified copays with income and/or net worth ABOVE the VA means Test threshold and income ABOVE the geographically based threshold for their locality • Subpriority a: Noncompensable 0% service-connected veterans enrolled as of January 16, 2003, and who have remained enrolled since that date • Subpriority c: Nonservice-connected veterans enrolled as of January 16, 2003, and who have remained enrolled since that date • Subpriority e: Noncompensable 0% service-connected veterans applying for enrollment after January 16, 2003 • Subpriority g: Nonservice-connected veterans applying for enrollment after January 16, 2003

Note: Veterans assigned to Priority Groups 8e or 8g are *not* eligible for enrollment as a result of the enrollment restriction which suspended enrolling new high-income veterans who apply for care after January 16, 2003. Veterans enrolled in Priority Groups 8a or 8c will remain enrolled and eligible for the full range of VA health care benefits.
Source: Department of Veterans Affairs: VA Health Care Overview.

there will be 2.9 million veterans receiving these benefits in 2007, a 24 percent increase.

Veterans who are "catastrophically disabled" by non-service-connected conditions have the next highest priority for VA health care services after those with service-connected disabilities (priority 4). This group of veterans has severely disabling injuries, disorders, or diseases that permanently compromise their ability to carry out the activities of daily living like feeding or dressing themselves. These veterans require personal or mechanical assistance to leave their bed or their home, or they require constant supervision to avoid physical harm to themselves or others. This group has generally been very small, much less than 50,000 individuals in any year.

The DoD disability compensation system compensates military service members rendered unfit for military duty as a result of service-connected disability. DoD only considers conditions making member unfit for duty and the compensation given is based on years of military service and disability rating. DoD rating is permanent. The compensation can be in the form of a lump sum or monthly payment. DoD allows the Army, the Navy, and the Air Force to implement their disability evaluation systems differently.

The VA compensates veterans for service-connected disabilities to make up for an average reduction in civilian earning capacity. The VA disability compensation depends only on the degree of disability and is not tied to the individual's level of income before disability. The VA ratings could change from time to time as the veteran's medical condition changes. The VA considers all service-connected injuries and illness and the compensation is based primarily on disability rating and the number of dependents. The compensation is in monthly payments.

Proposed changes to the military and veterans disability systems could consolidate their assessments, but DoD currently assesses a veteran's disability only once while VA can assess it multiple times (GAO, 2006a; GAO, 2006b). Reassessment may recognize that conditions that were not disabling when the veteran was young may become so with age. Official recognition that the disability is greater than in the past can raise the veteran's priority for VA health care as well as increase any monthly compensation payments he or she receives. As a result, the majority of the VA caseload in a given year consists of reassessments of existing disabilities rather than new cases. Each year, the VA processes hundreds of thousands of applications for disability ratings, either new or changes in old ratings. Not all the applicants qualify for a new rating, however.

In 2007, VA provided disability compensation to about 2.7 million veterans. Less than two-thirds of them accessed VA health care, however; service-connected disabled veterans make up only about 30 percent of the 5 million veterans treated through VA, about 1.5 million. The VA health care benefit is funded by discretionary allocations that Congress reviews every year. Disability compensation (along with pension benefits, vocational rehabilitation, and life insurance) is supported by mandatory congressional funding. Thus the level of VA funding for veterans' health care is not guaranteed and may change year to year. Since 2001, it has expanded from $21 billion to about $30 billion, a 43 percent increase (The Library of Congress, 2006a).

The VA operates the largest direct health care delivery system in the nation. It is divided into twenty-one Veterans Integrated Service Networks (VISNs). Each network includes between five and eleven hospitals as well as community based outpatient clinics (CBOCs), nursing homes, and readjustment counseling centers (Vet Centers). In 2005, VA operated 157 hospitals, 134 nursing homes, 43 residential rehabilitation treatment centers, and 711 CBOCs. In addition, the VA provides grants for construction of state owned nursing homes and domiciliary facilities. It also shares health care and resources with DoD for the Tricare and CHAMPVA health care programs for military retirees and for dependents.

Contrary to popular belief, not every veteran is automatically entitled to health care for life from the VA. The Veteran's Health Care Eligibility Reform Act of 1996, P.L. 104-262, expanded the eligibility categories to seven (later eight) priority levels. In addition, VA currently provides combat veterans free medical care for any illness possibly associated with service during a period of hostility for two years after the veteran's discharge. Once the veteran's priority status has been established, the veteran is placed in one of eight priority groups. Veterans eligible for Priority Groups 1–6 are regarded as high priority and are currently eligible for health services. Those in Priority Group 7 are evaluated for eligibility on a case-by-case basis. In 2003, the VA suspended enrollment of veterans in Priority Group 8, those with high income and without military related disabilities. Veterans with

Priority 8 who were already enrolled continue to receive VA care, but new Priority 8 veterans cannot.

By the beginning of 2007, the VA had provided health care services to 229,015 of the total of 686,306 OEF/OIF veterans (VHA Office of Public Health and Environmental Hazards, 2007). Of this number, only 3 percent (7,760 veterans) were treated on an inpatient basis. The other 97 percent were outpatients only. These proportions reflect the relative youth of these patients (56 percent under the age of 30, 80 percent younger than 40) and their low rates of disease and injuries. Even so, the health problems of these recent OEF/OIF veteran patients have encompassed more than 7,990 diagnostic codes with the most common problems (reported for 30 percent or more of the patients) being musculoskeletal (joint and back), mental, nervous system/sense organs, digestive system, and "symptoms, signs, and ill-defined conditions." This last category is a catch-all that is commonly used for outpatient diagnosis and consists primarily of common symptoms that do not have an immediate cause.

About 10 percent (70,000) of all OEF/OIF veterans are women and 27,500 of them have accessed VA care since 2002 (VHA Office of Public Health and Environmental Hazards, 2007). This number represents almost 40 percent of the women veterans of OEF/OIF, a somewhat larger proportion than for the men, a third of whom used VA health care. The reason for this difference is not known and may indicate differences in non-VA health care coverage after veterans reenter civilian life.

OEF/OIF veterans are receiving care in all of the VA networks around the country, but are disproportionately affecting VA medical centers in California, Texas, Florida, and the southeastern states. These include states with some of the largest veteran populations, but the OEF/OIF patient loads represent larger percentages of this veteran cohort than is true for other veterans. Florida, for example, was home to 7.3 percent of all veterans in 2005, but has treated 8.4 percent of all OEF/OIF veterans treated in VA nationwide. The reasons for this pattern may be that these states have more military bases where military families reside and to which the veterans return. This pattern has important implications for the future costs of care for OEF/OIF veterans because it may indicate the need to expand VA capacity more in these states than in other areas of the country.

VA estimates that in 2008 it will treat about 263,000 OEF/OIF veterans, an increase of 54,000 (26 percent) from 2007 and 108,000 (70 percent) more than the number treated in 2006. The number in 2008 represents 5 percent of all veterans expected to receive VA health care that year. Unless they are disabled from their military service, these veterans are categorized as priority 6 and pay no co-payments for any conditions related to their military service.

Signature Conditions

The OEF/OIF wars are the most sustained combat operations since Vietnam. Two major veteran health conditions stemming from these conflicts have received particular attention from Congress and VHA: traumatic brain injury (TBI) and post-traumatic stress disorder (PTSD). Neither of these is unique to OEF/OIF, but the needs of these two groups of patients have garnered attention. Congress, recognizing the special needs of OEF/OIF veterans, included funds for prosthetic research and increased funding for the Defense and Veteran's Brain Injury Center (DVBIC), the facility that coordinates treatment and research for traumatic brain injuries. Additional funding for programs for PTSD has also been made available.

TBI

While it is extremely difficult to obtain the number of veterans suffering from TBI, a rough estimate would be the number of troops with injuries to the face, head, or neck. Symptoms of TBI may not be evident on first examination since some cases of closed brain injury are not diagnosed properly at the time and may manifest later (Okie, 2005). TBI appears to account for a larger proportion of casualties among injured troops in OEF/OIF than in other wars. DoD reported a total of 1,179 TBI cases as of March 31, 2006, for OEF/OIF (The Library of Congress, 2006b; The Library of Congress, 2007). However, researchers have reported larger numbers of OEF/OIF veterans suffering from TBI. The difference in the estimates underscores the difficulty of obtaining reliable data for these injuries (Okie, 2005; DVA Office of Research and Development, 2006).

One estimate is that 22 percent of wounded OEF/OIF soldiers have TBI (Lew et al., 2006). This estimate would translate to an absolute number of about 8,000. VA and DoD have also reported TBI rates of 40 percent in two samples of wounded service members and a rate of 10–15 percent mild to moderate TBI in returning service members who had not been wounded. These estimates would translate to absolute numbers of approximately 14,500 for wounded veterans and 68,000 to 100,000 for returning veterans.

On average, veterans with a diagnosis of combat-related TBI suffer from a larger variety of symptoms than those with TBI that are not combat-related, which veterans of all ages may experience through falls, automobile accidents, and other injuries. This difference in symptoms may be the result of the interaction of the blast wave with fluid filled organs such as the brain and eyes. Vision impairment (post-traumatic vision syndrome), sensitivity to light or noise, sleep disturbance, and PTSD are among the symptoms experienced more by those veterans with combat-related injury.

The Defense and Veteran's Brain Injury Center (DVBIC) was established in 1992. It coordinates nine health care centers: two civilian, three military, and four VA sites. The four VA-operated Polytrauma Rehabilitation Centers (in Tampa, Florida; Richmond, Virginia; Minneapolis, Minnesota; and, Palo Alto, California) and another seventeen Polytrauma Network Sites have specific amputation, rehabilitation, and mental health expertise including Comprehensive Physical Medicine and Rehabilitation Service; Inpatient Rehabilitation Unit accredited by the Rehabilitation Commission (CARF); Prosthetic/Orthotic Lab accredited by the American Board for Certification in Orthotics, Prosthetics & Pedorthics (ABC) or the Board for Orthotist/Prosthetist Certification (BOC) and a certified prosthetist on staff; surgical expertise in the area of amputation care and polytrauma; specialized PTSD programming; Driver's Training Program present; and access to tele-habilitation technology.

While this policy places interdisciplinary expertise within each of the VA's twenty-one geographic networks, many veterans will find the cost of travel to these centers to be prohibitive. Improving the standard of care at the other 150 of so medical centers and the more than 800 community outpatient clinics will help some disabled veterans living far from the special polytrauma programs in a timely way. In the past, veterans have moved to be closer to the VA health care they needed. Some OEF/OIF veterans may also resort to this solution. Establishing additional clinics and contracting with local providers are other ways that the VA is making more services available, but there is a limit to the expansion that is possible for this type of care. The requisite skills do not exist in all towns and in some states the veterans requiring those services are too sparsely located to assure private sector providers of a livelihood.

Receiving timely treatment and rehabilitation may, at a minimum, help veterans adapt to the physical outcomes caused by mild, moderate, or severe TBI. For example, understanding the cause of physical symptoms like loss of hearing or feeling in the extremities and learning coping strategies may forestall a variety of negative feelings. In this way, getting treatment earlier is more cost effective than getting it at a later time.

PTSD

The VA has undertaken many efforts to improve PTSD care delivered to veterans. It has developed a guide for clinicians and implemented a clinical reminder to prompt clinicians to assess OEF/OIF veterans for PTSD, depression, and substance abuse. The VA has implemented a national system of 144 PTSD programs in all states and required all VA outpatient clinics to have either a psychiatrist or psychologist on staff full time. VA has also established Mental Illness Research, Education, and Clinical Centers (MIRECCs) to focus on issues of post-deployment health of OEF/OIF veterans such as PTSD and suicide prevention.

It is estimated that in the case of OEF/OIF, 15.6 to 17.1 percent of veterans deployed to Iraq reportedly displayed symptoms of PTSD and 11.2 percent of veterans deployed to Afghanistan reportedly did so (Hoge et al., 2004). Of the OEF/OIF veterans who have used VA services, however, almost 84,000 (37 percent of the total of 229,000) had a diagnosis for any mental health condition. Within this broad category, PTSD was the most common diagnosis listed (almost 40,000 patients), with substance use disorders, major depression, and neurotic disorders also reported for at least a quarter of the 84,000 patients (VHA Office of Public Health and Environmental Hazards, 2007). Among women OEF/OIF veterans, PTSD is potentially identified for at least as large a proportion of women as men.

Studies indicate that more frequent and more intense involvement in combat operations increases the risk of developing mental health problems (Office of the Surgeon Multinational Force, 2006). Due to the intensity of combat in OEF/OIF, returning veterans are at a high risk for mental health problems—specifically those resulting from TBI or PTSD. These two injuries often coincide. There is evidence that once veterans develop PTSD their symptoms remain chronic across their lifetime.

Because of its chronic nature, it is difficult to predict the pattern of utilization and therefore the costs for treatment of PTSD. Outpatient treatment is the norm in VA, but some specialized residential treatment programs do exist. However, these programs are not located in every state.

Future Costs for Care

The costs for care of veterans with disabling conditions vary as widely as the conditions themselves. They are borne by several different public programs, including the VA, in addition to the veterans and their families. Physical disabilities, such as amputations and TBI, require costly operations and rehabilitation even before the veteran separates from the military. For example, VA in-hospital care for patients with mild to moderate TBI (usually skull fractures) cost an average of $17,000 to $45,000 in 1999 (Amara and Hendricks, 2007). Given inflation in hospital costs since then, mild to moderate TBI hospitalizations would cost $23,000 to $61,000 in 2007. For severe TBI, the costs today could be $100,000 or more per hospitalization, not including the cost of any rehabilitative care. The immediate costs for disabilities that might not require early hospitalization (e.g., PTSD, hearing loss from mild TBI) might appear very low in comparison, but could still be considerable if the condition is chronic and requires intervention over time. Patients with PTSD, for example, may require frequent outpatient treatment for several years initially and then can still reappear throughout the veteran's lifetime.

About 30 percent of all veterans who are VA patients in a given year have a service-connected disability. Because they tend to be more costly than lower priority VA patients, their care probably accounts for more than 30 percent of the $31 billion VA medical care budget. Disabled veterans from wars of the last century receive 90 percent or more of the $9 billion of care, however. The resource constraints for newly disabled veterans are greatest in the very short run, as the veterans reenter civilian life and require immediate help.

It is currently difficult to quantify the costs and the amount of care that the OEF/OIF cohort requires because of all the unknowns:

- The nature and duration of OEF/OIF
- Politically mandated changes

- The nature, severity, and number of PTSD, TBI, and physical disabilities
- To which VA centers the veterans will turn for care
- How much the veterans rely on VA for care from one year to the next

Because the range of estimates for OEF/OIF veterans with disabilities is so large (15 to 40 percent of OEF/OIF veterans possibly have PTSD), even translating those lower and upper bounds into amounts of utilization or funding for more than a few years into the future is not policy relevant today.

Conventional wisdom holds that caring for returning veterans is placing a large burden on the VA system, especially for mental health services (Bilmes, 2007). However, demand for immediate post-deployment VA services by the OEF/OIF veterans will be overshadowed nationally by the demands of the aging Korean and Vietnam Wars cohorts in terms of the number of patients and the average cost of their care. The importance of the aging veteran cohort is apparent from Figures 2.1 and 2.2. In 2005, not only were more than half of all veterans over age 60, about two-thirds were 55 and older. The health care needs of these older veterans are those of most elderly Americans with complex chronic conditions such as diabetes or heart failure. Elderly veterans, however, often have additional complications from disabilities sustained during military service, including mental health disorders. These veterans will continue to comprise most of the demand on VA funding and services until the majority of World War II, Korean War, and Vietnam War cohort pass through the system in 2015. By 2030, veterans from OEF/OIF will be middle-aged or older and will have additional disabilities that are not service-connected, but that will require health services nevertheless.

Bibliography

Amara, J., and Hendricks, A. (2007) *The Deferred Cost of War: Short and Long Term Impact of OEF/OIF on Veteran Health Care*. Working paper.

Bilmes, L. (2007). *Soldiers Returning from Iraq and Afghanistan: The Long-Term Costs of Providing Veterans Medical Care and Disability Benefits (RWP07-001)*. Working paper by John F. Kennedy School of Government-Harvard University, Cambridge, MA.

Buddin, R., and Kapur, K. (2005). *An Analysis of Military Disability Compensation*. Santa Monica, CA: RAND National Defense Research Institute.

Congressional Research Support Report for Congress. (May 2006a). *Veterans' Medical Care: FY2007 Appropriations* (Order Code RL33409). Washington, DC: The Library of Congress.

———. (October 2006b). *Veterans' Health Care Issues in the 109th Congress* (Order Code RL 32961). Washington, DC: The Library of Congress.

———. (April 2007). *Veterans' Benefits: Issues in the 110th Congress* (Order Code RL33985). Washington, DC: The Library of Congress.

Department of Veterans Affairs Office of Research and Development, National Institute of Mental Health, United States Army Medical Research and Materiel Command. (May 2006). *Mapping the Landscape of Deployment Related Adjustment and Mental Disorders. A*

Meeting Summary of a Working Group to Inform Research. Rockville, MD: U.S. Department of Veterans Affairs.

Hoge, C., Castro, C., Messer, S., McGurk, M., Cotting, D., and Koffman, R. (2004). Combat Duty in Iraq and Afghanistan, Mental Health Problems, and Barriers to Care. *The New England Journal of Medicine,* 351 (1), 13–22.

Lew, H. L., Poole, J., Guillory, S., Salerno, R. M., Leskin, G., and Sigford, B. (2006). Persistent Problems after Traumatic Brain Injury: The Need for Long-Term Follow Up and Coordinated Care. *Journal of Rehabilitation Research Development,* 43 (2), 7–10.

National Center for Veterans, Analysis and Statistics, Assistant Secretary for Policy and Planning. (March 2003). *National Survey of Veterans.* Washington, DC: U.S. Department of Veterans Affairs.

―――――. (April 1995). *National Survey of Veterans (Depot stock no. P92493).* Washington, DC: U.S. Department of Veterans Affairs.

Office of the Surgeon Multinational Force, Iraq and Office of the Surgeon General, United States Army Medical Command. (November 2006). *Mental Health Advisory Team (MHAT) IV Operation Iraqi Freedom 05-07.*

Okie, S. (2005). Traumatic Brain Injury in the War Zone. *New England Journal of Medicine,* 352 (20), 2043–2047.

U.S. Government Accountability Office. (2006a). *Disability Benefits. Benefit Amounts for Military Personnel and Civilian Public Safety Officers Vary by Program Provisions and Individual Circumstances (GAO-06-04).* Washington, DC: U.S. GAO.

―――――. (2006b). *Veterans Disability Benefits. VA Should Improve Its Management of Individual Unemployability Benefits by Strengthening Criteria, Guidance, and Procedures. (GAO-06-309).* Washington, DC: U.S. GAO.

Veterans Health Administration Office of Public Health and Environmental Hazards. (April 2007). *Analysis of VA Health Care Utilization among US Southwest Asian War Veterans: Operation Iraqi Freedom, Operation Enduring Freedom.* Washington, DC: U.S. Department of Veterans Affairs.

CHAPTER 3

Injuries and Symptoms

Editors' Comment

What is wrong with me?
Why am I having trouble remembering things?
What are the symptoms of PTSD?
Where can I turn to for help?
Why is my family member or friend acting weird and what can I do to help?

If you recently returned from the war—or if your friend or family member did—you are probably asking questions like these. The amount of medical information out there can seem overwhelming and may be difficult to find, so in order to provide you with the critical information you need to quickly answer these questions, we have asked some of the contributors to this book to assemble information you will need to know in order to understand and immediately address different types of war-related injuries. This chapter focuses on the "signature injuries" of the current conflict that are affecting hundreds of thousands retruning service members: post-traumatic stress disorder (PTSD), depression, traumatic brain injury (TBI), and the physical wounds of war inculding loss of limbs, burns, pain, and paralysis.

The first table is a listing of the symptoms of PTSD. Veterans can use this list to see if they are displaying any (or how many) symptoms. The table also offers an explanation of each sympton so that family members and friends can understand what their veteran is acting in certain ways. The table also offers suggestions of what friends and family members can do to help the veteran with each symptom. Jaine Darwin, Psy.D., compiled this table. Dr. Darwin has extensive experience working and counseling with veterans with PTSD and their friends and family members as the codirector and a founder of SOFAR (Strategic Outreach to Families of All Reservists).

The next table answers the same questions about depression—What are the symptoms? Why would a veteran react this way? And what can family and friends do to help the veteran? It was written by John W. Klocek, Ph.D., a staff psychologist at the Central Texas Veterans Health Care System & Professor at Texas A&M College of Medicine. Dr. Klocek has experience helping many veterans and their families and friends as they cope with their injuries. His primary research interests are pain management, integrated health care, and the interactive effects that psychological illnesses can have on physical health.

Problematic or negative thinking styles can increase the number of symptoms you might experience and the level of pain that accompanies them. To understand when and how you might be thinking in problematic styles Dr. Klocek created the next table of problematic thinking styles and examples of each style. You can use this table to see when you are thinking this way so that you can stop yourself and reframe your interpretation of your situation and decrease potential negative thoughts, pain, and feelings of helplessness.

Dr. Klocek also created the next table—a list of the symptoms of traumatic brain injury. If you see yourself displaying any of these symptoms, please get checked by a medical professional.

Concluding this chapter is a list of some of the most common physical ailments affecting the veterans of the current conflict. Listed with each ailment is a Web-based resource that you can access to learn more about each ailment and what resources are available to help you receive help with it. These Web-based resources and more information to help you is available on the web site that was designed to accompany this book at http://www.warswounded.com The table was created by Lt. Col. Mark J. Bates, Ph.D. of the United States Air Force; LTC Stephen V. Bowles, Ph.D. of the United States Army; Maj. Jocelyn A. Kilgore, MD of the Air Force; and Lionel P. Solursh, MD of the Veterans Administration.

Dr. Ainspan, the editor of this book and a speaker on disabilities and accommodations and Dr. Bates have also assembled a table of some of the accommodations that are available for different types of disabilities.

The material in these tables is no substitute for a consultation with a medical professional and we recommend only using the tables as a starting point in your discussions about your injuries. And if you or your friend or family member have any thoughts about suicide or harming others, please contact 911 or either of these numbers—1 800 SUICIDE (800 784 2433) or 1 800 273 TALK (8255) and speak with a trained counselor immediately. For other symptoms, please speak with medical professionals as soon as possible. You had a team by your side while you were deployed and your recovery is no different: physicians, therapists, and counselors are available to help you with any of the symptoms on these pages.

Psychological Ailments

Every one talks about post-traumatic stress disorder (PTSD) and depression, but how does someone know if they have it? What does it mean to carry a diagnosis of PTSD or depression? A diagnosis is shorthand to describe certain symptoms appearing in a cluster at the same time. For many veterans and their family and friends, a diagnosis helps organize and make sense out of an assortment of behaviors, feelings, and thoughts that may have seemed both disturbing and random. Many returning veterans may have some of these symptoms but may not have enough of them to qualify for the complete diagnosis. Some symptoms will abate over time and others may require professional help to get rid of them, to lessen the severity, or to learn to live with them.

The National Center for PTSD (on the Web at http://www.ncptsd.va.gov/) defines PTSD as "an anxiety disorder that can occur after you have been through a traumatic event." Further in the chapter is a table that describes the symptoms of PTSD. If you are a veteran, you can go through the list and see which (and how many) of these symptoms you currently are experiencing. These lists of symptoms are compiled from information collected by the "Battlemind" program (http://www.battlemind.org) and the Center for Deployment Psychology (http://www.deploymentpsych.org).

In summary, symptoms of PTSD fall into three main categories: (1) repeated "reliving" of the event in the form of recurrent and intrusive thoughts or distressing dreams related to the trauma, (2) persistent avoidance of reminders of memories or feelings, and (3) persistent increased arousal (not previously present) including irritability, sleep problems, concentration difficulties, and exaggered startle responses, and/or constantly being "on guard." The symptoms may occur soon after a major traumatic experience, or onset may be delayed for more than six months after the event. In either case, the symptoms are persistent.

Friends and family members can use this table to try to understand why the veteran is behaving in certain ways and can read in the third column of the table for the things that they can do to help the veteran with that symptom. It is hoped that the information in this table will begin discussions about what the veteran is feeling and how the family and friends can help—or at least understand why their veteran is acting in certain ways.

The next table is a list of some of the symptoms of depression to describe what the veteran might be experiencing with a list of ways that family and friends can help with each symptom.

The presence of any of these symptoms for any length of time means the veteran should seek professional help. PTSD or depression does not mean a person is crazy. Both are ways of reacting when people have been exposed to unremitting stress and feelings of helplessness over an extended period of time. Veterans may need to learn skills to readjust their nervous systems. Some feelings and behavior that were normal and helpful on the battlefield (such as hypervigilance) are not needed in the civilian world and in the absence of imminent danger become symptoms of PTSD. Depression can be seen as a normal reaction to the experiences that veterans had in the course of battle. Cognitive behavioral therapies, talk therapies, and medication can also help and can follow some of the ideas and suggestions offered in this chapter.

PTSD and depression happen to the veteran but have an impact on the whole family. A returning veteran has to understand the problem is not the soldier's alone, but a problem for the whole family. Keeping symptoms a secret is probably not possible and burdens rather than protects loved ones.

With PTSD and depression, it is not "one diagnosis to a customer" since symptoms can vary between individuals (no two people will have PTSD or depression in the same way) and symptoms can vary within the individual as well—a veteran who has been home for over six months can still begin experiencing symptoms at any time. And a veteran who was physically wounded can also suffer from PTSD or depression and both can make the physical wounds more painful and difficult to bear.

While this material is presented to help the veteran and the family understand PTSD and depression and suggest ways of coping with the symptoms, it is not a replacement for a proper diagnosis by a trained professional and a treatment plan that a professional can implement with the family members. If symptoms seem severe, and especially if the veteran's behavior could be harmful to someone, please contact professionals (through the VA or in your community) for referrals to counselors and other professionals.

PTSD Symptoms and How Family and Friends Can Help

Symptom	Veteran's Experience	How Family and Friends Can Help
Secretiveness	Family and friends have the right to be curious about deployment experiences. Veterans have the right not to talk about them but also the freedom to talk if they choose.	Both family members and veterans should voice their interests and preferences. The family member could say, "I'd like to know what happened for you in Iraq when and if you are ready to talk. It is confusing to see how changed you are without knowing what factors account for these changes."
		A soldier may say, "I am not ready to talk about things I saw that were very upsetting or I'd like to tell you, but I'm afraid of what you will think of me."
		Let that begin the conversation and approach your interactions from these points.

(Continued)

Symptom	Veteran's Experience	How Family and Friends Can Help
Controlling behavior	The veteran is used to giving and obeying orders. But decisions at home are not conveyed from command down and are not always immediately obeyed.	While the soldier may fear that lives are put in danger if commands are not obeyed, this is rarely so in civilian life. Families could help by reminding the soldier that no one will be put at risk if the teenager plays one more video game before washing the dishes.
Hypervigilance	Feeling on duty all the time is exhausting. Veterans may find themselves jumpy, irritable, or awaking frequently during the night and being reactive to loud noises.	Families can be helped if they began to notice things that trigger the soldier so that they are not so surprised by the soldier becoming jumpy or fearful at certain times. This awareness may also help them comfort the soldier by reminding the soldier that those noises signified danger in the war zone, but do not signify this at home.
Emotional control	Holding in all feelings can cause isolation that is not helpful to the veteran or others in the veteran's life.	Family members can help the soldier by giving feedback such as "you scare us more by withdrawing than by anything you might tell us."
Need to be armed	While every one has the constitutional right to bear arms, they also have the responsibility that arms are safely secured, safely stored and not carried at inappropriate times.	If a veteran feels the need to be armed, the veteran has to do so responsibly. If this is a new behavior, both the veteran and the family must discuss what it means to have guns in the house.
Targeted aggression	Aggressive responses are not a good first reaction in civilian life. Veterans must check out the appropriateness of a response before snapping at someone or lashing out. Physical abuse is never justified.	Families can help by identifying positive coping skills and improved behaviors. "I appreciate how hard you've been working on controlling your temper since you returned home. We notice how much less you've been snapping in the last week."
Driving defensively	No IEDs are planted in the roads at home. Traffic jams, while annoying, are not ambushes.	Families must feel free to choose not to drive with a veteran who is prone to road rage or to unsafe driving practices such as swerving, driving too fast, or tailgating.
Guilt	Regret about some of our actions in life is unavoidable. But blame and guilt are counterproductive.	Families can help their veterans to understand that while fighting in a war one might be forced to harm others and may have feelings of regret. Although this can be painful to live with, it does not make the vet a bad person.

34

Symptom	Veteran's Experience	How Family and Friends Can Help
Fear and anxiety	A veteran may start feeling panicky or as if his or her heart is racing for what feels like no reason. This may worsen in public spaces like malls or restaurants.	Families may feel upset at the new fragility of the soldier who they saw as the tough one in the house.
Intrusive thoughts	A veteran may start having mental pictures of things seen in OIF and OEF that keep reoccurring even when he does not want to think about it.	Families may be troubled by a veteran's withdrawal, without understanding that he or she is trying cope with flashbacks.
Nightmares	Trauma nightmares feel like one is really experiencing the things that are happening in the dream. Veterans may thrash about physically or strike out at the partner with whom they sleep.	Families may not understand that for the dreamer these dreams feel like real events. Partners must never try to awaken the person by touching them. Partners are at high risk for unintentionally getting punched, choked, or attacked in other ways. If partners want to awaken veterans having a nightmare, they should do it using their voices from across the room.
Sleep difficulties	Sometimes veterans sleep fitfully or are afraid to go to sleep because they fear the nightmares they are having. Drinking alcohol to facilitate sleep is a bad idea. While they may "pass out," the quality of sleep is terrible and not restful.	Family members may need to balance the tension between the need to maintain a regular schedule and the need to offer comfort to the disregulated veteran.
Difficulty concentrating	Veterans may have trouble sticking with a task or remembering things they have to do. The may find it difficult to focus which makes planning and finishing jobs and tasks hard.	Families may strive to have reasonable expectations of what the soldier can and cannot do when the soldier first returns home.
Feeling jumpy and on guard	Veterans may feel like they are always on alert, scanning for danger. They may react strongly to loud noises or to anyone touching them when they don't expect it.	Families may feel upset by the soldier's behavior. They may confuse the soldier's sensitivity for rejection.

(Continued)

Symptom	Veteran's Experience	How Family and Friends Can Help
Feeling numb or detached	Veterans may feel as if they are separate from what is happening around them, as if they are viewing the world through a veil or a haze. They may have no emotional reaction to things in the past that made them laugh or cry. Sometimes when people feel this way, they are tempted to cut or hurt themselves just to feel something. That is not a good idea.	Some of the most painful things for a family is dealing with a soldier who is physically present and emotionally absent. Families may feel helpless and even angry when the soldier acts so emotionally unreachable.
Feeling angry, guilty, or ashamed	Veterans may feel irritable and want to lash out at people. They also may feel swamped with worry about things they wish they had done, like being able to better protect a comrade or with things they did do like hurting a civilian in the act of protecting a comrade.	Families may help by respecting the soldier's pain and listening to the soldier's anguish. Families may help the soldier to live with regret, but not self-blame and guilt.
Grief or depression	Most soldiers who served were exposed to or experienced loss of fellow soldiers. Wounded soldiers have undergone loss of the sense that they are invulnerable. Soldiers, while they served, missed out on important family events. These may cause depression or feeling helpless and hopeless. Veterans who are very depressed may feel bad about themselves. Sometimes the pain can be both mental and physical. See the table following for a more detailed discussion about symptoms of depression. This is another time when veterans may think about hurting themselves either to escape from the pain or to localize a pain that feels unbearable to one part of the body. This is not a good idea.	Families may have to decide if a veteran needs professional help if the grief and depression interfere with the soldier's ability to have good judgment about self-care.

Depression Symptoms and How Family and Friends Can Help

Symptom	The Veteran's Experience	How Family and Friends Can Help
Sad or depressed mood all day or most every day	The veteran may seem sad or down frequently. He will sometimes cry easily or at the smallest of things. Others may show this through heavy sighs, dwelling on how much better things used to be, or (especially for men) simply expressing the feeling that things just are not right.	Things as simple as offering support by being there for the veteran or giving her a chance to talk can be a big help. Try to let the veteran express how much she wants to have company or how much she would like to talk.
	Remember that everyone has ups and downs—depression is when those downs last more than two weeks and when they interfere with day-to-day life activities.	Be patient—it takes far more than "think happy thoughts" to overcome depression and continued support will be valuable.
		Being around someone who is down and sad is difficult. It can quickly wear on family and friends. People with depression often sense this and are worried that they are being a burden. Friends and family should recognize the cost it has on them and remember to care for themselves through breaks, seeking support elsewhere, or engaging in activities they enjoy.
Unable to enjoy anything	Virtually nothing brings a smile to the veteran. Even a favorite meal, visiting the special spot for fishing, or a surprise visit from an old friend cannot seem to help. The most common response to a question such as "Are you having fun?" or "Is that good?" is a flat sounding "Yeah," or "It's O.K," or simply a shrug.	Friends and family can help by continuing to provide opportunities for enjoyed activities, but not pressuring the veteran to participate—or to say that it was enjoyable. Continue to try these activities and stay active.
Irritability	This is one of the most common—and perhaps least expected—symptoms of depression. Seemingly upset by the smallest of things, a depressed individual can react with frustration and anger to just about anything. Often, there is a feeling of sadness and regret following an angry outburst.	Though difficult to do, try not to take the anger and frustration personally. It may be directed your way, but is probably more related to depression that anything you may have done. Still, you may feel as though you must "walk on eggshells" around the veteran. It can be helpful to try and reduce the situations that may be irritating to the veteran, but you may also want to work out a way to give the veteran "space" when he or she is feeling on edge. Try to talk about this

(Continued)

Symptom	The Veteran's Experience	How Family and Friends Can Help
		plan during a time when both of you are feeling good. Find a place or a signal that can indicate that either of you needs space. Also identify a way that you will come back together when ready. And remember to take care of yourself while taking care of others. If physical violence is involved, contact the authorities and seek safety.
Low motivation	Things around the house may not be getting done because you cannot figure out where to start. Or it may just seem like too much work to get everything together for that family trip to your sister's house. Whatever it is, you just cannot find enough reasons to go through all the trouble that would be involved.	Encourage the veteran instead of pestering and assist instead of criticizing. Help the veteran get started with tasks but do not do everything for his or her—this will only reinforce his or her feeling of not being able to do anything. Be patient, as things will take some time to get done as the veteran battles depression.
		As simple (and difficult!) as it sounds—start somewhere. Whatever you pick does not have to fix or solve everything. Start with one small thing that you can do that will result in you being able to look at something that you have completed—no matter how small—to demonstrate that you can get something done.
Fatigue—no matter how much rest you get	More than being a little tired, it feels like everything is just too much. You just do not have the energy and you may feel like you even lack the energy to get out of bed. Even if you sleep much more than usual, you still never feel rested.	As with low motivation, encourage the veteran to be active. As a friend or family member, his or her level of activity may not be same that you saw in the past. Rather than pushing too hard or letting the veteran spend days in bed, work side by side with her to be up and around during the day.
Sleeping too much or too little (especially waking early in the morning)	Some people who are depressed will find that they are sleeping much less than they had in the past. You may have difficulty falling asleep and then awaken for no apparent reason after a few hours of sleep. You may also find that you are waking up very early in the morning and cannot get back to sleep. On the other hand, some depressed individuals find they are sleeping a great deal more—but still never feel rested.	Try to help the veteran keep a regular sleep schedule. Our bodies strongly prefer a regular cycle. Try to help set up a routine at night that helps everyone wind down from the day. Avoid caffeine and alcohol late in the evening as it can disrupt sleep. Avoid naps (or limit them to 30–45 minutes) during the day. Work to set a regular waking time. To cope with the frustration of not being to able to fall asleep, get out of bed and find something quiet to do (like reading) until drowsiness sets in again. For more information of creating good sleep habits, visit http://www.sleepeducation. com. A physician may also prescribe a sleep

Symptom	The Veteran's Experience	How Family and Friends Can Help
		aid to assist in falling and staying asleep.
Changes in appetite (increase or decrease)	To someone who is depressed, nothing may taste good or she may simply forget to eat. Food no longer looks appetizing. You may find that you are losing weight even if you never intended to do this.	Encourage a friend or family member who is not eating to keep a regular meal schedule. Though things may taste bland—or the veteran does not feel hungry—it is important that the body continues to take in nourishment.
	On the other hand, the depressed person may also find comfort in food and find that he is eating constantly. Not surprisingly, weight gain may be the result.	In the case of overeating (or "comfort eating"), encourage the veteran to choose healthy snacks, limit portions, and eat more slowly.
		In either case, maintaining a level of regular activity and exercise can be beneficial.
Strong feelings of failure	It may be something you did today, last week, or 5 years ago. It may be a task you did not complete or it may be a feeling that you are not where you thought you would be at this point in your life. Whatever it is, you feel bad about it. You have regrets and question why things are not better for you. In some cases, you may even feel as though nothing will ever get better.	Help the veteran see her successes and encourage her to acknowledge every small daily success. Identify daily goals to help identify successes. Even small goals like taking care of one errand, making a phone call, or emptying the dishwasher are helpful. Your response to the completion of that goal should not be over the top but should encourage the veteran to continue to try to meet daily goals.
	Sometimes you may also feel guilty about your actions—or lack of actions. You may feel guilty about surviving an event—or being home while others are still in Iraq or Afghanistan. That feeling of guilt can be clear, but it may also show up in the little things. For example, it may be a feeling that you need to apologize repeatedly for not getting more done that day, or for doing too much. Despite your prior service, you may feel as though you could have done more to contribute. You may feel like you need to apologize for just about anything.	

(Continued)

Symptom	The Veteran's Experience	How Family and Friends Can Help
Strong feelings that you should be punished for your actions and failures	You may find yourself feeling like everything you do—or things you have done in the past—were things that deserved to be punished. Or that because it was not perfect, what you did was actually a failure and you really should be blamed for failing. Sometimes these thoughts go as far as blaming yourself or thinking you should be punished even though there nothing more you could have done. When others try to tell you that you should not be so hard on yourself, it may feel like a cop out. Family members may wonder why you get so frustrated when things are not right—or why you keep going back to events from the past just to describe how things did not go as well as they could have and why you are to blame for the outcome.	The feelings of guilt often come from patterns of thinking that leave the veteran vulnerable to feeling guilty about many things. These thinking patterns are usually very strong and may not even be noticeable. It will not help if family and friends say things like, "No, no—it's ok—you did all you could," or "Anyone would have done the same . . ." but they will probably say it anyway. Talk to the veteran and help him think through what happened carefully. Is he using thinking styles that make it more difficult to see the shades of grey that are typically present in any situation or its outcome? (See the following table on Problematic Thinking Styles for more information in this area.)
A desire to avoid others	Most requests to the veteran to go to a restaurant, visit family, go shopping, see a game, or almost anything social are turned down. The veteran may not feel like going or might be too tired. Either way, the veteran just wants to be alone and could become even more withdrawn around people. For the veteran, it is often a sense that being with other people is just too much work. In a social situation, you feel like you will need to talk, smile, and answer questions. You may feel like you do not want to inflict yourself on others and make them suffer through your company.	Though the veteran may say "no" more often than not to taking part in social activities, keep asking. Providing support is often as much about simply being there—not giving up on the depressed person—as it is about making sure that he or she has fun all the time. At the same time, do not pester the veteran to take part in activities. The veteran is often saying "no" because he or she does not want to be around anyone—not because he does not want to be around you specifically. If isolation becomes more frequent, make an effort to be around others more frequently. This does not mean say yes to every invitation for a social event. It may be something as simple as being in the same room as the family while watching TV after dinner or agreeing to one or two social events a week. As depression lifts, the desire to be around others will likely return to what is was previously.

Symptom	The Veteran's Experience	How Family and Friends Can Help
Loss of interest in sex or difficulty having sex	You may find that you are just not interested in having sex. Or you may find that no matter how much you would like to have sex, your body just will not respond. It might be pain, it might be anxiety, or it might be depression that is causing the problem. It might even be the sense that things are different now—that you no longer feel any real connection to anything or anyone. Whatever it is, an important part of your life (and your partner's life!) is gone. This can be as difficult for your spouse or girlfriend or boyfriend as it is for you. It can mean hurt feelings, suspicion, even feelings of rejection or inadequacy. You may feel misunderstood and your partner may feel unwanted when sex is much less a part of your relationship than before.	Many different things can cause problems with sex—and many different things may help. Speaking with your physician or mental health provider about what is going on is a first step. Depending on what is causing the problem, they may have some ideas to share with you and your partner, or even medications that may help. You should also talk with your partner about it. Sex may not always the easiest thing to talk about. This can be especially true for the person who is having difficulty as it can be very frustrating, embarrassing, and even humiliating. But if sex disappears from the relationship without a word, all your partner can do is wonder. A first step can be to stop putting pressure on yourself (or each other) when it comes to sex. Take some time to simply enjoy being together without worrying about sex. It may take some time to adjust to being together again—or for things to start to return to normal. But it is important that you approach the problem together.
Crying spells	You may find yourself crying at the drop of a hat. These crying spells may be a few tears or full blown crying. Either way, it is uncomfortable and sometimes embarrassing. Family and friends may find that they have to be very careful about what they say so as not to upset the veteran. This is often very difficult as it is difficult to predict what will start a crying spell. The veteran is definitely not who they used to be and may even seem weak.	Make an effort not to make a big deal out of the crying spells. Offering support through simply being there with him or her may help (as might a tissue). Avoiding some topics may be helpful—the topics to avoid will be different for each veteran. However, it may also be hard to avoid the topics that cause the veteran to tear up simply because they may vary from day to day. Rather than "walking on egg shells," it may be more helpful to be aware of the changes in moods associated with any particular topic or situation.

(*Continued*)

Symptom	The Veteran's Experience	How Family and Friends Can Help
Persistent thoughts of death	The veteran may talk about death or things related to death and dying frequently. You may even express a wish not to wake up tomorrow or that you want to be killed in a car crash. You may begin to notice or even be drawn to movies, books, music, or discussions about death.	Perhaps the first thing to notice is whether or not the veteran is talking about taking her own life. If the veteran is talking about suicide, see the section below. If the veteran is persistently talking about or thinking about death, family and friends may turn the discussion to other topics. Avoiding the topic or reacting strongly to it may change the focus in the short term, but the veteran will likely return to the topic and may now feel worse about his tendency to think about death. If the thoughts of death are frequent, make an effort to think of something (anything) else. Trying not to think about something does not work because you have to keep it in your mind while telling yourself not to think about it.
Thoughts of suicide	The most serious consequence of depression is suicide. The depressed individual may no longer feel worthy or continuing to live, may see themselves as a burden, or may simply want the sadness, pain, and loneliness to stop. Whatever the source, the veteran is thinking of killing himself. He may share these thoughts with others or he may keep them to himself.	Not every veteran who is depressed is suicidal—nor is every suicidal veteran depressed. If you hear the veteran talking about suicide, involve a medical or mental health professional (if available) as quickly as possible. If the veteran has made suicide attempts in the past, make sure that a mental health professional is involved in the veteran's care.
	The veteran who is depressed may be frightened by these thoughts. He or she may also be comforted by these thoughts as they offer a way to stop the current suffering. The thoughts may be fleeting and contain nothing more than knowing you could end it all. Or the thoughts may be more elaborate and include a plan for how to actually do it. If you are having suicidal thoughts, contact a mental health professional immediately.	Knowing that someone is thinking about suicide can be frightening. It can be difficult to overlook such thoughts. As noted throughout this table, providing support to the veteran can make a big difference. In the event of suicidal thoughts, it is very important to tell a physician or counselor about them. You can also call 1-800-273-TALK, the national suicide hotline. It is critically important to let someone know about suicidal thoughts or if they become more frequent and more detailed. The bottom line is: Let someone know—help is available.

Problematic Thinking Styles—And How to Reframe Them

Someone with PTSD or depression—or anyone who starts to feel down—can start thinking in problematic and nonproductive ways that will increase the feelings of helplessness and can make the problems even worse, creating a "doom loop" style of thinking. If you catch yourself using any of the thinking styles listed in the table below, try to reevaluate your situation, and see if you can reframe the problem to pull yourself out of the doom loop. If you find yourself experiencing any of these thinking styles with increasing frequency or intensity, talk to a health care worker about seeing a psychologist or other professionals who can help with reframing your style of thinking.

Problematic Thinking Style	Definition and Examples
All or none	Thinking in absolutes and not recognizing the small steps in between. Watch for when you use words like "always," "never," "everyone," "nobody," and other absolute phrases.
	Examples: "I'll never be able to overcome my injury." "It always turns out the same—why bother?"
Catastrophizing	Thinking of the worst possible outcome when faced with a difficult situation.
	Examples: "Because I cannot do what I once did, my spouse will have no use for me and will leave me."
Shoulds	Sometimes a sign of unrealistic expectations and sometimes a way of discounting any effort or progress you have made.
	Examples: "I should be able to do everything the same." "I ought to be able to walk further than that by now."
Ignoring positives	Looking at the world through grey lenses. You are able to see and identify all the negative events of the day but cannot recognize or spend time thinking about the small positives.
	Examples: Ignoring the call you received form a friend, or enjoying that you got a good parking space, or acknowledging that you made progress in physical therapy.

Symptoms of Traumatic Brain Injury

Traumatic brain injury (TBI) can be difficult to diagnose because so many of the symptoms can be symptoms of PTSD, depression, and other injuries. Also, many of the symptoms may be temporary, some may disappear temporarily but reappear over time, and others may not emerge immediately but may be seen after you return home. Note that not all of these symptoms occur in everyone who has experienced a head injury—and many of these symptoms may be a result of other problems or injuries.

TBI is created by injuries involving a blow or jolt to the head or a penetrating head injury that disrupts the function of the brain. Not all blows or jolts to the head result in a TBI. The severity of such an injury may range from "mild," a brief change in mental status or consciousness, to "severe," an extended period of unconsciousness or amnesia after the injury. A TBI can result in short or long-term problems with independent function. For more information on the Web about TBI, visit the Defense and Veterans Brain Injury Center (DVBIC): http://www.dvbic.org/.

Here are some of the symptoms of TBI. If you sustained some kind of explosion to the head and regularly experience any or some of the following, ask your medical provider to provide screening for TBI and discuss your concerns with the medical provider.

- Headaches
- Dizziness
- Ringing in the ears (tinnitus)
- Double/blurred vision
- Sensitivity to noise
- Sensitivity to light
- Nausea
- Fatigue
- Physical weakness
- Disrupted sleep
- Difficulty with memory
- Difficulty with concentration
- Irritability
- Short temper
- Anxiety
- Aggressive behavior
- Depression

Physical Injuries

This is a list of the most common injuries that service members are experiencing and some of the Web-based resources that are available to provide help and assistance.

Amputations

Definition: Injuries involving the loss of a body part
Considerations:

- In a partial amputation, some soft-tissue connection remains. Depending on the severity of the injury, the partially severed extremity may or may not be able to be reattached.
- The long-term outcome for amputees has improved due to better understanding of the management of traumatic amputation, early emergency and critical care management, new surgical techniques, early rehabilitation, and new prosthetic designs. New limb replantation techniques have been moderately successful, but incomplete nerve regeneration remains a major limiting factor.

Web-based resources include:

- Amputee Coalition of America (ACA): http://www.amputee-coalition.org/

Paralysis

Definition: Total loss of use of a part of the body.
Forms of paralysis include:

- "Uniplegia": total paralysis of one lower limb or one upper limb.
- "Hemiplegia": total paralysis of the upper and lower limbs on one side of the body.
- "Paraplegia": total paralysis of both lower limbs or both upper limbs.

Web-based resources include:

- Paralyzed Veterans of America (PVA): http://www.pva.org/.

Injury to Vision

Definition: Injuries involving visual disturbances. These include blurred vision, halos, blind spots, floaters, and other symptoms. Blurred vision is the loss of sharpness of vision and the inability to see small details. The most severe form is visual loss or blindness in one or both eyes.
Web-based resources include:

- Blinded Veterans Association (BVA): http://www.bva.org/.

Substance Use Problems

Definition: Can include abuse and dependence.

- Abuse: deliberate, persistent, excessive use of a substance without regard to health concerns or accepted medical practices.
- Dependence: desire or need to continually use a substance and associated with increased tolerance and withdrawal.
- Many substances can be misused including alcohol, prescription medications, common beverages and foods, and illicit drugs.

Web-based resources include:

- National Institute of Mental Health (NIMH) Fact Sheet on Depression: http://www.nimh. nih.gov/health/topics/depression/index.shtml.
- Substance Abuse and Mental Health Administration (SAMHSA) for information on all substance use disorders: http://samhsa.gov
- Also see the table in this chapter for a detailed description of depression symptoms and the ways that family members and friends can help you with each symptom.

Burns

Definition: The diagnosis of a burn injury is based on the depth of injury. These injuries are cclassified as first, second, or third degree burns.

Web-based resources include:

- Burn Recovery Center: http://www.burn-recovery.org/.
- Burn Survivor Resource Center: http://www.burnsurvivor.com/medical.html.

Disfigurement

Definition: Condition of the body that involves having one's appearance deeply and persistently altered, such as result from scars from burns, wounds, and surgical procedures. Permanent and significant changes in the body's appearance and functional ability may change the way the person views his or her body and identity. Disfigurement can be the main medical condition or related other physical injuries (e.g., amputation, head injury).

Web-based resources include:

- Let's Face It: http://www.faceit.org/.

Pain Conditions

Definition: Pain is an unpleasant, often disabling, highly individual experience. Experiencing pain is dependent on mental functions and personal appreciation and may be accompanied by a wide variation in measurable findings of damage or dysfunction.

Pain conditions can be the main medical condition or related to other physical injuries.

Web-based resources include:

- American Pain Society: http://www.ampainsoc.org
- American Academy of Pain Management: http://www.aapainmanage.org
- International Association for the Study of Pain: http://www.iasp-pain.org
- Pain Management Guidelines: http://www.pudue.ca/links/links_guidelines.asp

Injuries Requiring Aid with Toileting

Definition: Injuries to intestinal and urinary systems (e.g., as a result of gun shots or blasts) that require aid with toileting.

The terms ostomy and stoma are general descriptive terms that are often used interchangeably though they have different meanings. An ostomy refers to the surgically created opening in the body for the discharge of body wastes. A stoma is the actual end of the ureter or small or large bowel that can be seen protruding through the abdominal wall.

Web-based resources include:

• United Ostomy Association of America (UOAA): http://www.uoaa.org

Sources used in this section

To compile this table we used the MedLine Plus Medical Encyclopedia at the National Library of Medicine at National Institute of Health (http://www.nlm. nih.gov/medlineplus/encyclopedia.html) and the Web sites listed as resources under the different medical conditions in this table.

Assistive Technologies

Here are some of the assistive technologies available for different types of disabilities. Information about other types of assistive technologies can also be found at the Job Accommodation Network at http://www.jan.wvu.edu. In addition, the Department of Defense (DoD) Computer/Electronic Accommodations Program (CAP) provides assistive technology and support to returning wounded service members in their recovery, rehabilitation, transition, and employment phases. Information about the program is available at http://www.tricare.mil/cap.

This list was compiled with help from Lt. Col. (and clinical psychologist) Mark Bates, Ph.D., of the Air Force based on material from Kratzer (2006) combined with material from Brown (2000), and publications from JAN.

Blind or Low Vision

• Screen Readers
• Scanners
• CCTV (Closed Circuit Television)
• Magnification Software
• Glare Screen
• Braille Displays
• Portable Notetakers
• Braille Embossers

Cognitive (TBI)

• Assistive Listening Devices

- Text-Based Devices
- Scanners
- Word Prediction Software
- Speech Recognition Software
- Cueing/Memory Aids
- Screen Readers
- Scanner/Readers
- Dynamic Display Devices
- Others read materials to you
- Voice mail instead of written memos
- Tape recorders
- Having additional time (or a quiet place) to process materials
- Creating a chart of important information for the wall
- Utilizing organizational and storage strategies
- Calendars and date books
- "To do" lists with tickler files (that create reminders on your computer screen)
- Beepers or cell phones with an alarm

Communication

- Word Prediction Software
- Text-Based Devices
- Dynamic Display Devices
- Voice Amplifiers
- Ask people to repeat information or write it down
- Ask questions to clarify information or the intent of the person

Deaf or Hard of Hearing

- Signaling Devices
- Video Communication Devices
- Teletypewriters (TTYs)
- PC TTYs
- Network TTY
- TTY/Voice Carry-Over Telephones
- Assistive Listening Devices
- Amplified Telephone Equipment

Dexterity

- Alternative Keyboards
- Keyboard Trays
- Alternative Pointing Devices
- Wrist Rest
- Footrest
- Monitor Riser

- Lumbar Support
- Document Holder
- Headsets/Microphones
- Telephone Headset and Handsets
- Ergonomic Chair
- Speech Recognition Speech Recognition Software and Hardware

Bibliography

Brown, D. S. (2000). *Learning a Living: A Guide to Planning Your Career and Finding a Job for People with Learning Disabilities, Attention Deficit Disorder, and Dyslexia.* Bethesda, MD: Woodbine House.

Kratzer, N. (Fall 2006). "Program Helps Wounded Return to Normal Lifestyle: Assistive Technology Provides Real Solutions for Real Needs." *FHP—The Magazine of Force Health Protection*, 1 (1), 5–19.

CHAPTER 4

The Physical and Psychological Impact of Your Injury and Disability

John W. Klocek

Editors' Comment

Your war-related injury—or the injury of your friend or family member—is going to have a big impact on everyone's lives. Each injury is going to manifest itself in many ways—both physical and psychological, both noticeable and hidden, and in ways that the veteran may not even notice or acknowledge. Many of these symptoms may not emerge immediately while others may reoccur over time. And to make matters more difficult, most veterans will return with more than one type of injury and all of these injuries have a cumulative effect, with each injury piling symptoms on top of each other, adding to the pain and the complications that can develop. Physical injuries can create psychological illnesses and psychological injuries can intensify and even lead to the development of physical maladies.

The author of this chapter, John W. Klocek, Ph.D., presents a detailed overview of some of the most common injuries of the war: loss of limb, brain injury, burns, stress, psychological disability, pain, and the psychological impact of these injuries. Each injury is explained, with attention spent on the way that the injuries can intertwine. Dr. Klocek has spent his career understanding the pain that these injuries can cause and has worked extensively with veterans and their families to help them cope with this pain through the rehabilitation process. His research focuses on pain management and integrated health care. He has been a staff psychologist in the Central Texas Health Care System and Assistant Professor at Texas A&M College of Medicine since 2005. In addition to earning his doctorate in clinical psychology from Saint Louis University and completing an internship in medicine at the University of North Carolina–Chapel Hill School of Medicine, he also served a postdoctoral fellowship in pain management at the University of Virginia Health Sciences Center.

Introduction

Returning home involves a great deal of change and adaptation. As other writers in this book have noted, nothing is ever quite the same. You may return with memories you do not really want and you may also return from the combat zone with physical injuries. These injuries may be the result of mortars, small arms fire, or improvised explosive devices (IEDs). You may be injured from falling, while performing your duties, through a motor vehicle accident, or as the result of an illness or a disease. Your injuries might be visible to others, such as burns, an amputated limb, or a skin condition. Or your injuries might be harder for others to see such as a traumatic brain injury (TBI), damage to your back, or a stress related injury such as post-traumatic stress disorder (PTSD). Whatever the type of your injury, it is something that you may find can cause a number of problems in your day-to-day life and it can also remind you of your time in the combat area which can create an additional source of stress. Your injuries might require daily care, or they may only cause problems in one specific area of your life. But no matter what type of injuries you may experience, their impact on your life can be much greater than they might initially appear.

You may have experienced "mission creep" in the service as unexpected consequences extended the length and complexity of your missions. In a similar way your injuries and disabilities can create their own form of "mission creep" as they and their impact on your life interact and multiply with each other to create additional unforeseen problems. This chapter will highlight some of these impacts on daily life that your injuries or disability may create, and provide you with some ideas and possible solutions to cope with and resolve these problems. In the course of doing so, we will describe what is known about the relationship between physical health and stress, the impact of stress on behavior, and some ideas on limiting the "mission creep" of your injuries.

Please note that the material presented in this chapter is a general discussion and is for informative purposes only. It cannot replace the careful evaluation of your condition by a physician. Any changes you notice in your physical condition should be discussed with your physician as soon as possible.

The Current Situation

Battlefield medicine has progressed throughout the decades resulting in far fewer deaths due to battlefield injuries. In fact, it is estimated that currently nine in ten battlefield injures will be survived while only seven in ten survived in Vietnam—and fewer than that survived in Korea and World War II. In addition, soldiers, marines, sailors, and airmen are asked to perform their increasingly complex duties with exceptional precision under less than ideal and highly stressful conditions for long periods of time. The result is that more and more men and women who serve their country in a time of war return to noncombat active duty stations or civilian life with injuries that affect their ability to work, play, exercise, and take care of day to day responsibilities at home.

The Veterans Administration (VA) has made an effort to track the kind of disabilities seen in veterans who return to civilian life and seek medical care at VA hospitals. The most common types of diagnoses seen at the VA as of October 2007 were related to problems with muscle tissue, connective tissue, and bones that are usually painful conditions. These types of problems are often chronic and significantly impact how well you can conduct your daily life activities. Over 44 percent of returning Operation Iraqi Freedom/Operation Enduring Freedom (OIF/OEF) veterans received a diagnosis related to these types of problems. The next most common problems seen are related to mental health diagnoses with over 38 percent of veterans receiving care for things like depression, anxiety, PTSD, and substance abuse. These types of problems also tend to be chronic and have a significant impact on daily life activities. While other chapters address topics related to mental health, the current chapter is devoted to discussing the wide ranging impacts that long term or lingering medical problems may have—and how you might best deal with those types of problems.

Injuries, Disabilities, and How They Might Impact You

Each injury affects each person differently. Most of the time, however, an injury or disability that changes what you are able to do causes stress in many areas of your life. If you happen to return with more than one injury, the combined impact of all the injuries can go far beyond what could result from each injury alone. Of course, how an injury or disability affects each person is unique. And you will find unique ways to deal with the stress and changes in your life. What follows is a discussion of some of the things that you may be experiencing as a result of your injury or disability and some ideas about how to cope with what is happening to you.

First, we cover some of the physical changes you may be experiencing, as well as some of the additional psychological problems that may result from these changes. We then turn to the impact the injury may have on how you think about yourself and how that changes your approach and interactions with the injury and your family and friends, your work, and the future. Sometimes injuries can impact your psychological well being as well. The chapter will address some of the things to watch for especially when it comes to depression and anxiety. We discuss the impact that stress can have on your physical condition. Finally, this chapter will provide a few suggestions on how to overcome some of the challenges presented by your injury or disability. As each injury or disability is as unique as the individual who experiences it, this chapter can only describe general information and suggestions. It is hoped that it can provide a general guide and starting point to adapting to the changes you are experiencing.

Physical Challenges

Any injury or disability can cause a wide range of additional physical challenges in your daily life. Some of the most common injuries faced by veterans who served in Iraq and Afghanistan include the loss of a limb or appendage, an injury to the brain as the result of a blast or motor vehicle injury, burns and other skin conditions, stress related problems, and pain which persists for a long period of time as a result of any of the above injuries.

Loss of a Limb

An unfortunately common injury seen in OIF/OEF veterans is the loss of a leg, part of a leg, an arm, a hand, or other appendage. There is perhaps no more powerful daily reminder of the price of service than an injury like this. There have been many advances in prosthetics, and many injured veterans are able to use artificial legs to walk, arms to grab or lift, or to simply develop new ways of doing things that compensate for a missing limb. But while medical and technological advances have made a difference for many veterans, not everybody is able to return to the life they had before the injury. In fact, even for those who have found success through the use of prosthetics, using these prosthetics can be both painful and disturbing to the person using them.

The loss of a limb or appendage may change how you can perform every task. Suddenly, the simple act of getting out of bed, putting on a shirt, hammering a nail, or picking up your child becomes a real challenge. The potential for additional injury as a result of strains, pulls, or breaks occurring while trying to do what you used to do prior to your injury without difficulty is higher. Should you be facing the use of a new prosthesis to replace a leg, arm, or hand, there is the daunting challenge of how to use it. Using a prosthetic limb requires careful training and attention to detail. It also typically results in changes to how you walk, lift, hold, twist, and perform other actions. For example, the use of a prosthetic leg may change how you walk and place you at risk for hurting your back. If you walk quite differently than you did—say holding up one side of your back more than the other—you may strain the other parts of your back in a way that results in stiffness, tightness, and soreness in your back. This, in turn, may cause you to do less practice or exercise with the new limb that can then begin to contribute to deconditioning and losing strength in the limbs. More than just being "out of shape," deconditioning means that you have used your muscles so little that they have trouble just supporting you and may have even begun to atrophy. Being deconditioned makes it very difficult to get around to do anything and can result in less and less interaction with others and less and less activity.

Many veterans have trouble trusting their new prosthetic limbs and may be reluctant to actually use them. Surprisingly, this is likely to result in less practice with the new limb and less skill using the new prosthetic. This can sometimes lead to additional injury as a result of a fall or near fall when going somewhere new or difficult. Sometimes, veterans expect the new limb or prosthesis to be just as good as what it is replacing and then quickly become discouraged or angered when it is not. This can be a discouraging process and one that takes patience, persistence, and tolerance for pain—not to mention a great deal of guidance and assistance.

Physical therapy after getting a new prosthesis is extremely important in preventing further injury to other parts of your body. The physical therapists and people who fit your prosthesis are experts in helping you to figure out how to use your new device and how to minimize the risk of further injury. Physical therapists can also help you to better understand your body's sensations and reactions to the prosthesis. And through your physical therapy appointments and interactions with fellow veterans, you may also have the opportunity to meet other individuals who are fighting battles similar to yours. Do not hesitate to ask your fellow veterans to share what they have learned already. Many veterans probably have a long list of "I wish I would have knowns" that they will be able to share with you. And it certainly will not hurt to check-in with the experts in prosthetics and physical therapy a few months down the road after you work with them initially to see if anything has changed or if they have suggestions for continued improvement. If you have just left the military, or have just moved to a new area, ask your VA primary care physician about seeing a physical therapist at your medical center or clinic. If you are working with non-VA medical folks, you can also ask your primary care doctor about how you can make contact (or get a referral) to physical therapy. You can also, of course, seek out physical therapists in your community by looking in the phone book. It is helpful however, to learn if they have experience in treating people with your condition. Again, your physician—and sometimes your friends and family—can help you make a decision about who to see.

Brain Injury

If you have been close to a blast or involved in a motor vehicle accident during which you took a hard blow to the head, were knocked unconscious, or had your "bell rung" by a blow to the head that left you stunned or dazed, you may have suffered a brain injury. The terms sometimes used for these injuries are "mild brain injury," "closed head injury," or "mild traumatic brain injury." You may also have been told that you suffered a concussion. Again, each of these terms refers to an injury to the brain as a result of a blow to the head. Most of the time (70–80 percent), the symptoms you experience as a result of a mild brain injury resolve within a few weeks. Problems that result from a brain injury that last longer than six months can be considered chronic. Somewhere between 10 percent and 30 percent of individuals who experience a mild brain injury have long-term problems as a result of their injury. This kind of injury is both difficult to diagnose or identify, and difficult to deal with in the long term.

Physically, a brain injury is hard to see. Most of the time, there is no visible injury to the head—only a gradual realization that something is not quite right. The things you may notice first are problems with memory or concentration. Actually, others may notice this first! Family members may find themselves saying

"I already told you that" or "Did you do what I asked?" or "Are you listening to me?" on a regular basis. You may be surprised by their frustration or you may be just as frustrated as your family and friends. Your friends and family see you everyday (and knew you before the injury) and they are often the first ones to see you enough to recognize that something is wrong. At times others may even tell you that you are different—that your personality has changed, or that you are more irritable or say things you normally would never say to others. Because it can cause frustration and even conflict, it can be hard to see beyond the trouble the brain injury is causing or the arguments that ensue because of the conflicts, missed appointments, forgotten conversations, or "in one ear, out the other" moments you might be experiencing with them. You might want to let those times when things do not seem right or when others express frustration to be a sign that you may be having difficulties. Other signs that you may have a brain injury are symptoms and sensations that might be occurring. You may be experiencing headaches, dizziness, ringing in the ears (tinnitus), blurred or double vision, sensitivity to light and/or sound, nausea, and fatigue. You may find you're having difficulty sleeping or even find you are experiencing weakness. If you were knocked unconscious during your injury, you are more likely to experience more of the above symptoms.

A brain injury can affect your health in a wide range of ways. While it may not be something that you think of as having a direct impact on your health, the problems that a brain injury causes may make it difficult for you to follow up on medical appointments or to follow through with rehabilitation assignments. For example, if you are having difficulty with headaches and fatigue, you may decide that you really do not feel like keeping up with basic exercise. This can result in a series of health problems such as weight gain, increases in blood pressure, or increases in cholesterol levels. Problems with dizziness or your vision may result in falls or accidents that can cause new injuries or make old injuries worse. Research has found that people who experience a mild brain injury are at increased risk for suffering another brain or other physical injury. It appears that each injury to the brain lowers the amount of impact that will result in the next brain injury. That is why you sometimes see hockey or football players retiring from their sport as a result of too many concussions.

In some cases, a head injury can even result in the loss of your job. With all the symptoms described above, your performance at work may not be what it used to be, or what it needs to be. It can be tough to explain to family or friends why you can no longer concentrate or remember simple things like conversations or important dates—especially if you are not even sure why these things are happening to you. If sleep or headaches are problems, you may miss enough work that your employer finally says they have had enough and have to let you go. It is not clear to you or to others why you might not be able to do these things, only that you are not meeting the standard at your workplace. This can be both frightening and discouraging. While the Americans with Disabilities Act provides some protection for individuals with disabilities, it also permits employers to only extend "reasonable accommodations" to help you perform your job. If memory loss or other reductions in your mental functioning are impacting the work that you can perform, your employer may be legally able to fire you. If you are noticing these kinds of problems it may be a good time to ask that you be screened for a brain injury if you have suffered one or more serious blows to the head. You can also contact the Job Accommodation Network by phone at (800) 526-7234 or on the Web at http://www.jan.wvu.edu. Chapter 6 of this book and the Web page for this book (http://www.warswounded.com) has more information about locating and maintaining employment with a disability.

At this time, the treatment for long-term problems related to a head injury focus primarily on coping with the problems that a brain injury could cause. These interventions include education and support in coping with the frustrations, changes, and daily challenges encountered when experiencing the symptoms listed above on a daily basis. The treatment can also focus on the feelings of depression or anxiety that arise as a result of the frustrations and changes caused by a head injury. Research has also indicated that some antidepressants can be helpful in reducing irritability, depression, and headaches. If you find yourself experiencing the kinds of problems listed above, it is extremely important that you obtain an evaluation by medical professionals familiar with head injuries and the problems they can cause. Your local VA center will have these types of professionals and can provide referrals to places close to your home. When visiting these professionals, you need to be willing to listen carefully to their recommendations and follow their suggestions. You will also need to marshal the support of those around you in coping with the problems that arise as a result of a brain injury. Your friends and family can provide support, guidance, and help in recovering from the brain injury. As those who spend the most time with you, your friends and family can assist the rehabilitation team in taking the suggestions and activities developed in a treatment setting and moving them into your daily life. It is not a matter of just being strong enough to overcome a brain injury: you must be strong enough to begin to accept the change you have experienced and the commitment to live the life you want to live in the context of those changes.

Burns

Many veterans returning from combat will have experienced burns that have permanently altered how they look and how they feel. These kinds of injuries are among the most visible of injuries and can have a strong impact on how you look at or think about yourself. Burns can also cause additional health problems through reduced ability for the skin to fight off disease or infection, reduced ability to tolerate exposure to the sun, or the need for continued treatment and correction of ongoing problems.

Burns are described in three stages: *First degree burns* affect only the surface skin. They are red and sensitive to the touch, but with no blisters,

Second degree burns affect deeper skin layers and often leading to blistering with increased sensitivity.

Third degree burns are the most intense with all skin layers affected. The skin may be white or charred and if skin is destroyed skin grafts may be necessary. The treatment for the severest of burns is very painful and typically requires hospitalization. Afterward, a person's appearance may be very different and they may have difficulty with touch or withstanding hot or cold temperatures. It may also include the need to use antibiotics for a period of time since you may be vulnerable to infections.

Problems from severe burns can complicate additional medical challenges you might face over the long term such as making it much more uncomfortable or painful to engage in physical therapy for an injury. If you are worried about how others will look at you as a result of your changed appearance, you may also be less willing to attend medical or physical therapy appointments that are important for your overall health. If you have suffered both a severe burn and the loss of a limb or appendage, the burn may make it that much more difficult to use or control a prosthetic. Additional modification of the physical therapy program or specific manner in which a prosthetic is controlled may need to be modified. Again, the importance of following through with medical care and follow-up treatment programs cannot be emphasized enough.

Stress/Psychological Disability

Being in combat or in a combat zone for a long period of time can result in a disability that is psychological in nature such as PTSD. These disabilities are among those disorders that are not easy for others to see, but are among those that can cause the most problems in the most areas of your life. Problems caused by stress-related disability can be seen in decreased overall health, increased difficulty in managing other disabilities, and problems with work, family, and social life. Chapter 3 of this book contains detailed descriptions of the symptoms of PTSD and depression.

The consequences of stress-related disability on other physical conditions has been well documented through research. Both anxiety and depression are known to have a negative effect on compliance with medical treatments and recommendations, motivation, optimism about the future, and interest in being around others. Changes in these areas of your life can result in your being less able or willing to complete a course of treatment for your injury or to cope with the unique stressors that this kind of disability or an injury can create in your life.

In addition to potentially impacting how you manage an ongoing injury or disability, stress reactions may have their own unique, negative impact on your physical life. For example, we know that stress reactions and depression alike have strong physical components. Stressful situations, for example, can bring on the fight-or-flight response. This response can be especially strong in situations where the outcome is uncertain and which may involve physical injury or death.

Emotionally, we will often feel anxiety, fear, and anger. Physically, the body will release more cortisol, endorphins, and epinephrine—all of which help the body to respond more quickly and with greater strength. While this kind of reaction is useful in a stressful situation (such as when you were in the war zone) since it kept you alert and able to move quickly, it is counterproductive to your health if your mind and body activate it when you are trying to sleep at night at home.

When you experience anxiety, your nervous system responds in a way that looks much like the way it responds while you are exercising, helping the body move from storing energy to using it to respond to a threatening situation. Repeated activation of this system can begin to wear on an individual physically as well as mentally. The impact of long-term stress and frequent stress reactions can be seen physically in such problems as a weakened immune system and negative changes in cardiovascular health. Research in this area has begun to shine a light on the importance of the interaction between the mind and the body in dealing with chronic stress, injury, or disability of any type.

A veteran's health may also be impacted by how you do cope with the distress related to service in Iraq or Afghanistan. One way that some people cope with distress caused by PTSD, depression, or other stress-related disorders is through drinking excessively, smoking more heavily, using drugs, or engaging in fights, and fast driving or other "excitement-seeking" behaviors. These kinds of responses may help you to forget your problems for a while—or they may be a result of impulsive behavior made worse by high levels of frustration and anger. While there are a number of physical and psychological reasons why people find themselves responding to stress with these kinds of behaviors, our focus is to discuss the possible additive impact that these behaviors may have for a veteran who is already injured or disabled. The negative impact of those behaviors that result in additional injury to the veteran is obvious. However, these behaviors may make other injuries worse through a lack of medical compliance, the countering or diluting of the therapeutic effect of medications by drugs, tobacco, or alcohol, or a reduced capacity for exercise or endurance related to smoking.

Obviously, any one of these activities listed above has the potential to negatively impact your overall health. Whether it is the injuries related to a high-speed car accident, a reduction in the physical strength and resources needed to get through the day-to-day due to excessive drinking, or the physical (and possibly legal) consequences related to a particularly serious road-rage incident, ongoing psychological distress can be as challenging to cope with as the physical changes you experience as a result of injury or disability.

Pain

Injuries that result in chronic pain are another type of injury frequently seen in veterans of OIF/OEF. The pain may be as a result of an injury to an arm or a leg. It may be the pain that persists after a back or neck injury sustained in a vehicle accident, fall, or blast. Some veterans will experience phantom pain—the very real perception of pain in a limb or appendage that has been amputated. Whatever the source of the pain, it can be one of the most debilitating problems faced by anyone. Pain has a way of impacting everything that you do. It may result in you changing how you do the most simple of actions—like sitting down, opening a door, or tying your shoes. If simply putting on your shoes and sitting down in the car causes a great deal more pain, then you are less likely to be interested in, much less motivated to, get out and do much of anything. If the pain is added on top of another medical condition, that reluctance to do much of anything can change how closely you follow medical recommendations or if you continue to exercise as part of a treatment plan.

You may find yourself "compensating" for the pain—sitting or walking differently than you did—which can cause additional pain or even a new injury. For example, the veteran who has experienced a significant knee injury as the result of a Humvee rollover may compensate by favoring that injured knee while walking, thus putting added strain on the other side and placing that knee at increased risk for injury. Or, if you have suffered a back injury in addition to the loss of the lower part of your leg, you may find that it is extremely difficult to follow the physical therapist's recommendation for the correct use of the prosthesis. That may mean less use of the new device, or use that results in increased pain in other parts of your body.

Pain can also result in your doing less activity. In addition to difficulty following through with recommended treatments for other injuries or problems, you may even become inactive enough to actually cause additional health problems related to deconditioning and weight gain. Your inability to be active may also result in job loss or significant conflict in the home as a result of changes in what you can and can no longer do on the job or at home. As someone who is used to being very active, working hard, and supporting yourself and your family, pain can change how you look at yourself. It can make you wonder what good you are to those around you—or even yourself. Pain also has a way of stealing hope and optimism and may make ongoing medical problems and treatments seem endless or hopeless. In fact, any one of the medical challenges discussed previously can challenge how you look at (and feel about) yourself.

Sex

Something else that may be a problem is sex. Many veterans with physical disabilities or high levels of stress find that they have difficulty having sex because of pain, anxiety, feeling self-conscious about an injury, or simply feeling like nothing is the same—including their relationship. Sometimes they find that their body just does not respond the same way—even when you really want to have sex. This can be embarrassing and frustrating for both the veteran and the partner.

There can be many different reasons that cause problems with sex. As described above, it can be a physical difficulty or it can be a psychological difficulty that interferes with your ability to enjoy sex. A first step can be to talk with your physician or mental health provider about the problem. They will have some suggestions depending on what seems to be the reason for the problem. For example, if having sex causes your back pain to flare up, your physician may be able to help by referring you to a physical therapist who can recommend different ways to enjoy sex that will cause the least amount of pain. If a chronic medical condition is causing erectile dysfunction or impotence, your physician may be able to prescribe medications that can help. If the problems seem to be that you no longer feel connected to your partner—that everything is different and you are no longer the same, your mental health provider may be able to help. If anxiety or depression has taken your desire to have sex away from you, both your physician and your mental health provider may be able to help by collaborating to treat the anxiety or depression.

Sex is an important part of a relationship. Problems with sex are also pretty common. When it changes, it can have a big impact on the relationship. However, people can sometimes be embarrassed about talking about sex. This is especially true when there is a problem with sex. Often, a couple will not talk about a problem with sex until it has become a source of frustration or anger. It is best to try and talk about it sooner—before it becomes an argument. That is not to say that every little change in how things go in bed should be the topic of discussion—that can put too much pressure on each of you. But if you are both noticing a consistent change in the role sex plays in your relationship or your ability to have sex, it is worth talking about with each other and with your medical and mental health providers. As with so many other topics addressed here, patience and communication can go a long way to addressing the problem.

Impact on Self and Others

The physical challenges that accompany injury and disability may change your life and even create additional medical problems. Throughout your military career you have been taught that you can overcome anything but now you may find yourself in a situation that challenges that training. It may even seem that no matter what you do, you are just not the same person. Anytime that you are not able to do what you once did you may become frustrated and discouraged. In fact, you may even begin to wonder who you are or even what good you are to anyone. You may again try to do something that you were not able to do because of your injury—only to find out that you still are unable to do that task. Or you may find that you cannot return to the kind of job you used to have because of your disability. As someone who was trained to overcome adversity—to live by the motto "no pain, no gain"—the fact that an injury may cause significant trouble in many areas of your life may have you questioning your own toughness. How you view yourself has a very strong impact on how you cope with the changes you face. But as great a challenge these physical challenges can be, the psychological battle to accept the new you may be even more difficult—if only because it is a battle that is harder to see, harder to explain, and harder to ask for help.

For example, even though you are able to get used to your new limb or appendage, you find that removing the device each night and putting it on in the morning is a constant reminder of what you went through and how much things have changed. This can lead to thoughts along the lines of "I am not the person I was before" or "I am damaged and not as good as I was before my injury." Even if the change is not quite as obvious, for example, you may still find that you miss your index finger more than you thought you would whenever you try to play catch. This may lead to thoughts like "What good am I if I can't teach my boy to play ball?" The married veteran who returns from war with a visible burn injury may wonder, "Who would want be around someone who looks like me—much less love someone who looks like me?" You may wonder why anyone would put up with the emotional outbursts and forgetfulness that seem so common following a brain injury. During those quiet moments you may find yourself thinking that you are not someone who is pleasant to be around or someone that your friends want to have around—and you may start to wonder about why you subject others to what you have become. You might even wonder what good you are if you are unable to hold a job that provides well for your family. Many men strongly believe that they are only as good as their ability to provide for their family since "a man who does not work is not a man." Women also place a great deal of their self-worth in their ability to care for and support others. Suddenly finding that you are unable to do these things can be devastating and can lead to thoughts like "I am worthless" or "I am a burden." Any one of the above thoughts is not only common, but can be a real barrier to returning to a somewhat normal life. These types of thoughts can even lead to thoughts of committing suicide.

Some veterans may also begin to experience a great deal of frustration related to the reactions received from others. Many individuals who use prosthetics, wheelchairs or other assistive devices experience stares, questions, and being treated like a fragile object by others. It is important to let those around you know your preferences of how you would like to be treated. Some people who have lost a limb do not mind discussing how it happened or how their life has changed since the injury. Others prefer that nothing be said about it—and more importantly, that no special treatment be offered as a result of the injury. Taking in the idea that your new assistive device or visible reminder of time spent in a war zone is now a part of your life is difficult. Helping others to understand how best to relate to the new you may be just as difficult, but just as important.

Thoughts about injuries have their impact in an even less obvious way than other chronic injuries or problems. In fact, they sometimes have an impact without the person even knowing about the impact. For example, a veteran thinking that nobody would want to be around him because of his burn injury could lose his motivation to care for himself or for his injury, leading to additional medical complications. He may begin to withdraw from his wife by thinking that she does not want to be around him and then stay away from the rest of his family. He may even feel that it is for the better that she does not have to be around him in the future. The veteran is unlikely to ever say this to anyone. Rather, he is more likely to simply avoid being around his loved ones and find excuses to push them away. His wife (and family) is left to wonder why they are unable to get through and why the veteran has seemingly given up on caring for himself or for them. The additional stress related to family problems only serves to confirm the veteran's belief that his injury or disability is a permanent problem that is unlikely to get better and that he is a burden to those around him.

The veteran with a chronic back problem who suddenly believes that she is worthless because she can no longer do the same job she was able to before her injury may also begin to see additional complications as a result of this self-image. Rather than continue to try and follow a long course of rehabilitation and training to begin the pursuit of a different line of employment, she may simply believe that she is not worthy of such attention. As a result, she stops following through on care for her back and a number of additional complications can result. As you can see, the change in how you view yourself can impact those around you, what you do, and even what you try to do.

The challenge of dealing with something over which you may have little control is a tremendous challenge. That belief that you can face any challenge and succeed will certainly serve you well here. The first task is to accurately identify the challenge. You are already well aware of the physical challenge you face—identifying how you view yourself as a challenge is much more difficult. One way to do that is to notice your own feelings as you approach a situation like finding a new job or facing the challenge of rehab. Notice your feelings as you return home to your family, friends, and other loved ones. If you find that you are already feeling defeated or sad in the face of the challenge; if you find that you are regularly sad, withdrawn or even numb when you are around family or loved ones, or if you feel like you are undeserving of the attention given to you by health care staff, take a moment to see if you can identify the thoughts you are having about yourself in that situation. Ask yourself if you think you are worthy, capable, or deserving. If you get an answer to these questions that you do not like, the battle to maintain your health may also include work on how the injury or disability has changed how you think. The way you are thinking about your injury or disability and how you are thinking about yourself can either help you meet the challenge of change or make it much more difficult. How you think about your injury will have a direct impact on what you will be able to do or not be able to do in the future.

If those thoughts are indeed part of the problem, there are a large number of resources you can access. This book and its Web site at http://www.warswounded. com are a great place to start. Do not hesitate to ask for assistance in fighting this part of the battle—it is much more than a matter of simply "thinking happy thoughts" in the same way that overcoming memory deficits caused by a brain injury is much more than "just try harder to remember." It is helpful to have some assistance in identifying your views that are interfering with your ability to overcome the challenges presented by your injury or disability. In addition, you can begin to observe how your thinking might be working against your efforts to cope with the challenges of an injury or disability. In chapter three we list of some of the most common styles of thinking that can result in a change in how you think of yourself following a disabling injury. While most of us experience these styles of thinking to some degree in some areas of our life, they can be a problem if they remain strong and you remain focused on your self-worth. Some of these beliefs can be challenged simply by asking those around you if they are true. Others may require you to actually try something out to see if your prediction (such as "I'll never make any progress toward being able to use that artificial leg") actually holds up. ("Never," by the way, is a pretty strong word.) There are a large number of self-help guides that can provide additional assistance in working on these types of challenges such as *The Pain Survival Guide* by Turk & Winter or *Managing Pain Before it Manages You* by Caudill—both of which are available through your local bookstore or online. Even though each of these self-help guides is focused on pain, they can provide information and assistance in coping with a number of other challenges faced by those with a chronic injury or disability.

What's Needed for What's Next

Research has also begun to identify the importance of developing some level of acceptance of your current situation. That is not to say that you must accept where you are in your life right at this moment, but rather that you are able to accept that things are different and you may indeed be unable to do some of the things you might have taken for granted. It may be that the rules have changed and that these new rules shape what is realistic for you for the future. Your own values will guide you to where you place your energy in maintaining your health and returning to a normal life. An additional recommendation is to carefully examine your expectations about where you really want to be in the future. Identify what is important and how you might be able to attain that—and what resources you need in your quest to maintain your health and well being in the face of injury or disability.

Psychological Impact

When left unchecked, the stress and distress related to injury and disability can lead to depression or anxiety. Other reactions to the injury can cause problems as well. We often throw around the term "denial" in day-to-day life when describing people who do not seem to recognize they have a problem. It was a term initially used to identify people who literally were not aware that something was wrong but today we use it to describe people who might have an awareness of there being something different or difficult in their lives but are unwilling to change how they have done things in the past. Instead, they spend a great deal of energy "fighting through" the problems they are experiencing, stubbornly insisting that they can do everything the same way. A common thinking pattern here is the "all-or-none" thinking style that "either I can do it the same way as I used to or not at all." Acknowledging that something is different is not the same as giving up or giving in. It is at times a necessary step in developing a new approach to regaining as much of your life as is possible—recognizing that you still have much you can and will do, but it may happen differently. Toughing it out or fighting it through a stubborn insistence that nothing has changed will likely lead to additional frustration, anger, and even resignation. These in turn, often contribute to depression and a feeling of helplessness—and will push you toward the "none" end of the all-or-none spectrum. The strength is not in being able to do everything and do everything perfectly; the strength is in persisting in the face of challenge, change, and pain to do what is possible (and sometimes even a bit more).

Depression is much more than feeling sad or blue. Everyone experiences ups and downs in the course of their life. Common symptoms of depression are listed in a table in Chapter 3. If you find that you are experiencing a number of these problems and they are interfering with your ability to get through the day, talk to your physician or request an evaluation for mental health services. Depression is a significant barrier to your being able to do what you need to do to maintain your health and to get to a level of functioning that you are capable of achieving. Often times overcoming depression requires some assistance. Medications can help lift the feelings of sadness, fatigue, and hopelessness while psychotherapy can provide you with tools you can use to both overcome depression as well as fight it off should you find yourself feeling the same way in the future.

Chapter 3 has a list of the symptoms of depression. If you believe that you are experiencing these symptoms, speak with your family and friends about them—the third column of the table lists the ways that your friends and family can help you—and if you believe they are severe please speak with a professional who can help you with these issues.

At times you may even find that you are unable to see the point of going on. The pain is too great, the changes too much to overcome, the role you used to have in the family is forever changed so that you will never be the person you were or want to be. You may come to the point where you are considering suicide. It may simply be the thought that you would not mind if you did not wake up one morning. It may be a brief thought while driving: "What if I were to simply drive into that bridge. All this would be over." It may be more direct: "I am such a burden and I will never be myself again. I have a gun in the closet. It would be over quickly." While most people (research suggests as many as 90 percent) experience suicidal thoughts during their lifetimes, the presence of stress, distress, physical injury/disability, and other consequences of serving in a combat zone place you at higher risk for following through on these thoughts. While at times these thoughts are passing thoughts with no real intent tied to them, others are more serious, more persistent, more detailed. If physical injuries or disability have changed your outlook on life to the degree that you are considering ending your life, it is critical that you seek assistance immediately. Though you may be frightened or ashamed of these thoughts, your physician or therapist will know how to find help for you. If you are worried that you may act immediately on these thoughts, call 911, a local crisis hotline, or the national crisis hotline 1-800-SUICIDE

(1-800-784-2433) or 1-800-273-TALK (1-800-273-8255) and let them know what is happening. The urge to hurt yourself is very powerful, often very scary, but is also something that is treatable.

Anxiety can also significantly interfere with your ability to cope with and manage a physical injury or disability. This anxiety can range from concerns about how others will react to you to anxiety that engaging in physical therapy will cause additional injury or pain. Whatever the focus of that anxiety, it is likely to keep you from doing what you need to do in the face of that injury. For example, the veteran who must now use a wheelchair to get around may be worried that others will treat him as less than a whole person or a burden when he returns to work. As a result, he may decide that it is not really worth it to return to his previous place of employment—or that it would be just as easy to not exercise with the chair enough to be able to have the endurance for an all day trip outside the house. Similarly, a veteran who experiences additional pain as a result of physical therapy for a back injury may decide that this pain reflects additional damage or injury and decide that any activity which results in pain is bad. Not surprisingly, he may be unwilling to attend the physical therapy that is necessary for recovery or to work hard enough to make any progress in therapy.

In each of these scenarios, the anxiety will result in additional problems, complications, and potentially additional injuries. Anxiety is also something that is quite natural and, should it interfere with your day-to-day life, can be quite treatable. One way to begin to challenge the anxiety is to try to understand the specific reason for the anxiety. Is it a worry that you can test? For example, is asking if the assistance you need in opening doors too much trouble for others to tolerate? Is it a worry that you can seek additional information about to find the answer? You can ask the physical therapists if the pain you are experiencing after the therapy sessions signals a new injury. If you find that the anxiety continues to cause problems—or that easing those worries is not as simple as asking those questions, speak to a health professional about treatments for anxiety.

Meet the Challenge with a Team

As has been implied in a number of the previous sections, stress is something that can make physical disability worse—or even cause additional disability. It can be a vicious cycle. Injury or disability can cause stress through the challenge of coping with your not being the same person, difficulties in supporting your family, or pain. Stress can also cause injury and additional disability by interfering with your ability to follow through on medical recommendations and treatments, making choices that place you at risk for additional injury, or by leading to levels of depression or anxiety that cause additional disability. The increased disability which results can then worsen the stress you are experiencing and create another viscous circle. Coping with injury and disability is not for the faint of heart. All the strength you have demonstrated in your service to the country will be necessary in overcoming that challenges you now face. Just as you relied on the other members of your unit to overcome obstacles, you will likely need to rely on family, friends, and health care workers to form your new unit that will help you in overcoming the challenges you now face. If you are not sure how to do this, enlist the services of a behavioral health consultant who can help coordinate that team. Strength lies not in going it alone, but in identifying and gathering a team around you that can help you work toward what is important to you.

CHAPTER 5

Fitness for Duty, Recovery, and Return to Service

*Mark J. Bates, Stephen V. Bowles,
Jocelyn A. Kilgore, and Lionel P. Solursh*

Editors' Comment

Once you are injured in combat, going from being an active soldier to a patient recovering in a medical hospital is not an easy process. In the past, the assumption was made that with a major injury, your career in the military was over, whether you liked it or not. Today, however, with advances in prostheses and accommodation technology and changes in opinions and attitudes, service members with disabilities can return to active duty and continue to serve our nation even with missing limbs or other injuries.

This chapter takes you through these steps. It begins with a description of how an injury may impact veterans and their family members, then it explores options available, and describes the challenges you may face in the military as you go through this process. The chapter offers you practical advice and suggestions on how to stay organized and persevere through these steps as it lists the people and resources that you can utilize to help you through all the steps. Finally, if you are interested in remaining in the service, the chapter describes the ways that you can do this. Because each branch of the armed forces uses different terminology and has unique steps, processes, and programs, specific details about each branch are provided.

The authors of this chapter have assembled useful information in one easy-to-read format. Mark J. Bates, Ph.D., assembled a team of active duty military psychologists who work with and treat service members in all of the military's branches. As this work was compiled by military and VA personnel, it is expected that much of the extensive material assembled in this chapter will be used by the Uniformed Services University of the Health Sciences (the military's medical school) training programs for military psychologists. Dr. Bates is a licensed clinical psychologist and an active duty Lieutenant Colonel in the United States Air Force (AF). He is currently

the Training Director at one of the three AF clinical psychology intern-
ship programs at the Malcolm Grow Medical Center located at the Andrews
Air Force Base in Maryland. The other authors are: Stephen V. Bowles,
Ph.D., a licensed clinical psychologist and active duty Lieutenant Colonel
in the United States Army and Assistant Professor and Director, Division of
Military Psychology and Leadership at the Uniformed Services University
Health Sciences F. Edward Hébert School of Medicine. He also served as
Joint Task Force Command Psychologist in Iraq and as the Interim Chief
and Deputy Chief at Walter Reed Army Medical Center. Jocelyn A. Kilgore,
M.D., is a board certified psychiatrist and an active duty Major in the United
States Air Force currently assigned to the Department of Psychiatry and the
Center for the Study of Traumatic Stress at the Uniformed Services Univer-
sity of the Health Sciences F. Edward Hébert School of Medicine. Lionel
P. Solursh, M.D., PPsych, is a board certified Internist/Psychiatrist who has
authored forty-four papers in professional journals, twelve books or book
chapters, and numerous other materials. He works with the Mental Health-
PTSD team at the VA Medical Center in Augusta, Georgia, and is also a
Professor of Psychiatry at the Medical College of Georgia.

Introduction

Service members who return from the Operation Iraqi Freedom (OIF) and Operation Enduring Freedom (OEF) combat environment, as well their loved ones
and their communities, face complex decisions when considering their future.
The reintegration process can be especially challenging for members who are recovering from significant physical and/or mental injuries. These injuries can take
many forms, but they all can have a significant impact on the lives of the individual and the family members, friends, counselors, and members of the community
who must learn to cope with them and adapt with the changes associated with
the injuries.

Unlike in the past, there are increasing opportunities for service members to
continue military service, aided by advances in medical technology, increasing
emphasis on rehabilitation, and supportive views by the military leadership. This
chapter is a guide for injured service members who are either thinking about continuing military service or are in the process of returning to duty. It is written for
service members and their family members, unit members, medical staff, and others who support them. The guide is organized into sections that describe different
parts of the recovery and return to service process. Each section is introduced by
a question and includes information and coping tips. The following questions are
answered in this chapter:

1. What are my options after being injured?
2. What are the different types of injuries?

3. What are common stressors when recovering from an injury?
4. What types of services are available to help?
5. Who is available to help me with the recovery process?
6. How do I make sure that I get adequate medical care?
7. Am I having a "normal" (common and understandable) response?
8. What are some common steps in the recovery process?
9. What are some general coping strategies?
10. What are some ways to decide about continuing military service, and to feel satisfied with those decisions?
11. How does the medical fitness for duty process work?
12. What are some potential family issues?
13. What are potential long-term adjustment issues and how are they affected by returning to duty?

What Are My Options After Being Injured?

There are increasing opportunities for injured service members to continue military service for many reasons. These reasons include support from civilian and military leadership, advances in medical technology, and an increasing emphasis on rehabilitation.

President Bush told injured soldiers at Walter Reed in 2003: "Americans would be surprised to learn that a grievous injury, such as the loss of a limb, no longer means forced discharge. In other words, the medical care is so good and the recovery process is so technologically advanced that people are no longer forced out of the military . . . When we're talking about forced discharge, we're talking about another age and another army. This is a new age, and this is a new army. Today, if wounded service members want to remain in uniform and can do the job, the military tries to help them stay" (Miles, 2007). The general view is that injured service members who want to stay on active duty should be able to stay and do work within their capabilities in available jobs.

Advances in medical technology, like prostheses (artificial limbs), are enabling injured members to recover more capabilities and to continue to perform military duties (Kratzer, 2006). The medical services are also offering improved rehabilitation services to help service members become more familiar with these medical technologies and adapt to any functional issues. As SGT Steve Clark (U.S. Army retired), OIF amputee, currently Department of Defense (DoD) program analyst, points out, "After being wounded, one of the best things I did was realize that I couldn't do it myself and reached out for help."

Injured service members have several possible options for continuing service after an injury. The options largely depend on the individual's ability to satisfactorily perform the original or alternate military specialties. Military specialties have different titles in each service:

Army: Military Occupational Specialty (MOS)
Navy: Navy Enlisted Classification (NEC) or Designator (for officers)

Air Force: Air Force Specialty Code (AFSC)
Marines: Military Occupational Specialty (MOS)

The options for return to military service include:

1. Returning *to same duty position*. Please note that "return to duty" in the army means specifically returning to the same MOS.
2. Reclassifying *into another duty position*. The recommendation to reclassify is made by a MOS/Medical Retention Board (MMRB) in the Army. The MMRB is an administrative screening board that determines the ability of an individual to perform the duties of your military job satisfactorily.
3. Being *temporarily put in a nondeployable status*. Nondeployable status can be used on a temporary basis for continued treatment and reassessment.

If a person's functioning is impacted to the point that they may not be able to return to duty, a Medical Evaluation Board (MEB) will be conducted to assess suitability for duty.

What Are the Different Types of Injuries?

The recovery process will be different for each individual—no two service members will have the same injury or recovery process. As one service member we interviewed commented: "No two service members will have the same injury because there are many factors that affect each service member's unique situation." Service members can be recovering from a variety of physical and mental conditions. Also, there are many factors that can affect a service member's injury. For example, these injuries can have different levels of severity and impact on functioning. Service members can also be recovering from several of these injuries at once. In addition, other factors from each service member's life can have a big impact on the injury. Therefore, it is not possible to describe exactly how things will go for recovery and return to service for any particular injury.

However, it is possible to describe common adjustment, recovery, and reintegration issues for injured service members. Understanding these issues can help you have some idea of what to expect and how to make the most out of available resources.

Some of the more common types of injuries include amputations, paralysis, injury to vision, traumatic brain injury (TBI), post-traumatic stress disorder (PTSD), other mental health disorders, burns, disfigurement, pain conditions, and injuries requiring aid with toileting. Please note that your type of injury may not be listed in this chapter but the adjustment issues and advice in this chapter would still apply to your situation. For example, it is common for changes in mood to follow combat service that do not meet full criteria for the diagnosis of PTSD. The list in Chapter 3 contains brief descriptions of these "injury categories" and Web-based resources for each condition, while the list after it is a set of assistive technology that is available through the DoD Computer/Electronic Accommodations Program (CAP), which provides assistive technology and support to returning wounded service members in their recovery, rehabilitation, transition, and employment phases. Further information about CAP is available at http://www.tricare.mil/cap/.

What Are the Common Stressors When Recovering from an Injury?

The injured service member faces many possible stressors and adjustment issues. Here is a list of many of the potential issues you may face. The rest of the chapter will provide recommendations on how to address these issues.

Physical and mental stress. Injuries and treatments can lead to physical pain, disrupt sleep, create difficulties with concentration and memory, and contribute to strong emotional reactions. In addition, some prescribed medications can also lead to taking part in fewer healthy activities and difficulties making decisions.

Being injured and being a patient. Going from working as a service member to being injured and being a patient is a big change. It is understandable to feel like a "fish out water" and feel guilty for not serving with fellow unit members and knowing what they are going through. It can be a challenging part of the recovery process to lie in a safe bed looking at your injuries while also worrying about unit members still deployed.

Complicated medical system and treatment. You will now need to keep track of an enormous amount of information, appointments, and paperwork that accompany medical treatment in the military. Not being on top of this information can cause delays in your care. Some of the information that you will need to track and stay on top of include:

- Keeping multiple appointments
- Remembering to take multiple medications and keep track of doses and timing
- Completing lots of paperwork
- Keeping track of lots of paperwork
- Understanding unfamiliar medical terms and processes, as well as how these will help you heal and recover functioning
- Receiving care in more than one hospital or other setting, possibly at the same time

Keeping track of many resources. The DoD and Veterans Affairs (VA) have separately and together developed the best possible medical support services for our service members. They are also constantly changing or adding services that they hope will support injured members. However, all of these services and improvements also result in challenges for members and their families. The high number of support agencies and their differences can be confusing. It can be challenging to sort out which agencies can provide or coordinate various needed services. Even the information in this chapter can become outdated. For updates to this information, visit the Web site of this book at http://www.warswounded.com.

Slow recovery. Physical and emotional recovery often does not go as fast as you would like it to go. Many of the injuries require extended time and treatments for the body and mind to heal.

Treatment not going as fast as you would like it. The standard treatment strategy typically starts at the lowest, least invasive level even though you would be willing to undergo a more intensive treatment right from the start.

Changes in view of yourself and others. There are many possible changes to a service member's functioning and relationships with others. These can include self doubts because of not being able to do what one used to do, reduction in one's role as provider in the family because the partner has taken over much of this role even before the injury (especially after multiple or extended tours), and loss of partner after long absences (i.e., receiving a "Dear John" letter).

Changes in sexual functioning. Sexual and other dysfunctions may injure one's sense of control and satisfaction as well as contribute to tension with one's significant other. Many misunderstandings can also follow. It is very important to raise these problems with treatment personnel, despite an understandable feeling of discomfort.

Emotional stress. Service members can also be weighed down with depression and anxiety, which may increase the effect of medical conditions and decrease functioning. See the tables in this section of the book for a list of the symptoms of PTSD and depression and for ways that your family and friends can help you with these symptoms.

Financial stress. Family members may have to leave work to be with and support the service member and this will reduce the amount of money available to the family. Likewise, an injury may impact your employment prospects and result in decreased earnings for the family.

Family stress. Family members who are either at the medical treatment facility or left home alone will experience stress for a variety of reasons. The changing relationships among family members (as previously noted) can become another source of stress.

Uncertainty. Experiencing uncertainty about your health and future employment, finances, and relationships can aggravate symptoms and increase stress for the service member and family members.

What Types of Services Are Available to Help?

It is helpful to know which services are available and what they can do for you so you can ask the right questions and get what you need. The good news is that multiple medical and support services are available and these services are being improved all the time. The challenge is that these services can be called different things in each service and the names of the agencies can change. This section will give you a list of the primary services and the current agencies and specialists who provide these services in each military branch. As this information changes, we will maintain the updated information on the Web site for this book at http://www.warswounded.com.

The main medical and support functions available to you include case management, command and control, medical providers, fitness for duty, and patient advocate. The names of the agencies providing these medical and support services are subject to change as the military medical system works to improve its services (check with the http://www.warswounded.com Web site as things change over time).

Who Is Available to Help Me with the Recovery Process?

You will meet with a number of professionals from the DoD who will be assisting you and your family through the recovery process. Here is a list of some of their titles and their responsibilities and roles.

Case Manager. This is the central medical person who is with you from admission to discharge. This person assists the medical social worker in supporting you while you are an inpatient in the hospital. The case manager assumes primary responsibility once you become an outpatient or are transferred to another facility.

Chaplain. The military's ministry staff who provide spiritual support.

Command and Control for Patients. You will report to a unit that is part of the medical facility. This unit will be administratively responsible for you and can assist you with the local medical and other military resources you can access. As time passes and you move from inpatient to outpatient treatment you gain a great sense of control of your life and begin to consider if you want to return to duty. This continuing contact, after the acute or hospital phase, is an important support for you and is central to regaining and maintaining optimal function.

- Army: Army medical treatment facilities have created specific Warrior Transition Brigades for injured soldiers. A core feature is the Core Medical Team, which is described below. Also, the soldier's chain of command facilitates housing, meal cards, accountability issues, awards and decorations, leadership, transportation, finances *and* clothing, among other things.
- Navy: The original unit maintains control of the patient unless the patient is assigned more than 50 miles from the primary Military Treatment Facility (MTF). Then the patient may be transferred to Medical Hold.
- Air Force: Injured service members stay in the operational unit or the Patient Squadron or Medical Hold Unit depending on the severity and prognosis of their injuries. Patient Squadron is for members with the intention of returning to service. Medical Hold can be used to extend duty before a separation or retirement.

Core Medical Team. A sample core medical team is the Army TRI-AD program. This structure was created to ensure close coordination between the case manager, command and control, and medical specialties. The team consists of the squad leader, case manager, and primary care manager. These three parties meet regularly to make sure that they are providing injured service members with integrated care.

Judge Advocate (JA). Legal and judicial arm of all of the United States Armed Forces. JA officers can provide service members with a wide range of legal services free of charge. JA and legal-assistance attorneys can help soldiers review medical board findings.

Medical Social Worker. An individual who usually has a master's degree in social work. This person's job is to support service members and sometimes family members by providing an in depth understanding of how to navigate the hospital system and get medical support and devices.

Ombudsmen. The advocate for injured army service members and their family members who investigates and resolves complaints at the lowest and fastest level (by contacting the people directly involved with the issue rather than elevating it up the chain of command or initiating formal complaint procedures, and ensuring that the situation is resolved as quickly as possible). Issues include health care, physical disability processing, Reserve Component medical retention issues, transition to the Veterans Administration, pay issues, etc. They will also assist with issues that come through the Army-wide Wounded Soldier and Family Hotline. In all cases, Ombudsmen will attempt to link the soldier or family member with the appropriate subject matter expert.

PEBLO. The Physical Evaluation Board Liaison Officer (PEBLO) assists the service member throughout the entire Medical Evaluation Board/Physical Evaluation Board (MEB/PEB) process including counselling service members who have been evaluated by a Medical Evaluation Board and assisting with questions about disability policy and procedures.

Personnel Office. Assists with identifying and coordinating job options.

Patient Advocate. Helps each patient work with others who have an effect on their health care and outcomes, including doctors, chain of command, case managers, and lawyers. Helps answer questions and resolve issues about health care and other issues related to a patient's medical condition.

Primary Care Manager (PCM). The PCMs are considered to be the gatekeepers of the medical system because they are the first providers who most patients see and are then responsible for providing general medical care and referring patients to specialty care as needed.

Unit Liaison. This is typically a person from the service member's unit who acts as a liaison between the service member, unit, and medical community.

Veteran Service Organizations (VSOs). VSOs include the American Legion, Veterans of Foreign Wars (VFWs), Disabled American Veterans (DAV), and Military Order of the Purple Heart. These organizations can help represent you during the MEB and PEB processes and VA claims process. They can also provide a unique form of social support because they will understand and accept you as a fellow veteran. It is important to note that each of these organizations has different requirements for membership.

Veterans Affairs (VA) Liaison. Meets with all injured service members to assist with VA benefits and entitlements. Their offices are often colocated with the military medical treatment facility.

Medical Specialists

During the course of your treatment you may also meet up with specialists and doctors from different fields. Here are some of the fields that you may encounter and a description of their specialities.

- *Neurology* is a branch of medicine focusing on disorders of the nervous system. Physicians specializing in the field of neurology are called *neurologists* and are trained to diagnose, treat, and manage patients with neurological disorders.
  - *Neuropsychology* is a science (not a branch of medicine) concerned with the integration of psychological observations on behavior and cognitive function with neurological observations on the central nervous system (CNS), including the brain.
  - *Neurosurgery* is a surgical discipline focused on treating central and peripheral nervous system diseases amenable to mechanical intervention.
  - *Neurosurgeon* is a physician who specializes in surgery within the nervous system.
- *Occupational therapy (OT)* is a specialty that helps patients gain the ability to function in various activities of daily life.
- *Ophthalmologist* is a physician (with an M.D. degree) who specializes in disorders of the eye.
- *Optometrist* is a health care professional (without an M.D. degree) who specializes in nonsurgical eye conditions.
- *Orthopedics/orthopedic surgery* is a medical specialty concerned with the skeleton and its associated structures.
- *Orthotists* are individuals who specialize in devices, such as artificial limbs, designed to restore function or supplement a weakened part of the body.
- *Pain management* is a branch of medicine concerned with the relief of pain.
- *Pharmacologist* is a clinical professional concerned with the effectiveness and safety of drugs in humans.
- *Physical medicine and rehabilitation (PMandR)* is a branch of medicine focused on the functional restoration of a person affected by physical disability.
- *Physical therapy (PT)* is the provision of services to people and populations to develop, maintain, and restore maximum movement and functional ability throughout the lifespan.
- *Plastic Surgery* corrects disfigurement, restores function, or improves appearance.
- *Prosthetics* is the specialty dealing with designing and constructing artificial limbs.
- *Psychiatry* is the medical specialty treating mental illnesses.
- *Psychology* is a clinical specialty concerned with recognizing and treating behavior disorders and enhancing performance.
- *Rehabilitation nursing* is a specific field in nursing geared toward patients who have temporarily or permanently medical issues which impact lifestyle and functioning.
- *Sleep medicine* is a medical specialty concerned with conditions characterized by disturbances of usual sleep patterns or behaviors.

- *Social Work* is a specialty trained to help individuals in a myriad of ways. Depending on job function, duties may include facilitating placement in a facility or therapy.
- *Speech Pathologist* is a therapist who deals with disorders of communication, swallowing, and voice.

Titles of some of these professionals and some procedures with them may vary between the services. Here is a table that outlines the differences between the services.

	Army	Navy/Marines	Air Force
Case Management	RN Case Managers	Clinical: Primary Care Manager or RN Clinical Case Manager (for traumatic injuries)	Primary Care Manager
Command and control (C2) unit	Injured Warrior Transition units	Original unit maintains control of patient unless the patient is assigned more than 50 miles from the primary Military Treatment Facility. Then the patient may be transferred to Medical Hold.	Operational unit or Patient Squadron
Command and control (C2) primary point of contact	Injured Warrior Transition unit leadership.	If the unit, then the unit commander If Medical Hold, then the Fleet Liaison	The unit commander or Medical Group's Patient Squadron commander
Primary provider	TRI-AD physician	Primary Care Manager (PCM)	PCM
Point of Contact (POC) for MEB (Medical Evaluation Board) and PEB (Physical Evaluation Board) processing	Physical Evaluation Board Liaison Officer (PEBLO)	Limited Duty Coordinator oversees duty limitations. MEB office admin clerks support through MEB process. PEBLO tracks through the PEB process, not the MEB process. Medical Readiness does return to full duty assignments screener	PEBLO
Patient Advocate	Ombudsman	Clinical case manager for clinical issues. Fleet/Marine liaison for admin issues	Patient advocate
Military Personnel	Military Personnel	Personnel Support Detachment (PSD)	Base Military Personnel Flight (MPF)

It is vital that you know who your "support team" is and how to contact them.

	Name	Phone	E-mail
Case Manager	_____	_____	_____
Command and Control	_____	_____	_____
Primary Provider	_____	_____	_____
PEBLO	_____	_____	_____

How Do I Make Sure I Get Adequate Medical Care?

It is important to have some strategies to better understand the medical system and control your medical care.

Work closely with your case manager. This person is critical to keeping track and sorting out the complexities of your individual situation. Sometimes there are too many people trying to assist you, so be ready to insist that you have just one coordinator for this role.

You are your own best advocate. Take charge of your care when and where you can. Watch out for just going with the flow. Ask questions when you do not understand or need something more from the system. Be assertive in a polite way without being aggressive. It is often helpful to phrase concerns or needs in the form of a simple question.

Take care of yourself. Do self-care/social activities and avoid isolating yourself from people (e.g., schedule activities with friends), keep military bearing in your life (e.g., act professionally and keep a sharp uniform to show respect for yourself and your occupation), resist temptation to indulge in food and alcohol (e.g., limit the amount of junk food and alcohol in your room), and stay active.

Ask questions. Ask questions about anything you have a concern about or do not understand.

- Ask about your medical conditions and what these conditions mean.
- Ask about different treatment options for each condition, how well the treatments work, and the advantages and disadvantages of each treatment.
- Ask about correct doses and times for taking medications and possible side effects.

Take the time to review and question before signing. Read every document carefully, ask questions, and get clarification. This is especially important before you sign a document. Keep in mind that signing a document is legal confirmation that you have read and understood the document you are signing. To say later that you did not read the document will not help you.

Get copies of all documents. Get copies of your medical records and all other documents for your own files.

Get information in writing. When you ask for answers, also ask that the answers be given in writing with an e-mail or a memo. It is common to have a hard time remembering what someone told you, especially when key staff members (e.g., case managers) change. It is also important to be able to refer to written documentation when questions arise and there is confusion about previous guidance and staff positions have changed.

Keep information organized. Keep all documentation in one place and organize it chronologically. You never know when you will need to look up what you were told by someone. This is one of the simplest ways to be able to find information when you need it.

Prepare for appointments. Write down any questions or information that you want or need to have addressed at an appointment. Also, write down questions when you think about them so that you will remember to ask the questions. Remember that you deserve to have every question answered by the medical staff because you are the customer. Answers will generally be clearer if you can keep questions simple (KISS—otherwise known as "Keep It Simple Stupid"). Also, it helps if you keep your questions as specific as possible. An example might be to ask the doctor, "Can you please tell me about any lab results that were out of normal limits from the blood sample I gave last Tuesday" as opposed to asking, "How were my labs?"

Get familiar with federal and military guidance. It is helpful to become knowledgeable about US Codes, DoD regulations, VA policies, and service-level instructions about relevant topics (e.g., medical evaluation boards, disability, benefits). Service member and family members can find out about this information from case managers, PEBLOs, providers, military legal staff, and other support staff.

Talk with your providers about all concerns. Talk with your providers about the things that may not be comfortable to bring up (e.g., problems managing anger, economic stressors, use of alcohol or drugs to cope, domestic strain and any episodes of potential domestic violence, and taking unnecessary risks like driving recklessly and excessive gambling or spending). Consider that these types of issues may get worse if not addressed. You can ask yourself "if not now, when?" You can also ask yourself "what things am I potentially risking by not addressing this now?"

Involve your partner/significant other. Keep them informed by having them attend as many key interviews as possible. They can be a great help recalling and understanding critical information for your health care, as well as providing additional information to clinical staff. Family members and friends may help keep track of paper work, appointments, and medications. They may also help provide important medical staff with important information. A common example is when significant others help identify sleep disturbances that are treatable conditions but that you may not have noticed in yourself.

Have realistic expectations and a healthy attitude toward recovery. Healing may take a long time. The frustration of this process can cause you to be self destructive if you allow it.

Manage your time wisely. Use a calendar to keep track of appointments and goals. Use a filing system to keep track of documents. Ask questions and take notes. Use a contact book to keep track of different people and how to reach them. Develop a system to keep track if you are taking each medication on schedule. You can find many examples of different types of charts for tracking medications by searching the Web for "medication chart."

Manage your effort wisely. Identify your goals, actions to achieve goals, timelines to complete actions, and ways to regularly evaluate progress.

Be patient. Do not hurry. Remember that it might feel like a relief to make decisions quickly but these decisions may impact the rest of your life.

Be persistent. Do not accept the first answer if you do not agree. Ask again. Consider if you are entitled to a second opinion. Also consider documenting your concerns and getting a response in writing. For example, you could write a memo describing what you were told and asking for a detailed explanation.

Be professional and avoid discrediting yourself. Avoid unprofessional or emotional behavior like using profanity and yelling because it can discredit you and what you are trying to achieve.

Address and resolve problems step by step. When you need to assert yourself or make a complaint, make sure you have all the facts straight first. Then start at the lowest level, go through the proper channels, and exhaust all options before going to the next level.

Am I Having a "Normal" (Common and Understandable) Response?

Not only may you experience being overwhelmed in a medical system but also you may feel a range of conflicting emotions. You may feel frustrated about your situation and become angry with family and staff. You might feel guilty about leaving your unit behind. You can become frustrated that you are dependent on medications and on other people. These responses are often natural parts of the recovery process. The typical responses can include the following:

1. Shock, confusion, and agitation
2. Denial
3. Anxiety, suspiciousness, and avoidance
4. Anger, frustration, and blame
5. Bargaining
6. Depression, guilt, and isolation
7. Testing, and finally
8. Acceptance

These responses can be pretty intense and can be different from how you would usually react. These responses can also be very stressful for both you and your family members. No one is sure what is happening, how long it will last, and what is coming next. However, not everyone experiences all of these responses, they do not necessarily go in any order, and they can often be repeated. The good news is that most service members work their way through these responses naturally even though it may take a while. It can also help you and your family members to know what these responses look like and some simple coping strategies that you can use. In addition, it is important to avoid making decisions based on strong feelings instead of what is best in the long run.

Shock, confusion, and agitation are common first reactions to a major change. Some people can react with total disbelief and even "shut down" by being unable to carry on conversations with others or even remember things that happened. Some common thoughts are "This must have been a mistake," "My life is over," and "How will I explain this to others?" Others may experience strong confusion and agitation. This can be especially confusing when someone who is typically quiet becomes verbally or even physically aggressive.

People can cope with shock by giving themselves time and privacy to recuperate. They can realize that they may have strong reactions and now is a good time to limit making decisions and telling others how they are doing.

Denial, which often follows shock and confusion, can take many forms. For example, a service member who is recovering from a head injury may say, "*Yes, I can drive*" when family members know that it would be dangerous. Denial can be very difficult for both family members and medical staff. The person in denial may say that there is nothing wrong, even when directly confronted that there is something wrong. When someone is in denial, consistent and direct feedback needs to be provided. However, some people get really angry when they are constantly being told "NO." Factual feedback must be continually provided to help a recovering service member gain insight into the new situation.

Anxiety, suspiciousness, and avoidance are natural responses to having experienced a severe change that you could not prevent. You may be on guard for what next "bad thing" will happen to you. You may also mistrust the motives of others. As a result of fearing what might happen or feeling "out of place," you might start to avoid situations.

People can cope with fear and panic by increasing their understanding that having the worries alone will not cause harm. This can be done by setting a time of fifteen minutes each day for thinking about the worries. In addition, you can write the worries on paper and then rate how likely they really are. Once you have identified the worries that are reasonable, then you can decide what specific things you can do to address these worries.

Anger, frustration, and blame are also common responses. As you are struggling to deal with changes related to an injury, you may get angry with people around you. Some of these strong emotions may also be due to the injury, medications, or just being constrained to a medical room. These emotions can also be due to thoughts about what happened. Typical thoughts can include "*This isn't fair*," "*How could they do this to me*," "*How would they like it if it happened to them*." These thoughts may be justified, especially after being hurt by others in combat. Often the anger can build, especially when there are no outlets. The building anger can result in feeling frustrated and powerless, and in angry outbursts with others.

You can cope with anger by distraction (e.g., count to 40), walking away from a situation to cool down, doing physically strenuous activity to work through stress, and talking with someone for support and advice.

Bargaining is a form of hopeful denial that often comes after anger. People typically think that there is a way to "bargain" or do something special to change things back. Others make deals with themselves that if they make big changes in their life (e.g., be the most dedicated service member possible), then they will get back what they lost.

Coping with bargaining involves accepting that there is no way to change things back and accepting responsibility for creating a new life.

Depression, guilt, and isolation can be a factor when people realize that there is nothing they can do to change what happened. What can happen next is that they can blame themselves and become depressed, which can be thought of as a form of anger turned inward. A lot of people who are depressed will criticize and blame themselves with thoughts like *"I'm a failure. I can't do this. I'm no good. If I had only been more . . ."* When people have difficulty dealing with overwhelming situations, they often go back and explain what happened by blaming themselves. For example, people who either missed a critical mission or made a decision to put people in harm's way may feel guilty for many years. People may also become angry at the world or their religion. The may question their basic beliefs about the world and faith. Sometimes when you feel down, you feel like withdrawing from others.

You can cope with emotions such as anger and depression by reading about others' experiences, and learning about different perspectives and coping skills. One good example would be Harold Kushner's book *When Bad Things Happen to Good People*.

Testing is an important phase in which people find their new limits. This phase almost always follows after a period of recovery and improvement in thinking abilities. People think, *"I'm really close to the way I was, so I'll just act the way I was. I'll do things as I always did."* For example, many people with a head injury have a fatigue disorder. They know they get tired easily. But during this testing phase, they "forget" they have a head injury and say, *"Well, I've got a lot of friends visiting this weekend. I'm just going to stay up really late. I'm going to see if I just can't be the way I used to be."* For people with physical changes to their body, they may say, *"I am going to lift this object or exercise like I used to."* When you overdo and go beyond your abilities, you may spend the next several days paying for it. Sometimes, people will test themselves and fail. For example, they previously may have been an A or B student. They take a class and come out with a C or D, even though they put in twice the effort for that C. For many people, getting a C is a failure. There is usually a period of time when the injured person says, *"Why can't I be the way I used to?"*

Acceptance happens when people decide that they cannot change what has happened, accept the consequences of what has happened and their limitations, and decide to move forward. The decision to move forward is the opposite of giving up. In acceptance, people have learned that it is not possible to return to the old life after trying to return to it. They have also learned that they have had to adjust their lives for their new health status. These adjustments can include doing less, having more structure, changing work, and changing friends. However, you do not have to like having to make these changes, it is simply learning to accept them and start the process of moving toward a new life. For this reason, this phase has been called "uneasy acceptance" (Johnson). This phase has also been called "temporary acceptance" because it is not an end point, but rather a transition to a new direction in life (Birkel and Miller, 1997). This phase includes thoughts like *"the past is past," "I cannot change anything by criticizing myself and others," "why focus on what I cannot change," "it's time to move on,"* and *"what I do with my future is up to me."*

What Are Some Common Steps in the Recovery Process?

Here is a six-part model of the recovery process that injured service members have found helpful. The model was originally developed for amputees but applies to all forms of injuries. The model has been adapted from the Amputee Coalition of America (ACA; Isenberg, 2007) peer-training program.

Phase	Characteristic	Description
Enduring	Surviving initial injury, treatment, and pain that follows	Hanging on; focusing on present to get through the pain; blocking out distress about future—it is a conscious choice not to deal with the full meaning of the loss; self-protection.
Suffering	Questioning: Why me? How will I . . . ?	Intense feelings about the loss: fear, denial, anger, depression; vulnerable and confused; return to Enduring stage; emotional anguish about the loss of self adds to the pain.
Reckoning	Becoming aware of the new reality	Coming to terms with the extent of the loss; accepting what is left after the loss; implications of the loss for future—how will roles change; minimizing own losses in comparison to others' losses
Reconciling	Putting the loss in perspective	Regaining confidence, control, awareness of one's strengths and uniqueness—all an ongoing process; more assertive; taking control of one's life; self-management of illness and recovery; changed body image; need for intimacy
Normalizing	Reordering priorities	Bringing balance to one's life; establishing and maintaining new routines; once again, doing the things that matter; allowing priorities other than the loss to dominate; advocating for self
Thriving	Living life to the fullest	Increased confidence and trust in self and others; confidence; being a role model to others; working towards being more than you were before; not everyone attains this level of recovery

What Are Some General Coping Strategies?

(1) Admit to people that you have an injury and educate them about your injury.

(2) Understand the connection between emotions and thoughts. You are likely to experience a number of conflicting feelings and thoughts. It is useful to acknowledge the emotions and thoughts so that these thoughts do not have a negative effect on your decisions about your future career. It is also useful to evaluate whether there are alternate thoughts that may be less distressing and make you more confident. Below are some examples in a simple three-column table. The way to use this table is to first identify a painful feeling that might affect your decision, then identify the main thoughts tied to that feeling, and then see if you can identify other ways to look at your situation in a more realistic and more reassuring manner.

Emotions	Sample thoughts tied to the emotions	Sample alternate thoughts
Guilt	*"How did I truly serve my country if I had to return early?"*	*"Redeploying after being injured is fulfilling my duty."*
Sadness	*"I have nothing to offer because of my injuries."*	*"Being injured in a combat zone is a valuable experience that few have, especially when training junior service members."*
Worry	*"I won't able to adapt to a new job if allowed to continue service."*	*"I will be able to learn a new job easier because of prior military experience."*
Anger	*"If somebody is against the war, they are against me."*	*"I did what was right for me and others may not understand what I have seen or be in the same place."*

(3) Develop realistic expectations and perspectives.

(4) Anticipate normal distress like feeling anger/feeling powerless, accept the feelings as part of the process, and find ways to keep on doing valued and goal-directed activities.

(5) Figure out what you can and cannot control. Take responsibility for what you can control. Learn to let go of what you cannot control.

(6) Focus on one day at a time, one task at a time. Focus on what you can control and do today. Just do your best for today.

(7) Find reassuring and hopeful ways to view your situation. Consider if there are any benefits of the changes you are experiencing.

(8) Do not let your injuries blind you from your strengths. It is important to keep in mind your deployed experiences and injuries give you a unique perspective that others can only read about.

(9) Find ways to see humor in your situation. Sometimes people can make jokes about themselves; that is always a positive sign.

(10) Understand the connection between attitude and activities. Attitudes and activities influence each other. Keeping a positive attitude helps you stay active. Also, staying active can help you keep a positive attitude. See the diagram below as an illustration of the relationship between attitudes and activities.

The Connection between Attitudes and Activities

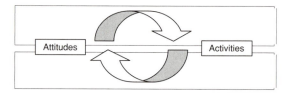

(11) Stay active just for the sake of staying active. Pick something to do with your time instead of isolating yourself and watching TV.

(12) Use goal setting to pursue goals and increase activity. Set goals, visualize how you would accomplish the goal, break the goal down into steps, set deadlines for each step, follow the plan, measure your progress, and adjust the plan as needed. If you are trying to change your activity level, SMART (specific, measurable, attainable, realistic, and time-limited) goals are easier to set, identify, and follow.

The SMART acronym can be helpful in identifying goals	
Specific	*Go to the gym at 5 P.M. and work out three days a week (Mon., Wed., Fri.) for three months*
Measurable	*Use aerobics equipment for at least twenty minutes each workout*
Attainable	*Have the physical condition to exercise for twenty minutes*
Realistic	*Have access to gym and time in the day to go to the gym three days a week*
Time limited	*Measure progress after three months*

(13) Identify what you value in life and schedule it into your week.
(14) Develop a routine and stick closely to it.
(15) Create time to talk and do things with your family and friends.
(16) Have a regular exercise routine.
(17) Keep encouraged even with setbacks: keep in mind that you are playing the odds, it is common to run into roadblocks, and a key to success is to "keep on keepin' on."
(18) Stay connected with others.
(19) Communicate with family members, doctors, and other support staff.
(20) Support other people with injuries. You can start with one person. Later, you can consider talking with groups. Your perspective will be invaluable when talking with others with similar injuries.
(21) Attend support groups to learn from others, support others, and be able to talk about challenges.
(22) Find ways to contribute to society and to people around you.
(23) Establish a new role for yourself in volunteer, religious, or other types of groups.
(24) Avoid making major decisions until you have had time to sort out your options.
(25) Ask questions about what you may not understand.
(26) Use problem-solving steps to work through challenging problems. Going step by step can help you get a better understanding of the problem, options, and best solution for you. In addition, problem solving helps keep you mentally sharp and helps avoid problems with memory and mental acuity that may develop long after the occurrence of combat-related injuries.

Problem solving steps

1. Gather information	Identify who, what, when, where, how the problem occurs.
2. Define the Problem	List at least 3 specific parts of the problem.
	1.
	2.
	3.
3. Brainstorm possible solutions	Ask yourself *"What are the different things that I would like in place of the problem and what are the different ways that I could pursue these goals?"* The goal is to list as many options as you can think of without thinking about how realistic each one is.
4. Consider likely outcomes	Think about which of the possible solutions you think are most doable, how confident are you that you can do each, and which ones are likely to make a positive difference.
5. Choose a solution	Pick an option that seems doable and likely to help.
6. Make a plan	Describe specific steps that you need to take to make your solution work. For each step, ask yourself, "If I do this will that take me one step closer to solving my problem?"
7. Plan for obstacles	Imagine carrying out your plan, what could get in the way, and how you could get around these obstacles.
8. Do the plan and measure results	Did you get the results you wanted? If not, go back through the steps and try again.

Top Things that I Learned from My Recovery Experience

This list is a compilation of good ideas that we obtained from a number of service members that have been through the recovery process.

1. Seeking out people that have gone through the experience I am going through.
2. Getting on the Internet and learn as much as I can about my condition and to reconfirm information with my health care providers. (See this book's Web site, http://www.warswounded.com for further updates.)
3. Going to support meetings for people with similar injuries to learn and teach others about this experience.
4. Making sure the paperwork I filled out before deployment is accurate. (For example, update the person/people you want to be contacted in case of emergency as they will probably be the people that are informed of your condition and greet you at the hospital. You may not want to use your ex-spouse or estranged parent to be your emergency point of contact.)
5. Making sure that I work closely with my support team (case manager, PEBLO, operational unit liaison, primary providers) to be on the same departure plan from the hospital to stay in the service.
6. Realizing medication may alter the way I think and feel in many ways. Medication may make it difficult to concentrate and remember, increase positive or negative feelings, increase fatigue, or make sleep more difficult.
7. Consider seeking advice from people I trust when making big decisions.

8. Knowing that time can be my enemy or my friend. Even though I want to get out of the hospital now, healing takes time so I need to be patient and let my body heal properly. I will also use time in the hospital wisely to prepare myself to hit the ground running when I am ready to return to my unit.
9. Knowing and accepting my limitations. Watching out to not overdo things because I am trying to do things the way I used to do them.
10. Making a copy of all paperwork and having a good filing system.

What Are Some Ways to Decide About Continuing Military Service?

The decision about continuing military service is very important. However, for some people, it may not be an easy decision. This can be frustrating as you may feel nervous having lost some of your mental or physical capacity and not knowing what the future will be like. Your past career in the military may have been in the infantry or in aviation, which may need to be reconsidered depending upon your capabilities. You may feel like you do not want to stay in the military if you cannot do what you were doing before. Others such as your wife, parents, children, siblings, coworkers, or peer visitor program of ACA may also be influential in your decision process. As it becomes clear to you that there are options in the service based on your medical condition, you will begin to move forward perhaps with a little supportive push from others.

It is important to make a big decision like this for the right reasons and in a realistic way. Therefore, it helps to use a careful decision-making process. This process takes some careful thought but is worth the extra time and effort. To help you with this process, below is a list of common considerations and some decision-making tools. Please note that the some of the suggested steps may seem overwhelming. It may help a lot to seek out professional assistance (e.g., job counselor) or a workshop that can support and guide you through the process.

(1) *Knowing your employment options.* There are three basic areas to consider job options. These include in the military, public sector outside the military, and private sector. It is important to note that military members have preferred status both with public and some private sector jobs. For more information about your employment options, check out the next chapter in this book.

(2) *Identifying military job options.* Your case manager, unit liaison, and personnel staff can help you find out more about jobs. For example, you can ask for the information on the duty descriptions for jobs. Also, find out more about job possibilities by talking with people in those jobs.

(3) *Identifying public sector job options.* Federal and state governments both have veteran's hiring preferences for jobs. You can learn about these options through programs such as:

a. *Department of Defense (DoD) Job Search* is an associate Web site of the US Department of Labor's (DoL) America's Job Bank. (Statement source: The Department of Defense (DoD) Job Search.) http://dod.jobsearch.org/

b. *USAJOBS* is provided at no cost and offers information on thousands of US government job opportunities worldwide. http://www.usajobs.opm.gov/
c. *Veterans Preference in Federal Jobs* lists federal government jobs for which veterans who served during major campaigns for which a campaign medal has been authorized or during any war declared by Congress receive preference. http://federaljobs.net/veterans.htm

(4) *Identifying private sector job options.* Some private sector companies are "veteran friendly" employers that also have veteran's hiring preferences. Here is information for some of the programs that assist military members in this area:

a. REAL-Lifelines is dedicated to providing individualized job training, counseling, and reemployment services to wounded service members. http://www.dol.gov/vets/programs/Real-life/main.htm
b. Hire Vets First helps employers find qualified veterans, as well as help veterans to make the most of a national network of employment resources. http://www.hirevetsfirst.gov
c. Veterans Employment and Training provides veterans with the resources and services to succeed in the twenty-first century work force. http://www.dol.gov/vets/
d. E-Vets Resource Advisor assists veterans preparing to enter the job market. http://www.dol.gov/elaws/evets.htm

(5) *Assessing your capabilities.* It is very important to take a hard look at your current abilities and skills.

a. Accepting your symptoms and knowing your capabilities and limitations. This can be as simple as making lists of both your capabilities (things you can do) and your limitations (things you can no longer do).
b. Identifying "motivated abilities and skills" (MAS) (Krannich, 2005). This approach starts by listing at least five of your most meaningful experiences in life. These experiences include things you enjoyed doing as well as things you have accomplished. Then ask yourself for specific details about what you did and what was the most enjoyable or valuable part to you.
c. Exploring all of the possible accommodations either by changing the way you do things or by using mechanical devices such as prostheses (see the list of assistive technologies in Chapter 3).

(6) *Assessing your interests and values.* Probably the most important part of the decision process is deciding what is most important to you. These can be thought of as both what interests you about a job and what you think is most important or valuable about a job.

a. Make a list of all your previous jobs in order. Then compare work experiences by asking the questions below (Birkel and Miller, 1997).
   i. Which one did you enjoy the most and why?
   ii. Which one did you enjoy the least and why?

    iii. What got in the way of your career goals?

    iv. What would you do differently if you could do it again?

b. Write what you would like your obituary to say about how you led your life.

c. Make a "before I die, I want to . . ." list of the most important things you would like to do or experience.

d. There are several tests to measure interests and values. You may be able to get these tests through the education office or books like *The Guide to Occupational Exploration*. You can also find many tests and other helpful resources at career counseling Web sites like http://www.marion.ohio-state.edu/career/career/internetresources.html.

e. List what you want from a job. Divide the list into what is essential and what you might be willing to give up.

(7) *Comparing job options*. Of the jobs available to you, which jobs are the best "overall" matches for you? When looking at "overall" match, it is useful to look at the full range of pros and cons as well as short term and long term ones. A three-column chart can help you compare the short- and long-term pros and cons for each option. When weighing pros and cons, it is helpful to consider the full range of impacts. These impacts can include your interests, values, work responsibilities, working conditions, pay and benefits, and opportunities. You can use the table below to help you with the decision making.

Decision-Making Matrix

		Pros	Cons
Choice one	Short term		
	Long term		
Choice two	Short term		
	Long term		
Choice three	Short term		
Pursue job in public sector: _____			
	Long term		
Choice four	Short term		
Pursue job in private sector: _____			
	Long term		

(8) *Assessing additional factors impacting your choices.*

a. Some factors you will need to consider include your career direction, the state of your finances, your immediate and short-term healthcare coverage, any family preferences, and family resources that may impact your decision of returning to service or look for employment outside the military. Also, your decision to remain in the military can be affected by the time you have spent in the military that can be applied to federal service or it can impact the cost of your healthcare. You can explore these factors with the help of your support services. For example, if you are on active duty orders as a Reservist or

National Guard service member you may decide that you are better off taking a medical retirement if you are eligible and unable to stay on active duty.

b. For many active duty, National Guard, or Reservist service members, financial issues can be a big factor in decisions about whether to try to continue on medical service, retire medically, or make other choices. Often service members find that the income from disability, and the time it takes to maximize the income, is far below what they were earning before the injury.

c. Even if you need to reclassify into a different specialty, it may be important to return to your old unit, especially if they were very supportive prior to and during your hospital stay.

d. The time you spend in the hospital may become an important factor. For a below the knee amputation, for example, the earliest you may be able to get out of the hospital is five to seven months while complicated blast injuries may keep you in the hospital healing for a couple of years.

How Does the Medical Fitness for Duty Process Work?

The medical return to duty process includes multiple medical decisions and options. The most common topics are:

1. Profile and duty limitations
2. Fitness for duty questions
3. Medical Evaluation Board (MEB) and Physical Evaluation Board (PEB)
4. Line of Duty (LOD) determination
5. Disposition recommendations
6. Return to service and reclassification
7. Disability ratings and determinations

Profile and Duty Limitations

After an illness or injury that results in a decrease in functioning, a service member is put on a profile. The profile is a system for documenting that a person has a condition that impacts his or her ability to perform duties or requires a geographic assignment limitation. The profile is typically initiated by the primary provider when it is evident that the service member has a duty-limiting medical condition. The profile also lists duty restrictions including that the service member is not worldwide qualified.

For Army and Air Force personnel, a profile can be initiated which addresses any duty limitations, including deployability.

For the Army, if you are given a permanent profile of 3 or 4, then you will need an MOS/Medical Retention Board (MMRB) (IAW, AR 40-501, AR 600-60) or an MEB if indicated.

For the Navy/Marines, individuals who require a limited duty status due to physical disability (except pregnancy) are placed on Limited Duty (LIMDU) status. Enlisted personnel may have two periods of six months where LIMDU status may be approved locally. Otherwise, the change in status must be approved by service headquarters. All changes in status for officers must be approved by service headquarters as well.

For most cases in all services, if a member is not deployable, or worldwide qualified, beyond a year, then a Medical Evaluation Board is initiated to evaluate fitness for duty. This may vary according to service policy of the branch involved and the injury sustained.

Fitness for Duty Questions

Ultimately, the military needs to answer the question, "Is this member fit for duty?" What does fitness for duty mean? A member is considered fit for duty if they are able to fulfill the obligations of their grade and occupation.

Medical Evaluation Board (MEB) and Physical Evaluation Board (PEB)

MEB is an informal process comprised of at least two physicians who compile, assess, and evaluate the medical history of a service member and determine if the member's duty is affected by their medical status ("fitness for duty"). MEB is *not* a duty reclassification board. Psychiatric MEBs require three physicians with at least one psychiatrist. In the Army, MEBs may be required merely because the service member has a medical condition that requires a referral. See Figure 5.1 for a diagram of the MEB and PEB process.

The MEB documents a service member's medical condition(s) and duty limitations. It consists of a thorough summary of all medical conditions. The MEB refers service members to PEB when the findings and recommendations suggest that the service member does not appear to meet fitness for duty standards based on their medical conditions. However, this does not mean an individual will be automatically separated from the military. The PEB takes into consideration both the medical issue and job performance and determines whether an individual is fit for continued military duty. The service member under review may still be able to be retained and do another job within the military or request "COAD/COAR" (An Army term for Continuance on Active Duty/Reserve). Administrative documentation will be used in the PEB as it provides the board with a picture of each service member's military career and duty performance.

The MEB process begins once optimum medical care has been achieved or if return to duty is questionable. Optimum medical care is defined as "the point of hospitalization or treatment when a member's progress appears to have medically stabilized and when it can be reasonably determined that the member is not capable of performing the duties of his office, grade, rank, or rating" (Under Secretary of Defense, 2007).

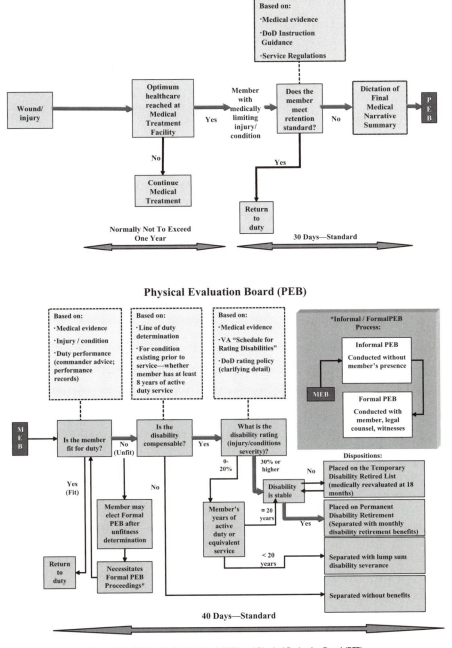

Figure 5.1. Medical Evaluation Board (MEB) and Physical Evaluation Board (PEB).

The MEB process can be initiated in multiple ways depending on the service:

- In *all services*, physicians can initiate MEBs based on timelines as specified in DoD and service regulations or if initiating a medical board is in the service member's best interest.
- *Army*: MEBs can be initiated by the physician and MOS Medical Retention Board.
- *Navy/Marines*: MEBs may be initiated by the physician, the MTF Commander, Chief of Naval Operations, the Commandant of the Marine Corps, or the Chief of Navy Personnel.
- *Air Force*: Physicians must initiate the medical board process.

Once a MEB is initiated, all medical documentation pertaining to the case must be submitted as one package. The tricky part is that all of your evaluations must be "current." This is tricky because it is possible for earlier documentation to no longer be "current" if too much time passes. To insure that your paperwork remains current, remain aware of the dates of each of your evaluations and share this information with your PEBLO and other providers. Ask your PEBLO and providers to help identify what paperwork needs to be completed and how much time until evaluations are no longer current.

- For the *Navy/Marines*, the definition of "current" is six months from the date the board was written. The goal of Navy MTFs is to get the MEB package to the PEB within thirty days of writing the MEB. Please note that complicated (polytrauma) cases are often an exception to the thirty-day goal.
- For the *Air Force*, the definition of "current" is thirty days from the date the board was written or ninety days for tri-service boards.
- For the *Army*, the definition is described in a memorandum of agreement with the Office of the Surgeon General and US Disability Agency and is condition-dependent.

The MEB process can be quite lengthy as it includes the time it takes to start the MEB process (to include documenting the necessary evaluations) and the time needed to address any rebuttals throughout the process, as well as any other MEBs that are being evaluated. Expect a general timeframe of approximately six months, though this could be much shorter or much longer.

The package of information is then forwarded to the informal PEB (iPEB), which determines fitness for duty, disposition, and disability ratings. If the member disagrees with the findings, they have a right to request a formal PEB (fPEB). In the Army and Navy, the member may also rebut prior to the fPEB. They may request reconsideration or rebut findings (they would need to supply new medical documentation), and these actions may take place at the iPEB level and never reach the fPEB.

The Web site http://usmilitary.about.com/od/theorderlyroom/a/medseparation. htm includes a generalized summary of the process.

Line of Duty (LOD) Determination

MEBs may include a Line of Duty (LOD) determination. In accordance with DoDI 1332.38, E2.1.18, LOD determinations are dependent on "whether an injury or disease of a member performing military duty was incurred in a duty status; if not in a duty status, whether it was aggravated by military duty; and whether incurrence or aggravation was due to the member's intentional misconduct or willful negligence." Basically this means that the military needs to determine whether the injury occurred while the member was on duty status, was aggravated by duty status, and was not the result of misconduct. This could potentially play a role in how the case is resolved.

All injuries and diseases that occurred on active duty are presumed in line of duty. However, for questionable incidents for reservists who are not active duty for over thirty days, a written LOD finding is always recommended to ensure future care and possible compensation.

What Can Happen to the Service Member? A PEB can result in multiple potential recommendations:

1. Return to service in same or different specialty.
2. Return to service with or without assignment limitations (e.g., some people cannot be worldwide qualified).
3. Medical retirement, which is based on being found unfit for duty and either twenty years of active service or receiving a disability rating of at least 30 percent. Two types of retirements are available:
   a. A service member could be temporarily retired and placed on a *Temporary Disability Retirement List (TDRL)* if there is a chance the condition might improve with time such that the service member could return to duty or if it is likely that the condition's disability rating will increase or decrease over a five-year period.
   b. *Permanent Disability Retirement List (PDRL)* is permanent medical disability retirement with lifetime retired pay, military health care, and other benefits.
4. Separation from active service, possibly with a one-time, lump sum severance payment. This would be the case when the disability rating is less than the 30 percent cutoff for medical retirement and the member has less than twenty years of service. The PEB will only rate disability in 10 percent increments.
5. Separation without benefits for a variety of reasons (e.g., separation for disciplinary issues).

Return to Service and Reclassification

Army. For Army members, permanent profiles with 3 or 4 will drive a MMRB. An MMRB selects from four possible recommendations to the general court martial convening authority: (1) return to duty, (2) return to duty with reassignment, (3) probation, or (4) recommendation for an MEB. If the MMRB recommends a return to duty with a reassignment, this process is coordinated with the member's local unit and the personnel office. If the service member goes before the MEB/PEB, they are determined fit or unfit in their specific MOS. If found fit, they are maintained in the preexisting MOS. It is only via MMRB that a potential for reassignment exists.

Marines. Once a combat wounded OIF/OEF Marine is found unfit by the PEB, the Marine may submit a Permanent Limited Duty (PLD) request using the MARADMIN 228/06—Active Duty Career Retention and Permanent Limited Duty Policy for Combat Wounded Marines as a reference. It is important for members to review this document for eligibility criteria. This is also driven by the Marine's desire to stay on duty and the medical community's approval for continued service but the individual must still be found fit for continued duty. Reassignments are coordinated through HQ MC at Quantico. Once approved, the Marine will see a career specialist who enters the request into the system. The monitor (the individual that assigns Marines to their duty or job) offers another MOS for the member.

Navy. Navy members can talk with their local career counseling shop about Navy Enlisted Classification (NEC) options. This discussion includes a review of Armed Forces Vocational Aptitude Test (ASVAB) scores and disability ratings. Then the member requests a change in NEC through local career counseling shop, who submits it to the detailer (the assignments person) at Bureau of Personnel (BUPERS). The detailer at BUPERS coordinates the change if it is possible. If a Navy member has over eighteen years of service, a disability, and goes through PEB process, then the sailor can request to stay in through service HQs and remain in the service until they have accumulated twenty years in the service. Otherwise, if a billet were available that the member can fulfill after being returned to duty, that decision would be coordinated with the detailer. For more information, check out the CNPC (Commander, Navy Personnel Command) Web site (at http://www.npc.navy.mil).

Air Force. If an Air Force member is returned to duty and the medical provider changes the member's Duty Limiting Condition (DLC) to one which is not compatible with continuing the current Air Force Specialty Code (AFSC), disqualification paperwork is sent via the Commander's Support Staff (CSS), if available, or Military Personnel Flight (MPF) to Force Management at Air Force Personnel Center (AFPC). It must be processed and the member officially disqualified from their current AFSC in order to submit retraining application through virtual MPF (vMPF). Once vMPF is engaged, the member can coordinate directly with AFPC, who is the point of contact.

Disability Ratings and Decisions

The military and VA have different standards for making disability decisions. The military awards disability payment only to conditions that are found unfitting (e.g., how an injury affects your ability to perform your military duties) by a PEB. The VA rates all medical conditions related to service. For example, the military may not rate you on a scar that was the result of surgery but the VA likely will. Also, the size and location of the scar may impact this decision. Both DoD and VA rate each service-connected disability separately, and then assign a global rating of disability (in multiples of 10's). The global rating is a "combined" rating and not the sum of the separate disability ratings. This is critical to understand, as many veterans assume that the components should be added to each other to determine overall disability. For example, if a service member has four unfitting conditions, each rated at 100 percent the service member would not receive 400 percent disability rating. An individual cannot be more than 100 percent disabled. If a service member had two unfitting conditions rated separately at 40 percent and 20 percent, the combined rating would be 40 percent combined with 20 percent of the remaining 60 percent or 12 percent for a total of 52 percent, which is rounded to the nearest 5 percent. The service member's 40 percent initial disability actually leaves 60 percent left over than can be affected by a second condition. The second condition causes a 20 percent increase to disability of the remaining 60 percent or 12 percent. This is based on the "whole person concept." It is usually confusing to service members and requires explanation by someone such as the PEBLO, VA representative, or legal counsel.

In some cases, disability ratings have exceeded 100 percent for compensation purposes. This can be confusing. Be certain to ask for details from VA personnel or your case coordinator. Also, take note that the VA may establish compensation awards or supports that are not directly related to level of disability. There may be additional supports, in some circumstances, to assist someone to help care for a disabled veteran.

It is important to note that the disability system is undergoing changes. At the time of this publication, the recent National Defense Authorization Act of 2008 resulted in significant changes to the DoD Disability System. Also, on November 26, 2007, a one-year pilot of the Disability Evaluation System Pilot Program was launched. As of the start date, this pilot program only applies to patients assigned to specific hospitals in the National Capitol Region (Army's Walter Reed Army Medical Center, Navy's National Naval Medical Center, and Air Force's Malcolm Grow Medical Center). These changes will affect services members in that they will receive a joint DoD-Veterans Affairs physical performed by the VA. In addition to the PEBLO, an additional coordinator will be assigned to assist service members undergoing an MEB during the VA process. The service PEB will determine fitness or unfitness for duty, and the Department of Veteran Affairs will assign the disability rating. The intent of this process is to facilitate an easier transition from military to civilian life. Further information and updates about this new program will be provided on this book's Web site http://www.warswounded.com.

Top Things to Remember about the MEB and PEB Processes (Compiled from Interviews with Service Members across the Branches)

1. The timeline for treatment and MEB processes are dependent on each individual's injury. You should discuss your own timeline with your physician and treatment team.
2. An MEB is designed to address retention standards and impairment based on each member's medical condition, and PEB is designed to determine fitness for duty and disability.

3. Refer to service-specific resources describing the MEB and PEB process. For example, the Army Physical Disability Evaluation System (PDES) is described at the following Web site: http://www.cs.amedd.army.mil/APDES/purpose.aspx. This Web site includes overviews of each process, governing regulations, forms, and a handbook on the PDES.
4. It is important to keep track of your paperwork and where it is in this process.
5. The PEBLO should be your primary resource for the status of your MEB and the PEB.
6. Ask about anything you do not understand. Also, ask providers how certain they are about diagnoses and other medical decisions and what are the reasons for these decisions. You have a right to know how your medical care is being decided.
7. Make sure you understand what you are signing. It is wise to double check that you understand the short- and long-term impacts of anything you sign.
8. Make it clear to your support team (case manager, physician, and PEBLO) whether you want to stay in the military or not.
9. Keep in mind that you may not be able to return to your previous job and you may need to be reclassified and obtain a new occupation (e.g., may not be able to go back to infantry).
10. Have a military lawyer/legal counsel review the results. Please keep in mind that Veteran Service Organizations (http://www1.va.gov/vso/) can arrange counsel for you. Also, if you choose a civilian lawyer, make sure that they understand the system.
11. Continually track your MEB and PEB (e.g., use Army MyMEB Web-based MEB database and tracking tool).

What Are Some Potential Family Issues?

Families face many potential challenges. These challenges may include:

- Being uprooted from their current home and moving to entirely different parts of the country to be with their loved ones in the hospital.
- Adjusting to unfamiliar areas, starting children in new school systems or leaving the children with their parents or family.
- Finding new jobs if they are able to work or taking a temporary leave of absence from current jobs.
- Developing new support systems while navigating through the sometimes difficult-to-understand medical system for their spouse.

Most medical treatment facilities should have a family assistance center that can assist with family issues (to include such things as child care and locating resources for children and spouses) and locating work. Your unit should also have a local family readiness group or some sort of local support through the garrison command that may assist with family or medical issues. If challenges occur during the hospitalization, speak with your caseworker or unit liaison.

Lessons Learned from the Experience of Spouses and Caregivers

1. Spouses worry about what to expect in the way of future physical, emotional, cognitive and behavioral outcomes.

2. They wonder what is wrong and benefit from hearing definitions and explanations.

3. They need the wounded service member to share just enough with them so that they can understand and be supportive. They do not want or need to upset an avoidant service member, but they resent and cannot adapt to silence, which is perceived as lack of respect and trust.

4. They need to know that they can be part of the ongoing rehabilitation and decision-making process.

5. They need to know that the angry, frustrated warrior understands that they must get help and not dodge accepting responsibility for his actions including angry outbursts, substance abuse, and various sleep disorders (e.g., nightmares, restless limbs, sleep breathing disorders, sleep walking and other activities in sleep). This may well require that they be treated as a couple for a while. Also, the spouse may need to be understanding of certain behaviors, such as being on guard, feeling sad or irritable, avoidance, and social withdrawal. These behaviors may be the warrior's understandable attempts to deal with stressful adjustments rather than being disrespectful towards others.

6. There may be a barrier in couple's sexual relationship. The role of medications, distractibility, anxiety and depression can be defined, and problems with drive or function can be resolved.

7. The power balance between the couple may have shifted the moment the service member went off to war, even before any injury occurred. This needs to be "on the table", defined, understood, and adapted to. Also, the "dependent" partner may no longer be so "dependent" as they may start to understand this large system better and manage the paper work.

8. Humor is important to perspective and balance. Do the things you can both enjoy, with the people whom you both enjoy. Take care of yourself.

9. The spouse who returned from war is mentally or physically different from the spouse who left for war.

10. The service member goes to war and so does the family. The service member goes through recovery and so does the family.

11. For spouse and children, it is challenging to move to another area and to care for the service member.

12. There may be financial challenges not only with a service member's pay but with the resources for family caregivers. Work with your unit liaison to access emergency relief funding (need-based loan/other nonprofit resources), reimbursements (for certain types of required travel), and pay issues (e.g., ironing out any difficulties in receiving pay). In addition to the liaison/case worker can provide or direct you to resources to educational materials regarding personal finance management and understanding military pay, among other related topics.

Lessons Learned from the Nondependent Caregivers Experience

Nondependent caregivers are family members or friends (such as parents, siblings) who are not official dependents of the service member. They do not have the same privileges as the official dependents (including ID cards, specific rights on military installations, and legitimate excuses to miss work). However, they might be the primary point of contact and may make the same sacrifices as dependent caregivers. Below are some suggestions offered by others who have been in this situation of how to cope as a nondependent caregiver:

1. You may be used to your service member being self-reliant and even taking the lead in many areas but after the injury you might find that the person is less assertive and more dependent on you and others.
2. Your service member may feel uncomfortable or even resent being dependent on others for help. Let the service member take charge of his own recovery. For example, the service member may not want you to help her get out of bed.
3. Be patient, take a break, do something you enjoy, then you can be more supportive without resenting it. Do not feel bad about going out to a movie without your spouse, since you will need to get away from the situation occasionally.
4. Find someone else (not yourself) to dictate what the wounded warrior can no longer do. Someone else needs to be responsible for clinically assessing and setting the new boundaries.
5. You need perspective and humor as much as your service member needs these skills. Lighten up, and play or attend games.
6. You may feel frustrated if the adult dependent caregivers are not assisting in helping the service members.
7. Seek support from other dependent caregivers.
8. Watch out for comparing your situation with others – each situation is different for many reasons.
9. You may need to assist the spouse as he reacts to the physical or mental change of the service member.
10. It can be doubly difficult for nondependent caregivers (e.g., a service member's father, grandparent, brothers caring for the service member or other service members) who are provided limited support by the military to assist service members that are recovering in the hospital. This constitutes an additional stressor for the service member as well as the nondependent caregiver. Chaplains, nonprofit organizations, and retired military organizations may assist nondependent caregivers in this process.

What Are Some Potential Long-Term Adjustment Issues, and How Are They Affected by Returning to Duty?

(1) Getting used to potentially being in the minority, depending on your medical condition, once you leave the hospital and are no longer surrounded by other injured service members. This is an adjustment for you and others around you

in a culture that may be less accustomed to seeing someone who has a visible scar, prosthetic, or someone who needs to come to meetings in a wheelchair or on crutches.

(2) Getting to an acceptance of your medical condition as it is after working through being angry and depressed and feeling like giving up. Become focused on where you can go from where you are currently.

(3) Rebounding from setbacks, some of which may feel like starting recovery all over again with your medical condition.

(4) Finding time to take care of yourself. Make the time in your busy schedule at work for prosthesis maintenance and take time away from work for establishing back your quality of life with family and friends.

(5) Ensuring that you have extra medications on hand to deal with recurring pain (e.g., amputees can have phantom limb pain or pain flare ups when changing prosthetics).

(6) Preparing for military training activities. You may need to work with physical therapists and others to prepare for the physical fitness test or taking an alternate event and achieving the same or better fitness score. You may also need to do extra training to prepare for weapons qualifications and other typical military training.

(7) Working through the potential impact of unrated time (time not performing duties) on promotion and job opportunities.

(8) Working through sexual issues that may contribute to other problems of self-image and of misunderstandings in key relationships.

(9) Being careful not to let physical and mental changes make you become dependent on medications.

(10) Becoming familiar with assistive technologies. Use the technology as often as possible so that they become routine in your day.

(11) Ensuring regular maintenance and follow up assistance for assistive technologies like prosthetic devices.

(12) Be prepared—it is hard work to stay on active duty. You have to love serving your country and make quite a commitment to adjust mentally and physically.

(13) An important adjustment is learning to take pride in being a survivor and an injured veteran with the unique knowledge gained from your injury and recovery.

Conclusion

It is important to note that the military medical system and the military policies are constantly changing to provide better and better services so the names and processes mentioned in this book will undoubtedly change too. However, the common adjustment issues and coping strategies for successful recovery and reintegration will likely remain the same. We hope this chapter is a useful resource in your taking pride in being a veteran, appreciating the unique knowledge you have from your injury and recovery, and developing a full and meaningful life.

Disclaimer: The conclusions and opinions expressed in this chapter are those of the authors. They do not reflect the official position of the US Government, Department of Defense, Department of Veteran Affairs, US Air Force, US Army, Malcolm Grow Medical Center, Uniformed Services University of Health Sciences (USUHS), or Augusta Veterans Affairs Medical Center.

Acknowledgments

This chapter would not be possible without the contributions from many people dedicated to supporting injured service members. Our deepest gratitude goes out to SGT Steve Clark (U.S.A. retired OIF amputee currently DoD Program Analyst), Dr. David Armitage (MD, JD, Senior Medical Advisor to U.S. Army Physical Disability Agency), and CPT Stephen Aycock (RN Case Manager in the Able Troop of the Injured Warrior Transition Brigade at WRAMC) who made substantial inputs to this chapter. Our heartfelt thanks also goes to Senior Chief John Crabtree (USN Explosive Ordnance Disposal blinded vet, currently DoD Program Analyst), CPT Bradley and CPT Gamble (RN Case Managers in the Able Troop of the Injured Warrior Transition Brigade at WRAMC), SGM Thompson (Sr. Liaison for SOCOM at WRAMC), Dr. Jim Staudenmeier (psychiatrist at Ft Drum, NY), Dr. Maria Mouratidis (neuropsychologist at National Naval Medical Center, Bethesda, MD), Mr. Roy Naraine (MCPO USN RET, Office Manager of the Military Patient Personnel Div, Medical Boards, National Naval Medical Center, Bethesda, MD), Ms. Carrie Woodward (PEBLO at Malcolm Grow Medical Center, Andrews AFB), Mr. Sarles (Army Public Affairs Office), Mr. Jason Kaar (Associate General Counsel at USUHS), George and Norma Davis, Dr. Denise Evans (Executive of MH and G Service Line at VAMC, Augusta GA), W. E. York (Deputy Director, Marine Casualty Services Branch, Limited Duty Coordinator, HQBn, HQMC, Henderson Hall), Jacqueline Floyd (DAC, Lead, PEBLO at Walter Reed Army Medical Center, Washington, DC), Robin Ferdinand (Career Progression Division (PERS-8), Navy Personnel Command in Millington TN), LTC David M. Benedek (Assoc Prof/Asst. Chair, Dept. of Psychiatry, Uniformed Services University School of Medicine), Mr. Dennis Brower (JD, Agency Legal Advisor to the Army Physical Disability Agency at Walter Reed), COL (Ret.) Robert K. Gifford (Center for the Study of Traumatic Stress, USUHS), TSgt Alethea Bard (NCOIC, Relocations and Employments, Military Personnel Flight, Andrews AFB, MD), and Dr. Seth Messinger (Anthropologist at Department of Sociology and Anthropology at University of Maryland, Baltimore County).

Public Domain: Materials within this chapter were produced at government expense and are not subject to copyright and lie in the public domain.

Bibliography

Birkel, J. D. and Miller, S. J. (1997). *Career Bounce Back.* New York: American Management Association.

Dole, B. and Shalala, D. (2007). *Serve, Support, Simplify: Report of the President's Commission on Care for America's Returning Wounded Warriors*, http://www.pccww.gov.

Isenberg, P. (2007). *Military Peer Visitor Manual*. Amputee Coalition of America.

Johnson, G. (n.d.). "Emotional Stages of Recovery," http://www.tbiguide.com/emotionalstages.html (retrieved October 8, 2007).

Krannich, R. L. (2005). *Change Your Job, Change Your Life: Careering and Re-Careering in the New Boom/Bust Economy* (9th ed.). Manassas Park, VA: Impact Publications.

Kratzer, N. (Fall 2006). Program Helps Wounded Return to Normal Lifestyle: Assistive Technology Provides Real Solutions for Real Needs. *FHP—The Magazine of Force Health Protection*, 1(1), pp. 5 and 19.

Kushner, H. S. (1981). *When Bad Things Happen to Good People*. New York: Schocken Books.

Miles, D. (2007). Severely Wounded Troops Find Meaningful Ways to Continue Serving, http://myarmybenefits.us.army.mil/EN/View/Article.aspx?articleId=1d513d6ecbed44b494ee742c21d05653 (retrieved November 8, 2007).

Under Secretary of Defense (May 3, 2007). Policy Guidance for the Disability Evaluation System and Establishment of Recurring Directive-Type Memoranda. Washington, DC: Department of Defense.

CHAPTER 6

Finding Employment as a Veteran with a Disability

Nathan D. Ainspan

Editors' Comment

Until only recently employment was seen as the last step in rehabilitation for wounded veterans. In the past, treatment providers and therapists worked to treat disabilities first and then found jobs for veterans only after they were "healed." But new developments and changes in thinking about disabilities are changing that sequence so that employment is now considered part of the rehabilitation and treatment program for virtually all types of disabilities. Research, including the work of Bandura (such as Benight and Bandura, 2004) and Seligman (1998), is starting to show how employment can provide positive feelings of "self-efficacy" to counter the negative feelings of "learned helplessness." Employment can help a veteran continually reframe negative thoughts by demonstrating competence, providing meaning to life, and providing a daily network and social support. And thanks to assistive technology and changes in attitudes, people with disabilities can work in more types of jobs than was thought possible in the past.

As the previous chapter demonstrated how a veteran with a disability can return to military service, this chapter will show you how you or your friend or family member can find a great job. This chapter also describes the benefits that military service and disability can bring to a potential employer and how a veteran can overcome questions and issues that might come up about military service or a disability. Nathan D. Ainspan, Ph.D., this chapter's author, is an industrial psychologist in the Washington, DC area. He has conducted research and written on issues impacting the employment prospects of people with disabilities, especially veterans and returning service members with disabilities. Dr. Ainspan was previously with the Office of Disability Employment Policy at the Department of Labor in Washington, DC. He has also led numerous seminars and workshops on finding employment. We hope that you will find this chapter helpful in your own successful job search, so that you can enjoy the rehabilitative and other benefits of a great job.

―――――――――――――――――――

Introduction

Do any of the following apply to you?

- Your rehabilitation and recovery from your war-related injury are far enough along that you are now thinking about going back to work—but you wonder what types of jobs you can do with your injury.
- After being in the service since you were a teenager, you have been discharged with a disability and for the first time in your life you need to find a job outside the military.
- You were with the Reserves or Guard and need to reenter the workforce but may have difficulty performing the tasks you did previously in your job because of your injury.
- You might be wondering if and how your injury will affect your ability to find and hold a good job. Or you may even wonder if you can still work with your new disability (or how you can work with a missing limb or with post-traumatic stress disorder)—or you may wonder if any employer will be willing to hire you with your new disability.

This chapter will help you answer these questions and others that you may have about finding and holding a job with your injury. This chapter will help you through the entire process of looking for a job with a war-related injury, from figuring out what interests and motivates you in the workplace to learning how you can accommodate your disabilities, to speaking with potential employers or interviewers who may have questions about disabilities and your experience in the military, to finally getting that job offer. This information will help you gain a better sense of what you want to do, where you can do it, and how to land a great job that interests you and makes full use of your skills as it accommodates your disabilities.

Hundreds of thousands of individuals with all types of disabilities—from missing limbs to blindness or deafness to quadriplegics to people with "invisible disabilities" such as traumatic brain injury (TBI) or post-traumatic stress disorder (PTSD)—have found well-paying jobs they enjoy with employers who appreciate the work that they perform. Every day thousands of people with disabilities go to work and earn their paychecks. Advances in technology and changes in employers' understanding of how to accommodate employees with disabilities have increased the number and types of opportunities for people who were previously seen as "disabled," including many who were recently seen as "unemployable."

However, you will need to consider your injury in your decisions about your future employment. While you will be capable of doing many things, you may still be limited in other areas. Also, you may meet many people and employers who have no experience with the military and it may feel like you are speaking a foreign language when you communicate with these civilians. And unfortunately, a number of managers and employers still retain negative perceptions and stereotypes about disabilities and military service and you will need to deal with these misconceptions in order for you to display your talents, sell yourself, and enable these employers to understand the benefits and skills you bring to the workplace.

This chapter will provide guidance, resources, and suggestions on the questions you may have about reentering the workforce with your injury—or getting a job for the first time outside the military.

1. What advantages (as a returning service member) do you bring to the employer?
2. What resources are available to you as a veteran?
3. How do you figure out what you want to do and where you want to do it?
4. How does your injury affect what you can do?
5. How can you accommodate your disability at work?
6. How much do workplace accommodations cost?
7. How do you find employers who will want to hire you?
8. How can you create a resume and translate your military experience into something that civilians will understand?
9. What happens when you meet with employers during the interview?
10. What concerns could employers have about your military service?
11. When and how do you discuss your disabilities?
12. What fears, uncertainties, and doubts could employers have about your disability?
13. How do you address these concerns?
14. If you were interested, how could you start your own business?

What Advantages (As a Retuning Service Member) Do You Bring to the Employer?

You may not realize it, but no matter what you did in the service, your time in the military and the skills you gained will be appreciated by many employers and will be seen as a competitive asset at many places. Not only did you learn a number of technical skills (such as computers) while in uniform, but you also gained a number of intangible skills and character traits employers will appreciate.

Some of the traits and skills that you probably developed during your time in uniform include:

- *Loyalty*. You stood for something and remained by your colleagues in difficult times because you were devoted to a cause. When things got difficult, you did not quit but persevered.
- *Selflessness*. You have given up personal gain and making money because you cared about something beyond yourself. You chose to put yourself on the line—and were willing even to sacrifice yourself—to protect the safety of others.
- *Respect for rank and authority*. You respect those who have earned positions above you and will follow orders when your superiors give them.
- *Disciplined*. You are trained to follow through on things and to be effective and will do the right thing when no one is watching.
- *Training and Experience*. You have received years of training and experience in your specialty.

As you read this list you probably wonder why these skills are such a big deal to employers—since most of the people you met in the service probably displayed these traits. But while these traits might be standard among your colleagues in the military, companies in the civilian world regularly complain that they have the hardest time finding people with them. Talk to hiring managers and company leaders and across the board, you will hear them complain that job candidates today are self-centered, spoiled, untrained, ungrateful, have little respect for authority, are unable to work in teams, lack many basic skills, and have no loyalty to the organization. Ask any employer ranging from the small store looking for hourly workers to a large corporation hiring executives and they will all say that they want employees who will come in on time, put in a full day's work, and follow directions from their bosses. All of these skills that were second nature to you in the service and became part of your character are now assets that you need to emphasize as you apply for jobs outside the military. Your mission now is to let your interviewers know that you have these critical skills—so feel free to mention them during interviews or emphasize in your cover letters to potential employers.

Additional Advantages You Bring to Employers as a Returning Service Member

Your time in the military has provided you with a number of important skills that employers are interested in hiring. Written from the employer 's perspective, The Department of Labor's Hire Vets First (www.HireVetsFirst.gov) program lists the following "Top 10 Reasons to Hire Veterans" on their Web site:

- *Accelerated learning curve.* Veterans have the proven ability to learn new skills and concepts. In addition, they can enter your workforce with identifiable and transferable skills, proven in real-world situations. This background can enhance your organization's productivity.
- *Leadership.* The military trains people to lead by example as well as through direction, delegation, motivation, and inspiration. Veterans understand the practical ways to manage behaviors for results, even in the most trying circumstances. They also know the dynamics of leadership as part of both hierarchical and peer structures.
- *Teamwork.* Veterans understand how genuine teamwork grows out of a responsibility to one's colleagues. Military duties involve a blend of individual and group productivity. They also necessitate a perception of how groups of all sizes relate to each other and an overarching objective.
- *Diversity and inclusion in action.* Veterans have learned to work side by side with individuals regardless of diverse race, gender, geographic origin, ethnic background, religion, and economic status as well as mental, physical, and attitudinal capabilities. They have the sensitivity to cooperate with many different types of individuals.
- *Efficient performance under pressure.* Veterans understand the rigors of tight schedules and limited resources. They have developed the capacity to know how to accomplish priorities on time, in spite of tremendous stress. They know the critical importance of staying with a task until it is done right.

- *Respect for procedures.* Veterans have gained a unique perspective on the value of accountability. They can grasp their place within an organizational framework, becoming responsible for subordinates' actions to higher supervisory levels. They know how policies and procedures enable an organization to exist.
- *Technology and globalization.* Because of their experiences in the service, veterans are usually aware of international and technical trends pertinent to business and industry. They can bring the kind of global outlook and technological savvy that all enterprises of any size need to succeed.
- *Integrity.* Veterans know what it means to do "an honest day's work." Prospective employers can take advantage of a track record of integrity, often including security clearances. This integrity translates into qualities of sincerity and trustworthiness.
- *Conscious of health and safety standards.* Thanks to extensive training, veterans are aware of health and safety protocols both for themselves and the welfare of others. Individually, they represent a drug-free workforce that is cognizant of maintaining personal health and fitness. On a company level, their awareness and conscientiousness translate into protection of employees, property, and materials.
- *Triumph over adversity.* In addition to dealing positively with the typical issues of personal maturity, veterans have frequently triumphed over great adversity. They likely have proven their mettle in missions and critical situations demanding endurance, stamina, and flexibility. They may have overcome personal disabilities through strength and determination.

(This list is reprinted from http://www.hirevetsfirst.gov/10reasons.asp?format=txt.)

What Resources Are Available to You as a Veteran?

As a returning service member, you have a number of resources and programs available to help you with your job search. I encourage you to use as many of them as you can. Here is a brief list:

Transition assistance. Every service member is required to attend the Transition Assistance Program (TAP) briefing on your base, which is a three- or four-day workshop available to all separating military members and spouses. Professionally trained workshop facilitators from the State Employment Services, military family support services, and the Department of Labor present the workshops. Information about the TAP program is located at http://www.dol.gov/vets/programs/tap/main.htm or at the TAP Online portal at http://www.taonline.com/. You can also download the TAP materials off the Web (at http://turbotap.org or http://www.taonline.com/). The TAP program was created as partnership among the Departments of Defense, Veterans Affairs, Transportation, and Labor to provide employment and training information to armed forces members within 180 days of separation or retirement. As a service member with a disability, you are also eligible for the Disabled Transition Assistance Program (DTAP), which provides individual instruction for you in addition to the TAP classes offered to all transitioning service members.

The program features an extensive manual that will walk you through every step of the job search process described in this chapter, from figuring out which skills you want to use in your next job to providing advice on negotiating the salary and getting the job offer. It also includes sections on dealing with stress during the job search and writing a resume. The manual provides you with worksheets that will help you figure out your skills, compute your costs, and keep track of your information every step of the way. The manual can be found at http://www.taonline.com/tappages/tapmanual.asp.

Each military base also has a transition office known by different names in each of the branches. It is called the Career and Alumni Program in the Army, the Family Support Center in the Air Force, the Work/Life Center in the Coast Guard, and the Fleet and Family Support Center in the Navy and Marines. For a complete list of these offices, go to http://www.taonline.com/tappages/. The quality and amount of information and the resources available to you will vary by each base. Some bases have staff that are more knowledgeable and will have more resources than other bases. The military has created other Web sites as well that can provide you with information and leads as well: The Department of Defense (DoD) TransPortal (www.dodtransportal.org) has information about the TAP and other useful information. Operation Transition has the Transition Bulletin Board (TBB) at http://www.dmdc.osd.mil/ot with lists of job opportunities and other information.

Relocation costs. The government will pay the cost of one relocation for you and your family as you transition out of the service to your new home. This benefit can be useful in negotiations with potential employers since the company will not have to pay the expenses to move you to a new job. Feel free to mention this benefit in your conversations with employers.

Nonprofit organizations. As a service member and as a veteran with a disability, you are eligible to join a number of organizations that can provide services to you. Some of these groups include Veterans of Foreign Wars (VFW), the Military Officers' Association of America (MOAA), Paralyzed Veterans Association (PVA), and the Disabled American Veterans (DAV). The resources on this book's Web page at http://www.warswounded.com list organizations and their Web sites. In addition to providing useful information and services (including financial benefits), these groups can also be instrumental in your job search, as explained below.

Corporate Gray. All transitioning active duty soldiers, sailors, airmen, and Marines receive a free copy of either *From Army Green to Corporate Gray*, *From Air Force Blue to Corporate Gray,* or *From Navy Blue to Corporate Gray* (which includes the Navy and Coast Guard) written by Carl S. Savino, a retired Major from the Army Reserve and Ronald L. Krannich, Ph.D. Make sure to pick up your copy—each version is filled with helpful information about the job search and transition process, and each book contains forms and checklists, exercises you can use to learn more about your skills, and even lists of military-friendly employers looking to hire veterans. The publisher has a Web site with most of this information at http://www.corporategray.com and they also have a transition service that will allow you to post your resume, search employers, and seek guidance about your transition. I have used the books extensively as I wrote this chapter and spoke with Mr. Savino directly and have found both him and his books to be enormously helpful.

One-Stop Centers. In every community, the Department of Labor operates "One-Stop" centers to provide information about the job search process and provide listings of local employers. Each One-Stop should have a Disabled Veterans' Outreach Program (DVOP) coordinator and Local Veterans' Employment Representative (LVER) available to assist you with this process, and to help you find employers that interest you. Locate your nearest One-Stop center at http://www.servicelocator.org/ or call them at 1-877-US-2JOBS. You can find a local DVOP or LVER through this site: http://networker.nvti.cudenver.edu/. In addition, every state has employment offices and programs that can provide assistance and ideas to you as well.

EARN. Another Department of Labor resource available to you as a person with a disability is EARN (which stands for the Employer Assistance and Recruiting Network) which can connect you to service providers that are working with employers interested in hiring employees with disabilities. You can contact an EARN Employment Specialist at: earn@earnworks.com or call them toll-free at 1 (866) 327-6669.

RecruitMilitary. RecruitMilitary, the country's only nationwide, full-service, military-to-civilian recruiting firm can also help you in your transition. The company is a veteran-owned, veteran-operated, and veteran-advised business that connects employers in all industries with men and women who are transitioning from active duty or Reserve and Guard service to civilian life (as well as veterans with a wide variety of business experience, and military spouses). All of their services are free to you and your spouse (the employers pay the company for conducting the search for them). The company was started when the founders realized that the experiences that they gained as recruiters for the armed forces could be directly applied to the private sector as recruiters for companies. The company's advisors will not only place resumes in front of employers, but they will also work with any veteran to help write a resume and provide advice on the best way to describe military service in ways that the civilian world can understand and appreciate. A number of consultants at RecruitMilitary advised me as I wrote this chapter and I found them knowledgeable about every step of the job search transition process. They can be reached at http://www.recruitmilitary.com or by phone at (513) 683-5020.

The Sierra Group. The Sierra Group is a national authority on disability policy and practices for business. The group runs a sourcing service linking employers and employees with disabilities. This service can be reached at http://thesierragroup.com/services.htm#candidate_sourcing and by phone at (800) 973-7687.

Federal government veterans preference. As a veteran, and especially as a veteran with a disability, you qualify for special hiring preferences in the federal government when applying for a job. Under the Disabled Veterans Affirmative Action Program (DVAAP), most departments and agencies in the federal government are required to have an affirmative action program for the recruitment, employment, and advancement of disabled veterans. War-disabled veterans receive preferences in hiring decisions and extra points in the process so you will have an easier time than others in finding employment with the federal government. For information on these programs available to you, check out this page at the Office of Personnel Management (https://www.opm.gov/veterans/). The "VetInfo Guide" is located at https://www.opm.gov/veterans/html/vetsinfo.asp. To see what jobs are available in the federal government, go to http://www.usajobs.gov.

How Do You Figure Out What You Want to Do and Where You Want to Do It?

If this is your first job after being in the service for a while, you may never have had the chance to think about what you really like doing on the job since in the military you were assigned your tasks. Or you may have taken jobs in the past just to pay your bills and never had a chance to explore what would really excite you in a job. You now have an opportunity during your transition to explore this question and find out what you want to do (to see which skills and talents you enjoy using) and where you want to do these things. This process may feel overwhelming but the more that you work to understand your skills and preferences, the better you will be at selling these preferences to potential employers—and the better your chances will be at getting a job offer. And in the end, you will be more content in a job that aligns with your preferences.

As a service member with a disability it is even more critical that you understand yourself and your preferences because you may encounter misconceptions from people about your prospects and about what you can and cannot do with your disability. But if you understand yourself, you will be able to defend yourself better against these kinds of comments and secure the right job for your interest, your skills, and your disability.

If you take the time to understand yourself, you will know what motivates you and you will have a better chance of finding a job that satisfies your motivating factors and thus you will be able to find a job you truly enjoy. There are far too many people out there who are working for the weekend and waiting until 5 P.M. so that they can go home and do what they really want to do with their lives. When you find a job that uses your top skills in an environment that matches your interests, work is no longer a four-letter word: you actually look forward to going to work in the morning and feel engaged all day. The sense of mission and purpose you felt in the services can be achieved in civilian life if you know what you want to do and where you want to do it and can find an employer that provides you with the right type job in the right type of environment.

As part of this process, Carl Savino, the coauthor of the *Corporate Gray* series of military-to-civilian career transition books mentioned above, recommends that you make your employment interests clear to the employers and explain how the skills and experience you bring to the table will help them deliver their product or service better, faster, or cheaper (which are the top goals of virtually every organization). A number of resources are available that can help you figure out the answers to these questions.

You can start this process by talking to career counselors and with other veterans. You can also take "skills assessment tests" that explore your interests and abilities and are able to tell you what kinds of skills you have and suggest potential careers you could explore. (I have taken many of these tests and have found their suggestions helpful in my own career planning.) Some of these tests include the ASVAB offered by the military (the acronym refers to the Armed Services Vocational Aptitude Battery), the Myers-Briggs Type Indication (MBTI), the Strong Interest Inventory, the ISEEK Skills Assessment, the Career Assessment Inventory, and the Vocational Preference Inventory. Transition centers and other locations can provide and interpret these tests, sometimes at a fee. If you do not currently have access to a transition center, conduct an Internet search on these tests to find out places that provide them. The One-Stop centers mentioned earlier can also provide information about these tests as well. Savino suggests the following commercial sites that also provide skills assessment. Links to their products can be searched through Google or through the *Corporate Gray* Web site.

- Career Lab
- Self-Directed Search
- Personality Online
- MasteryWorks
- MAPP
- Personality Type

The "bible" of skills assessment resources is the book *What Color Is Your Parachute* by Richard Nelson Bolles. The book is available in many libraries but I would recommend purchasing it at a bookstore or buying it online because you will want to write in your copy and refer back to it repeatedly. The author also has a Web site about the book at http://www.jobhuntersbible.com which contains information and links to other job search materials. The author has a supplement to the *Parachute* book, written specifically for people with disabilities titled *Job Hunting for the So-Called Handicapped or People Who Have Disabilities* to help you figure out how to accommodate your injuries as you work through the *Parachute* exercises and your job search process. The book was coauthored by Dale Brown, a woman with a learning disability, the director of the world's largest Web site for people with learning disabilities (www.ldonline.org), and a self-help leader in the learning disability movement who has helped hundreds of people obtain employment. Another useful book to check out is *The Job Search Handbook for People With Disabilities* (2004) by Daniel J. Ryan.

I recommend that you purchase the *Parachute* book, take the time to read through it, and work through the exercises. I bought the book the first time I looked for a job and I found the exercises it contained to be an enormous help. I have used it in each subsequent job search in my life and continue to access it and refer to it regularly. Here is a brief summary of what you will do in the book: The exercises ask you to think about when you felt happiest and most fulfilled doing something either at work, with your family, or in one of your activities and then describe these situations in writing. Next, you work through a detailed step-by-step process that dissects these stories to locate the skills and other things that you will need for a job to engage your interests.. It takes a few hours to go through this process but do not try to skip through the process. When I went through the book, I was tempted many times to take shortcuts, but I did not, and in the end I was rewarded with a thorough understanding of who I was and what I needed to look for in a job that I would enjoy. Over the years, I have gone back to the book and to the notes that I made about my interests and I continue to use the exercises to reevaluate what I need to be happy in my next job. I have also been surprised at how little these elements have changed over time—the things that were critical to me at high school are still important to me decades later. When you complete this process, you will have a good idea of what you will need in your next job in order to feel successful and productive at work. You will also have a good sense of the environment in which you will do your best work. Based on this information, you will then be able to seek out potential employers that offer this kind of environment and determine if they have jobs that fit your qualifications.

How Does Your Injury Affect What You Can Do?

As you compile your list of your skills and the type of environment in which you want to work, you will have to give serious consideration to your disability and if and how this changes what you can do and where you want to work. Your injury may permanently impact some of the skills that you enjoyed using or affect the types of tasks that you were able to do in the past. If you enjoyed driving in the past but lost your vision, you may need to find jobs that do not involve driving—or figure out ways to have another person do the driving so that you can perform other tasks that do not involve your vision. If you had supervised dozens of people in past jobs but now have memory issues because of TBI, you will need to factor in your changed intellectual capability into your decisions about your next job. Or if you were used to working in fast-paced situations before the war but now find this difficult because of PTSD, you will need to adjust your thinking and expectations about what you want to do at work (at least for now). As you work through the exercises in *What Color is Your Parachute* or the other tests mentioned earlier, you will need to realistically access your situation and adjust your list of skills so that you will know what you will be capable of doing as you go forward with your working life.

But before you cross too many things off of your list because of your injury, make it a point to learn about accommodations that are available to you and can help you perform these tasks. Improvements in technology and changing times have opened up more opportunities for people with disabilities and allowed those with disabilities to do things that would have been thought of as impossible only a few years ago. Computers can read books to people with visual impairments, prosthetics allow amputees to take part in sports, and people with brain injuries can use miniature tape recorders to help them remember things. The VA and other places will also provide training and rehabilitation that can help you accommodate other disabilities as well.

The Department of Labor runs a service called the Job Accommodation Network (JAN) that I describe in detail in the next section that can provide you with suggestions specific to your injury. (JAN can be reached at http://www.jan.wvu. edu or by phone at (800) 526-7234.) I have seen many veterans with disabilities performing tasks that many would have thought their injury would have prevented them from accomplishing. I have seen amputees ski down hills and run marathons, I have spoken with hearing-impaired coworkers and presented PowerPoint shows to blind colleagues. Before you eliminate skills or activities off of your list, talk to others and do research on the ways that your disability can be accommodated. From what I have seen, with the right accommodations, the only barrier that prevents veterans with disabilities from achieving their goals is the individual's own attitude and determination—and veterans have some of the most determined attitudes I have ever seen.

And as you evaluate your skills and strengths against any disabilities, remember that while you have a more visible, pronounced, or severe disability, everyone on this planet has some type of disability and everyone—including those with disabilities—has unique strengths that outweigh their disabilities. And most important, everyone is capable of working in spite of—and because they have—these disabilities. Everyone—not just individuals with "disabilities"—uses accommodations. I am five and a half feet tall and need to push my seat forward in my car. At my office I do not put things on the top shelves above my desk and I bought a footrest that raises my feet up, since they cannot touch the floor. Some of my employers have ordered a chair for me that fits me better. These are all "accommodations" that either I have made for myself, purchased, or had the employer purchase for me. Your accommodations for your injury, for your wheelchair, or for your PTSD or TBI are no different.

Job Hunting for the So-Called Handicap, or People Who Have Disabilities reminds us that "everyone is disabled and everyone is employable . . . If you speak of yourself only as free, capable, and as a person with abilities, you are denying the other side of your nature. Or if you speak of yourself only as handicapped, disabled, and as a person with disabilities, you are denying the first side of your nature. Each and every human being has both sides. In interpreting yourself to an employer, it is crucial for you to know this and emphasize this during an interview. You can put it quite simply: "It's true I have a disability; all of us do. Every one of us has things that we cannot do or cannot do well. But I am here because there are many things I can do well. This is what they are."

In an interview with me for this chapter, Dale Brown, the book's coauthor adds that many people with disabilities have succeeded in getting jobs through selling themselves and telling their stories. She says "It is your abilities, not your disabilities that get you the offer. Emphasize your strengths and how you can meet their needs. Explain clearly and calmly about how you will get around the challenges. Help the employer overcome their fears about disability. Then you will be offered the chance to start work."

But as you think about the skills that might have been impacted by your injury and consider jobs you can do and what you might not be able to do in the future, reread the attributes listed under the "What advantages do you bring to an employer" section above (i.e., your loyalty, determination, and willingness to follow orders). You earned all of these traits while you were in uniform, and now none of those traits will ever be affected by your disability—and all of them will always remain strong assets that any employer will appreciate and will want to hire. Your injury may have affected your leg, your face, or your memory. But it will never touch your loyalty, your desire for hard work, and your selfless character. And all of these will be assets to your next employer regardless of what injuries you may have received in your service to the nation.

How Can You Accommodate Your Disability at Work?

The best source of information about workplace accommodations is the Job Accommodation Network (JAN), located at the University of West Virginia. The federal government funds JAN and their services are free to anyone with a question about accommodating disabilities. You can call them at (800) 526-7234 or visit them online at http://www.jan.wvu.edu. JAN has a team of consultants with years of experience in this area. Many specialize in working with veterans and their employers to accommodate their injuries. Call or e-mail JAN and describe your disability and the type of work or tasks that interest you. One of JAN's consultants will answer your questions and provide you with recommendations and suggested appliances or technology you can use to accommodate the activity you wish to pursue.

I have called JAN many times and spoken with their consultants on many different types of disabilities and have been impressed with the amount of information that they have collected and their ingenuity in figuring out solutions. The consultants are particularly creative in coming up with low cost solutions or even no-cost and free solutions tailored to each client's particular needs. One veteran with PTSD, for example, had difficulties in his office whenever people approached him from behind and was at risk of losing his job. JAN suggested that this man purchase one of those over-sized rear view mirrors at the local big box store (the kind you put up inside your car to see things behind you) and affix it on his computer monitor. This way he can see whenever someone enters his cubicle and thus he will not be startled if he is approached from behind.

JAN has more examples of how to accommodate PTSD available at the Web page http://www.jan.wvu.edu/corner/vol03iss02.htm.

For information on accommodating the symptoms of TBI, check out Dale Brown's *Leaning a Living: A Guide to Planning Your Career and Finding a Job for People with Learning Disabilities, Attention Deficit Disorder, and Dyslexia* (2000).

How Much Do Workplace Accommodations Cost?

One of the biggest concerns that employers have about the employment of people with disabilities is how much the accommodations are going to cost them in order for them to make their workplaces accessible. Most envision that the accommodations will cost them thousands of dollars and many suspect that accommodations will be difficult to implement and will disrupt their offices, their workflow, and their schedules.

But when you look at the actual numbers involved, you will see that most workplace accommodations are inexpensive and not disruptive to the company or other employees. And frequently, a number of tax breaks and other programs are available that can help defray most of the costs of making the accommodation.

To counter the idea that accommodations are expensive, JAN surveyed companies that had made accommodations for employees with disabilities. After speaking with more than a thousand employers, JAN found that for almost half of all companies, the cost to accommodate employees with disabilities was nothing. That's right—zero, no cost whatsoever. According to the data, 46 percent of the companies surveyed provided accommodations at no cost to the company. These employers accommodated disabilities without having to spend anything on tools or on any extra equipment. Sometimes, a change in schedule was all that was needed to accommodate an individual with PTSD. In another example, relocating furniture was sufficient to allow someone in a wheelchair to get around the office. When employers spent money on the accommodations, the costs were minimal. Only 7 percent of the respondents said that the accommodation required an ongoing annual cost to the company. The remaining 45 percent experienced a one-time cost, and the typical cost to the company was $500. And when companies were asked how much they paid for an accommodation beyond what they would have paid for an employee without a disability, the employers said that the typical cost was $300.

In exchange for spending a few extra hundred dollars, the companies reported that they gained a great deal in return: they reported a number of benefits from making the accommodation including the ability to retain a qualified employee, a way to recruit additional employees, a chance to improve the morale and diversity of their company, increase worker productivity, and eliminate the need to find and a train replacement employees when employees become disabled. On average, the companies estimated that they "got back" about $10 in benefits for each dollar that they invested in disability accommodation costs.

Even if a cost is involved in the accommodation, JAN's consultants are knowledgeable about sources of funding that can pay for these accommodations. A company that wants to hire a person in a wheelchair and wants to install a ramp can learn about many options and tax breaks that are available for them to help pay for the cost of this accommodation. In addition, funds are also available through Vocational Rehabilitation and Employment services through the VA and local state agencies—check out http://www.vba.va.gov/bln/vre/ or http://vetsuccess.gov/ for information.

A number of other financial incentives are available through the government to help employers reduce the cost of hiring you and paying for accommodations you may need on a job. The Sierra Group's foundation funds a Web site that lists many of these incentives at http://www.employmentincentives.com.

Here are just a few examples of the tax credits and other financial incentives that an employer could receive to accommodate your disability and offer you a job.

- *Work Opportunity Tax Credit (WOTC)* can provide a company with up to $2,400 in tax credits for each new qualified hire
- *Disabled Tax Credit.* Small businesses (those with less than 30 employees) that make accommodations can receive 50 percent of the expense as a tax credit
- *Architectural Transportation Barrier Removal Tax Deduction.* Companies can claim up to $15,000 per year in deductions for making their premises more accessible to people with disabilities and the elderly

Most employers are not aware of these tax credits and the other programs. Some may not even want to take the time to learn about accommodations that are available and could save them money in the short term and help them locate and keep good employees in the long term. Therefore you will need to be aware of how your own injuries can be accommodated and what technologies, programs, and tax benefits are available to help you and your employer. As you locate potential employers and work to sell yourself to them, you will need to know about these programs and benefits so that you will be able to effectively convince employers about the low cost and financial benefits of hiring employees with disabilities such as yourself. JAN's report—*Workplace Accommodations: Low Cost, High Impact*, available online at http://www.jan.wvu.edu/media/LowCostHighImpact.pdf.—is a great place to start looking for this information. For information about your specific disability, call JAN and explain your disability and what type of work you would like to do and see what kinds of recommendations and information they can provide.

If you encounter an interviewer or an organization that seems overly concerned about accommodation costs, you can present this data to counter misconceptions and help you make the argument that the company should hire you. You can explain that for a few dollars in investment (or no cost at all), the company will have access to a dedicated and skilled employee with your skills, background, and military experience

I have worked with many people with disabilities and have been surprised and impressed with how the right accommodations can allow them to do almost any task. I have read about a blind doctor practicing medicine at a hospital because he can use technology to read reports and X-rays. Many of his patients believe that his blindness makes him a better physician since he had to become a better listener and thus hears things from his patients' conversations that other doctors overlook. People in wheelchairs are able to work on manufacturing production lines with special tools or benches that lower the production line or raise them to meet the work. And veterans with PTSD or TBI and other injuries that impact their psychological and emotional functioning are able to fully interact in work environments with their coworkers because they were able to use accommodations.

Except for employer misconceptions and attitudes, the only limitations I have seen on employment for those with disabilities are the ambition, drive, and creativity of the person who uses the accommodation. If you have the desire to seek a job, want to work around your injury, and have the knowledge and creativity to accommodate it, the only barrier that stands in your way is the ability to find an employer that can focus on the skills and background that you can bring to their organization rather than looking at your disability and not seeing beyond it.

How Do You Find Employers Who Will Want to Hire You?

Once you have a better understanding of the skills that you would like to use and the type of place in which you want to use them, you will need to find employers that are interested in your collection of skills and will want to make you an offer. When you think of looking for employment, you probably think of the traditional ways to find jobs—looking through the "Help Wanted" ads in the newspaper or going online and looking through job boards such as Monster.com and others. While this is the way that many find jobs, it is not the most effective way nor is it the most efficient use of your time. Estimates suggest that only around 10 percent of job searchers find jobs through these "passive" techniques. And passive techniques are less effective for anyone with a background that might be slightly different from what an employer was originally expecting—and this includes both people with disabilities and transitioning service members. Richard Bolles and Dale Brown call this passive system "the numbers game" and remind us that the purpose of this system is to bring to the employer a huge number of résumés to let them screen out as many candidates as possible. This is why it is not the most efficient approach for an individual job searcher like you. Many employers dislike using this numbers game as well since they have to take the time to place the ads and then read through piles of resumes that each ad generates (sometimes hundreds of people will send in resumes for one opening) just to find one person who they hope will work out well for them.

If you use an active job approach like the one described here, you approach the employer directly and have a better chance to sell yourself and your skills to the people making hiring decisions. These active techniques will also provide you with a chance to learn more about yourself, hear about openings at companies that are not widely advertised, and stand out in the hiring manager's mind since you approach the employer directly with a demonstrated interest in the company and not in response to a job advertisement. You will also have a better chance to explain your disability and military experience to the employer. In addition, you will be able to save the employer time and money since they too can avoid the numbers game in their search for good employees.

Unlike civilians without disabilities, you have two elements in your background that employers might not understand and this could make it more difficult for you to find employment. First, a number of hiring managers and organizations might not understand your military background or appreciate the resources and benefits that your time in the military could bring to their company. Second, many organizations and individuals out there may have misconceptions about how people with disabilities can do jobs. To find a job, you will need to work your way past these companies and individuals or try to convince them to change their minds. In an active job search your mission is to find the employers and the people out there who appreciate your service to the country and will look at your strengths and skills rather than seeing your injury as a disability. This chapter will tell you how by describing resources that are available to help you with your search and by explaining the active job searching technique called "informational interviewing." The *Parachute* book describes this technique in detail so I will summarize it here.

As you start the job search process, you will realize how looking for a full time job is a full time job in itself. The time and effort that it takes and the emotional toll it can take on you are virtually the same, if not more than what you will encounter in a regular job. Therefore, take the job search process seriously and devote the time and energy to your job search process. And if you are still working through your rehabilitation and recovery from your injury (through physical therapy or counseling appointments), understand that it will take you even more time to go through the search process.

The secret behind an active job search is to mine every contact and every resource you have to learn about potential employers and potential openings. The most important resource you can draw upon is yourself and the network of people that you know. Tell everyone who you know that you are looking for work (and let them know what kind of work you would like to do) and ask each contact to spread the word to other people and see if these people can also look for jobs for you. In this way, you will have multiple pairs of eyes on the look out for you to let you know of any opportunity that might become available. When you talk to your friends, family, neighbors, fellow service members and veterans, members of your house of worship, and even people you meet at parties or as you go about your daily chores and errands. Tell everyone that you are looking for a job, and tell them about the work that you would like to find. Ask each of these contacts if they know anybody who is working in this area. If they do, ask for the name and contact information and ask if you could use their name to contact them for information. And also ask each person in your network to keep you in mind just in case they think of anything else in the future or meet anyone else that could be helpful to you. To help with your networking, I would recommend joining the veterans' organizations such as the VFW, MOAA, PVA, DAV, and the other organizations mentioned on this book's Web site, http://www.warswounded.com. In addition to the other benefits and services that they provide, they can also provide you with contacts for your networking.

This approach does work and will help you find out about jobs that are not advertised in the paper or online. I can verify from my own personal experiences about the effectiveness of these techniques. I used them in my own job searches and have found most of my jobs this way. As an example, when I graduated from school I was looking for a job in Washington, DC, even though I was living in upstate New York. My friend's mother was flying back from Florida and was sitting next to a woman who ran a company in DC who complained to her about how hard it was to find employees for their company. Fortunately, my friend's mother knew that I was looking for work in DC and asked this woman for her card. My friend forwarded the information to me and I made contact with that company. I started working with them about a month later.

Once you get a person's contact information, you will want to speak with him or her in an informational interview. Informational interviews are based on the premise that people like to talk about themselves. In an informational interview, you approach a person (either one of your contacts or someone that you learned about through one of your contacts) and ask that individual not for a job but for information about his or her own work experiences. Since you are not asking people for a job, people will usually be interested in speaking with you. But even though you are not directly asking for a job, many times informational interviewing will lead to real jobs because the contacts that you approach will keep you in mind and alert you to positions if they hear of any that are available. Through this informational interviewing process, you can learn more about yourself, your interests, and where you would like to work. With each interview you learn more about yourself and can better adjust your search to your interests. You will also learn about more places that hire people with your skills (including some you may never have heard about previously) and you will learn how you can best approach these places. Since you are developing and expanding the network of people that you know as you look for a job, this approach is also called "networking."

You can also conduct research online or in the library to help expand your network and to learn about places that may be interested in hiring you. There is a wealth of information on the Web that you can explore, but I encourage you to use your local public library or college libraries in your community to locate better information. Most libraries have reference librarians available who have extensive training on locating the best sources of information for you. Most public library reference librarians are available to serve the public and many reference librarians in college libraries will also help you out. I have worked closely with reference librarians in my job searches and I have found them to be important allies. In addition, the reference librarians will be able to access databases and other sources of information that you will not be able to find online by yourself.

As an example, virtually every industry has trade publications and industry magazines and a good reference librarian will be able to help you find the publications for any field you wish to explore. Read through these publications at the library, see if you can obtain them online, or even purchase them or subscribe to them if they are affordable. Not only will you learn more about the industry you want to explore, but you can also learn about people who write a lot about this field or are active in the field. If someone seems knowledgeable about your field of interest—either the person writes about your area of interest or an individual is interviewed in one of these publications—contact this person and see if you can have an informational interview (or at least get suggestions for other people to contact). I have had done this myself and found great leads by contacting people I read about and asking them for informational interviews or phone calls.

Many people have difficulty with making these kinds of contacts since most of us were raised to be modest and shy about approaching people for favors. It will initially feel awkward to overcome these feelings but it will become easier with each contact. So do not be bashful: feel free to write an e-mail (frequently the publication will print the e-mail address of authors or individuals profiled in the story) or look up the contact information on the Web for the person you wish to contact. (If no information is provided, you can look up the main phone number for the company on the Web, call their main number, and ask for the mailing address and title for the person you wish to contact.) I have found that most people are willing to provide you with information and in the twenty years that I have been making these contacts I have experienced only a small number of rejections and only a handful of people who were rude to me. But I have found dozens of others who helped me learn about jobs and fields and even provided me with the information that eventually led to my job offer.

The number one rule of approaching someone for an informational interview is to respect this person's time: remember that each contact is doing you a favor. Be respectful and grateful for whatever the person does for you. The second rule is never directly ask the contact for a job since doing this will probably lessen the contact's interest in speaking with you. Although the contact knows that you are looking for a job (and will probably mention it to you if openings are available) you still do not want to directly ask for the job. If you do this, the person may forward you to the HR department, where you can easily get lost in the crowd.

What do you say in your letter or e-mail to this contact? If you have any connection to the individual (through one of your contacts or because you share something in common) feel free to "name drop" and mention that connection immediately in your letter or e-mail. And if the person you wish to contact has any connection to the armed forces, mention this at the beginning of your letter as well. People like to interact with individuals with whom they share something and if you can connect to someone through a mutual contact or through your shared time in the service, feel free to exploit these connections. If you share anything else with the person (such as your veteran status or the branch in which you served), this will also increase the likelihood of receiving a positive response from them as well.

In your e-mail or letter to your potential contact, introduce yourself with a few sentences (but do not make it too long since you may lose the interest of the individual and you do not want to seem like you are bragging) and give your reader a sense of who you are and why you are contacting him. It never hurts to mention how you know or read about the person and to praise or compliment her for her achievements. The most important purpose of this e-mail or letter is to get a face-to-face meeting or phone call with the person, so keep the letter or e-mail focused on that mission. Remember to conclude the letter by asking the individual for a phone call or meeting and offer some suggestions of when you can meet or talk. It is harder to share information and respond to comments via e-mail, which is why ideally you want a phone call or a face-to-face meeting. But if the person is busy and e-mail is the only option, then pursue that option.

Below is a sample introductory letter to a contact of a neighbor to ask for a meeting.

TO: John Watson, Baker Street Corporation　　　johnwatson@bakerstreet.com
FROM: Morris Karakofsky　　　　　　　　　　　　mkarakofsky@gmail.com

RE: Referral from Leopold Bloom

Dr. Watson,

My neighbor, Leo Bloom, suggested that I contact you. I am transitioning from service with the Marines in Iraq and I am interested in a career in logistics and acquisitions. Leo mentioned that you are a logistics planner with Baker Street for the past ten years and that you also served with the Marines. If your time permits, I would like to meet with you to learn more about the logistics field and how I might be able to transition from the military into civilian companies.

I recently returned from Baghdad where I oversaw the logistics and acquisitions for my platoon. I am DAWAI certified (level III) and was responsible for managing a staff of twenty.

If your time permits, I would like to speak with you about your experiences in the field and hear your suggestions for someone wishing to enter this field. Would we be able to arrange a time to meet in person or speak by phone? I look forward to speaking with you and will call your office next week to see if we could set up a time at your convenience when we might be able to meet or talk. Thank you.

Semper fi,
Morris Karakofsky

Here is a "cold call" letter that you can use to contact someone you read about in a publication (or online)

TO: Arthur Dent   adent@logisticsquarterly.com
FROM: Morris Karakofsky   mkarakofsky@gmail.com

RE: Your comments about military acquisitions officers from Logistics Quarterly

Mr. Dent,

In the column you wrote for the recent issue of *Logistics Quarterly* you mentioned that many private companies have found it useful to hire former military acquisitions officers to handle their logistics work since these individuals have received extensive training and have recent certifications.

I was interested in your comments because I am a transitioning veteran with a background in acquisitions and I am interested in utilizing my experiences in the field with a private company. I recently returned from Baghdad where I oversaw the logistics and acquisitions for my Marine Corps platoon. I am DAWAI certified (level III) and was responsible for managing a staff of twenty.

If your time permits, I would like to speak with you about your experiences in the field and hear your suggestions for someone wishing to enter this field. Would we be able to arrange a time to meet in person or speak by phone? I look forward to speaking with you and will call your office next week to see if we could set up a time at your convenience when we might be able to meet or talk. Thank you.

Sincerely,
Morris Karakofsky

If your contact does not respond to your e-mail or letter, wait about a week and then follow up with them to see about setting up a time to speak or to meet. The contact may not be ignoring you but might be planning to respond but procrastinating. (I have to admit that I have been guilty of not getting back to people when they have contacted me for informational interviews.) So a follow-up phone call can help to remind them and may help you to get the meeting. When speaking by phone remember to be polite and to respect the person's time. And also remember that since informational interviews frequently lead to real job interviews, treat the informational interview process and each informational interview—including this phone call—as if they were real job interviews

If you do get a face-to-face appointment, dress professionally, carry yourself properly, and come prepared to the meeting. Be polite to everyone you meet, especially secretaries and support staff. Many senior people in organizations will notice how you treat the support staff and respond to how you treat the staff members. I have heard of people who have gotten or lost jobs based on how they treated the administrative staff members. Also, it is helpful to show up a few minutes early just to give you time to settle in before the meeting. The other advantage of arriving early is that it gives you some time to observe the office environment, which can help you learn more about the organization and if you would like to work in a place like that.

To help you prepare for the interview, here are some questions that I have found helpful to ask during informational interviews. Feel free to use them as a starting point and add to the list

- How did you get interested in this work?
- How did you get hired?
- What are the most interesting aspects of your job?
- What are the least interesting aspects of your job?
- What is a "typical day" like for you? (Or what did you do today?)
- What kinds of challenges do you face on this job?
- What skills do you find most useful to meet those challenges?
- If the meeting is going well, you can ask the person if they know of places that are hiring in this field.

Conclude each meeting or phone call by asking if the person can think of anyone else that could help you in your search. Ask your contact if you can use his name when you reach out to this new contact. This last step expands your network, increases the number of people looking out for opportunities for you, and gets you closer to finding a person and a place that will want to hire you.

The Goal of Your Informational Interview

The *Corporate Gray* books suggest that you remember and utilize these 5R's as the goals for what you want to get out of your informational interviews:

- *Reveal* useful information and advice to help in your job search
- *Refer* you to others
- *Read* your resume
- *Revise* your resume (based on their comments)
- *Remember* you for future reference

After every meeting or phone call, remember to send a thank you letter to every person that helped you. Even though the thank you letter is one of the most effective and easiest ways to make a good impression, I am constantly amazed at how infrequently people send them. Your letter is an easy way to stand out from other job searchers and will help you be remembered. I have actually received thank you letters from my contacts after I sent them thank you letters for spending time with me. In your thank you letter, thank the person for their time, reiterate some of the points that the person made during the conversation (to show that you were attentive during the meeting or phone call), and remind the contact of anything that promised to do for you (again, the person may have gotten busy and forgotten to do these things—the letter is a good way to remind them). Here is a sample thank you letter that illustrates these points.

TO: John Watson   johnwatson@bakerstreet.com
FROM: Morris Karakofsky mkarakofsky@gmail.com

RE: Thank you

Dr. Watson,

 I want to thank you for taking the time to meet with me on Friday to discuss my interest in using my skills as a Marine Corps acquisition professional in private companies. I am especially grateful that you took the time out of your schedule while you were under a tight deadline to deliver an article to your publisher.

 Your comments about the types of employers that want to hire military veterans and how difficult it has been for these companies to find the right employees were particularly interesting to me. As we discussed during the meeting, I have had a hard time finding employers that are interested in my skills and it seems that employers have had similar difficulties as well. It was reassuring to hear from you that there are companies that are looking for these skills.

 During our meeting you mentioned that you would check your files to locate the person you know at Allied Industries who said that he wanted to hire a DAWAI III certified veteran. When you get the chance, please forward the name to me and I will be happy to contact him.

 Again, thank you for meeting with me yesterday and for sharing your ideas with me. I look forward to remaining in touch with you and will keep you posted as things develop for me in my job search.

Thanks again.
Sincerely,
Morris Karakofsky

 With each subsequent interview and phone call you will continue to get more referrals and with each referral you will expand your network. Each new contact, phone call, or interview will allow you to learn more about yourself, the skills that you want to use, and the types of places that would hire someone like you. At some point, the informational interviews will lead you to companies and people that are looking for someone with your skills and then these visits will lead you to job interview. Eventually you will meet the individual who will have the power to hire you—and will want to hire you.

How Can You Create a Resume and Translate Your Military Experience Into Something that Civilians Will Understand?

 Based on the amount of time you spent in uniform, this could be one of the most difficult elements of your job search. If you entered the service when you were right out of school and are just now transitioning out you may never have had to compose a resume in your lifetime. It is a tough skill to learn and it will take some time—and multiple drafts—to get it right. Even seasoned writers have a hard time creating their own resumes since resumes force you to summarize your life down to a page or two. And not only do you have to summarize your life, you also have to have artistic lay-out skills to insure that the information is easy to read and effectively summarizes your life and sells you to a potential employer who is only quickly reading it. In addition, most career fields have preferences on what information you will need to include, ways of formatting and laying out the resume, and buzzwords and catch phrases that are widely accepted—but you might not be aware of these preferences if you are just leaving the service. Even though I helped many people write their resumes, I chose to hire a resume writing service when I wrote my first resume when I graduated from school and looked for a job.

Resume writing is a skill and an art that you will need to learn. In addition, you are going to translate your military experiences into terms that a civilian employer will be able to understand. But you do not have to go through this process alone. A number of good books are available in the library and bookstores (one of my favorites is *Resumes That Knock 'Em Dead* by Martin Yate). I also highly recommend that you show your resume to friends and relatives (especially if they work in your field of interest) and ask them to proofread it and offer suggestions on ways to improve it. You will be surprised at the number of things that you miss when you have written and reread the document too many times. And you can show your resume to your contacts during informational interviews and ask them for their feedback and ideas as well.

Drew Myers, the CEO of RecruitMilitary (and previously a captain in the Marines), comments, "99.9% of companies value military service and want to hire employees who have served," adding, "not just because it's patriotic, but because they also value the technical skills and the leadership gained in the service. But most veterans do not know how to make the right argument about the benefits of their service to these employers. They need to know what skill sets they possess that will appeal to these companies. They also need to know how to package these skills and market themselves to the right employers. But the veterans who have been in the service for a while can't speak their language or know what to emphasize to civilian hiring managers. This is where RecruitMilitary fits in—we've served in the military and we work with private companies every day. We can speak both languages and translate between both worlds."

Joe Vroman, the Leader of RecruitMiltitary's National Recruiting Center (who also served in the Army and reached the rank of first sergeant) has worked with many veterans to translate their skills and improve their résumés. He recommends that you make a point to do more than just translate your acronyms and phrases into something that civilians can understand. Flesh your résumé out, and add more details to describe what you did in the service. As an example, after writing that you were "Platoon COR on MRE distribution," do not just expand the acronyms ("meals ready to eat," "contracting officer's representative") but explain what those phrases mean. In this example, add that you were the chief procurement officer and that you ordered food supplies for your platoon. And since most civilians are unaware of the size of divisions in the military insert these numbers into your résumé descriptions (as hiring managers like to see numbers in résumés, so that they have a sense of the size of your responsibilities). Instead of writing that you were a platoon leader, tell the reader how many people you supervised, and describe your responsibilities in this post.

Vroman also warns against going too far and "de-militarizing your military experience." He adds, "Most of the potential employers reading your resume probably understand something about military ranks and certain broad terms and will respect these terms. These terms also carry certain cachet as well so you should proudly use them in your resume. As an example, most people will know what a sergeant is and will have some sense of the types of responsibilities it entails. But remember to include the details about what you did in the service so that you do not under-sell yourself in the eyes of the person reading the resume. Make sure you provide the details so that civilians will understand why you are proud of these honors."

In addition, a number of resources and services are available to help you translate your military experience into civilian equivalencies. Translating military jargon and terminology into something that civilian bosses will understand—and making the military experiences of a veteran more attractive to an employer—is one of the strengths of the staff at RecruitMilitary. They have worked directly with thousands of veterans and helped them navigate the road from the military to employment. As fellow veterans, they speak your language and jargon, but as recruiters working for civilian companies, they also know how to speak the language of business.

The Department of Defense has a form that can make this resume translation process easier for you. The Verification of Military Experience and Training (VMET) form was created to help your transitioning process by providing verification of the skills and training you received in the military and translating this information into civilian terms. You can obtain the form at http://www.dmdc.osd.mil/vmet.

Another useful resource is O*NET run by the Department of Labor. O*NET is the nation's primary source of occupational information containing detailed information on hundreds of types of occupations. O*NET has a military to civilian converter which they call the Crosswalk (http://online.onetcenter.org/crosswalk). If you know your MOC (military occupation code), you can type it into the Web page and it will tell you what the equivalent civilian job is for that code. The database will also tell you about working conditions, the knowledge, skills, and abilities you need to succeed, the average expected salaries, and what the future looks like for each job listed in the database. Each job description concludes with a list of trade groups and associations for that occupation that you can use to find contacts for informational interviews. Feel free to visit the Web sites of the organizations listed to learn more about these occupations and then contact some of the names listed on the groups' Web page for more information and for potential informational interviews.

In the first section of this chapter I described some of the strengths that you bring from your military service that will appeal to employers. These intangibles of military service should be used to your advantage and will appeal to hiring managers and employers. But you will have to make this argument yourself to each employer you meet and connect the employer's needs for these skills with your unique background and skills. And this is another area where a service like TAP or RecruitMilitary can help you. RecruitMilitary's Vroman admits that this is a difficult process and one that takes time to learn and understand. After spending years in the service, the ability to think like civilian employers, to understand their needs, and to know how to speak their language is not an easy process for someone new to it. That is why he recommends that you do not do it alone.

Carl Savino of *Corporate Gray* adds that areas with large military installations will usually have more military-friendly and military-aware employers in the community so it may be easier to find a job in these areas as many companies will have worked with veterans in the past. These areas include Washington, DC, and suburban Virginia and Maryland; San Antonio, Texas; Tampa, Florida; and San Diego, California. But as more veterans return from war and go to work at more companies, word of the benefits of hiring veterans will spread and more will seek out veterans in their recruiting efforts. One by-product of employers realizing the benefits of recruiting veterans is the growth in the number of career fairs that are geared for veterans. RecruitMilitary sponsors a number of these fairs each year, as do organizations like the Washington Post, ClearedJobs.net, the Departments of Labor and Defense, the VA, and other organizations across the country. All of the organizations that sponsor booths at these fairs are reaching out to find veterans. I recommend that you make a point to attend these fairs in your area. Even if specific companies at the fair do not interest you, you can gather information about available fields and other organizations.

What Happens When You Meet Up with Employers During the Interview?

Congratulations—this is what you have been working toward. If you have been in the military for a while you might not have sat for an interview for quite a while and may have questions about what to expect. There are a number of good books that offer advice on how to do well in an interview. In addition to the *Parachute* book, check out *301 Smart Answers to Tough Interview Questions* by Vicky Oliver; *201 Best Questions To Ask On Your Interview* by John Kador; the *Corporate Gray* series, *101 Dynamite Answers to Interview Questions: Sell Your Strengths!* by Caryl Rae Krannich and Ronald L. Krannich; *Knock 'Em Dead 2008* by Martin Yate, and *Great Answers to Tough Interview Questions* by Martin Yate. You can also check the Web (including *Corporate Grey's* Web site at http://www.corporate-gray.com) for tips and suggestions on interview skills and questions.

The advisors at RecruitMilitary and your transition office will also work with you to help you through this process. The job interview process will seem like a strange and unfamiliar world. Check out the books mentioned above, work with a counselor, and even ask your friends or family members to engage you in a "mock interview" (where a friend pretends to be a hiring officer at a company and asks you typical questions to give you practice in answering these questions and polishing your responses).

Unfortunately, one disadvantage of the interview process is that the system frequently rewards candidates who have the best interviewing skills rather than those who have the best skills for the job. If you can imagine the military determining who will be the best rifleman based on how well someone talks about firing a gun then you have a sense of how poorly the interview can predict the success on the job. Research has shown that the interview is the worst predictor a company can use to determine who will do well on a job, but it is the one that is used the most often. Some companies are starting to use tests and other measurement techniques to determine how well you can execute the tasks of the job, but these companies are in the minority. Individuals who are transitioning from the military and people with disabilities can have a particularly difficult time with interviews if the interviewers cannot understand the relevance of the military experience to their needs (and if the veteran cannot effectively translate their experiences so that they are understood in the civilian world). The acronym FUD refers to the "fear, uncertainties, or doubts" that a hiring manager could have with making a job offer to an individual with a disability. The following sections will tell you how you can answer these questions, address these concerns, and "close the deal" with employers so that you can get the job.

Questions That Employers Like to Ask during Interviews

Be prepared with answers to typical employer questions. Courtesy of Carl Savino of *Corporate Gray*, here are some typical questions that employers like to use during interviews. Think about how you would answer them and practice the answers so that you sound confident with your responses.

1. Tell me about yourself.
2. What are your three greatest strengths and weaknesses?
3. What do you know about our company?
4. Why would you want to work here?
5. What about your background makes you a fit for this opportunity?
6. What sets you apart from other candidates we're considering for this position?
7. Where would you see yourself five years from now or ten years from now?
8. You've been working for the military in a service environment. We're a for-profit company; how are you going to make us more profitable?
9. Tell me about an instance where you disagreed with the direction from your boss and how you handled it.
10. What are your salary requirements and what are they based on?

Timing

If you are still in rehab, in a foreign country, or removed from your hometown (in a military hospital for instance), your timing and availability need to be considered as you start interviewing. If you are conducting informational interviews, you can make contact with potential employers at any time. But according to Joe Vroman of RecruitMilitary, most companies do not look beyond a forty-five- to sixty-day time frame in their hiring decisions. So if you think you will not be available in two months to start a job (either because of your service duty or because of your rehab schedule) focus more on informational interviews. If there appears to be interest in your application, let the other side know about your time commitments.

Even if you are recovering at Walter Reed, Bethesda Naval, in Germany, or at another military base far from home, you can still do research on the Web and in the library about employers and your job interests. You can also start the informational interview process while you are away from home even if you are not in the same time zone (or even the same continent). Even away from home you can use the Internet to visit the Web pages of local chambers of commerce, check out the local newspapers to see which companies are expanding or making promotions, or read about local companies to see who might be hiring. And with e-mail you will be able to reach out to any contacts any time of day. But remember when you do set up times to talk to people over the phone to confirm the right time and time zone—and always set up times that are convenient for that person rather than for you.

Salary Negotiations

There is great salary variation outside the military. Regrettably the highest salaries frequently do not go to the best qualified but to the best salary negotiators. This is another area where your life in the armed forces could not prepare you for what you must face in the private sector and your coaches and counselors with expertise in this area can advise you. A number of books can help you with this process, including *Negotiating Your Salary: How To Make $1,000 a Minute* by Jack Chapman and *Secrets of Power Salary Negotiating: Inside Secrets from a Master Negotiator* by Roger Dawson. One thing to remember is that many of the perks and benefits provided by the military will not be available in the civilian world. This can impact salary comparisons between your past salary and your future one. Unlike the military, you will not have access to a commissary or exchange to purchase items at a discount, you will only receive around fifteen days of vacation a year to start, you will not have a tax-free housing allowance, and you will need to factor in the benefits such as health insurance, dental benefits, and retirement programs that companies offer (which vary among employers).

What Concerns Could Employers Have about Your Military Service?

While most employers will respect and desire your military service, some individuals and some companies may have concerns or questions about your military service and could question how well you might fit into their corporate environment. During job interviews every interviewer fears that the candidates they hire will not fit in or that they will not be able to do the work and the company will have to endure the extra costs and headaches of firing the employee and finding a replacement.

To help reduce their fears and uncertainties, interviewers look for clues in anything that they can see about each candidate and will use these clues to make assumptions that affect their hiring decisions (these mental shortcuts are called "heuristics" by psychologists). Your military record may become fodder for the interviewer's incorrect assumptions about you. Some might think that a veteran might be too rigid for today's flexible workplace, might want to come in early when everyone else comes in at 9:30, might not know how to follow orders if the veteran was an officer (or work under a younger manager), or be knowledgeable about the latest technologies, tools, or processes. During the interview, your mission is to figure out what misconceptions the interviewer might have about your background, your military service, or your disability and directly address these concerns by speaking the organization's language. Explain how you can help the organization meets its goals.

As an example, if the employer seems to be concerned that you are not flexible, talk about a time in the service when you displayed flexibility. If the concern appears to be your perceived lack of understanding of current technology, describe some of the technologies that you have used in the past. If the interviewer does not raise issues, you can always bring them up as hypothetical examples. You could say something like "Some employers would see my years in the military and think that a veteran would be too inflexible for a private sector company. That is not the case, let me tell about a time when I had to show flexibility leading my squad." And continue with the story to illustrate how flexible you can be in a tight situation.

When and How Do You Discuss Your Disability?

The question of when and how to reveal your disability is tricky. If you talk about it too soon, you may be dropped from consideration. But if you wait too long, then the employer may think that you are trying to hide it or possibly pulling a "bait and switch" on them. The question is especially difficult if you have an invisible disability like PTSD or TBI. There is no right answer and you will need to judge each situation as it arises. The counselors at JAN, TAP, The Sierra Group, and RecruitMilitary can all advise you on when and how you can do this.

Kendra Duckworth, a counselor at JAN who has worked with many returning disabled veterans advises, "Deciding when to disclose a disability can be a difficult choice for a person with a disability who is job hunting. And if you have a hidden disability (such as a learning disability, PTSD, and TBI) then the question of when and how to disclose your condition can be a real dilemma. The Americans with Disabilities Act prohibits potential employers for asking medical or disability related questions so the choice to disclose is clearly up to the individual. If you decide to disclose, remember to talk about your abilities, not your disabilities. Employers need qualified, capable individuals to fill positions. Find a way to show that you are that person. Sell them on what you can do, not on what you cannot do and the interview will go better than you expect. Be positive about yourself and be honest."

One advantage of informational interviewing is that it helps mitigate this question of when and how to reveal your disability. Since you have met with people before you sat for the formal interview, most of them will already be aware of your disability.

Dale Brown has dealt with this issue both directly (as she sought employment with her learning disability) and as she advised other individuals. She explains that bringing up the disability while you are still competing for a job is "like tying a weight around your leg before you run a race." She adds, "In order to be covered by the Americans with Disabilities Act, you must disclose your disability. This is because the law covers only the 'known' disability of the applicant or the employee. So, if you need a specific accommodation, such as extended time on a pre-employment test, disclosure will often be the only way to receive it. However, disclosure opens you up to discrimination. When applying for a job, it is usually impossible to prove that you were rejected because of a disability, it can be risky to mention it in the application, resume, or job interview. After you are offered the job, it is safer to disclose, since the discrimination would be more obvious. A good time to request an accommodation is after the employer has selected you. This is the period where your leverage will be the highest. You can negotiate your accommodations along with issues such as salaries, benefits, and work hours. It may not be necessary to label your needs as accommodations. Flexible hours, extra clerical help, the ability to work at home at times, a quiet work station, and selection of your supervisor are often requested for reasons having nothing to do with disability. If you negotiate a high enough salary, you may be able to pay for some of your accommodations yourself. Consider asking for an offer letter that puts important matters in writing."

What Fears, Uncertainties, and Doubts Could Employers Have about Your Disability?

Just as many potential employers will use heuristics about your military service to reach incorrect conclusions, many interviewers will have questions and misconceptions about your disability and your ability to do the work. Companies have concerns about employing people with disabilities ranging from the costs of making accommodations to potential lawsuits to a personal level of discomfort with a specific disability. These concerns have been called the "FUD (fear, uncertainty, doubt) Factor" and you may need to address and disarm this FUD Factor in your interviews in order to convince a potential employer that you are able to do the job. The FUD Factor is apparently prevalent in companies: One recent survey found that 10 percent of the managers who were polled actually admitted that the main reason why they have not hired more people with disabilities is because of their own negative attitudes and discrimination against people with disabilities. Another 10 percent of respondents to this survey cited their fear of the costs of accommodations as the main reason for their not hiring people with disabilities (Dixon et al., 2003).

Research suggests that one of the reasons for the FUD Factor is that many people are scared of disabilities because they remind them of their own mortality and fragility. A person without a disability today could be involved in a car accident tomorrow and be in a wheelchair the rest of his life. Virtually all of us will lose our hearing and vision and become disabled over time through the natural aging process. These are not pleasant thoughts and many people try not to think about them. Some people will try to avoid thinking about these matters by avoiding people who have disabilities and either consciously or unconsciously keep them out of their offices and workplaces.

Research has also shown that many people have a "hierarchy" of comfort levels with disabilities. Based on the type of disability that you have, this will impact the way that some people respond to you and their comfort level in offering you a job. People are generally more comfortable with physical disabilities such as blindness and deafness where the person's body appears fully intact. Next on the list are disabilities where the individual has something different with their body such as missing limbs or using a wheelchair. "Hidden" or psychological disabilities including PSTD or TBI may scare people the most since they are the least understood and are still stigmatized. I mention this to let you know that the type of disability you have may generate a different type of reaction from the person who might be interviewing you.

Janet Fiore, the CEO of The Sierra Group (http://thesierragroup.com), a national authority on disability policy and practices for business, comments that the FUD Factor sometimes causes the interviewer to be as afraid as the candidate. "And when fears meet fears at job interviews," she adds, "job offers rarely follow. Fears also make people lose track of their common sense so that people and companies may fail to do the things that are in their best interests." She thus recommends that you try to do everything you can to make a potential employer feel more comfortable with you as a person and with your disability and your ability to do the work with your disability in order to raise your chances of getting an employment offer.

The ADA was signed nearly twenty years ago. Many people in the disability community felt that this law would help improve the employment prospects for people with disabilities, but some have suggested that the law could actually make things more difficult by making companies afraid that they will be sued. To avoid lawsuits, this reasoning suggests, companies will avoid hiring people with disabilities in the first place. EARN conducted focus groups about opinions on hiring people with disabilities among different employers across the country. The fear of lawsuits permeated all of the discussions, especially among owners of small businesses. One lawsuit can cost a company tens of thousands of dollars in legal fees—not to mention the time that the company has to spend defending itself as well as the negative publicity and the headaches that accompany a lawsuit like this. Most small business leaders said that they would rather find some reason not to hire a person with a disability than subject themselves to the potential costs and problems of having to defend themselves in court.

Employer's Concerns and Questions about Your Disability

This is a list of concerns a potential employer may have about hiring employees with disabilities. It combines material from the Bolles and Brown book with findings from the focus group research conducted by EARN. If a candidate with a disability is interviewing for a job, the interviewer is probably at least thinking some of these questions. Below we present some of the ways that you can answer these questions and address the interviewer's FUD:

- What is the person's disability? (This is especially pertinent with hidden disabilities such as PTSD or TBI.)
- What are the limitations of this person? Can they do the work and are they being honest with me about their skills during the interviews?
- Will this person be able to do all the tasks I need him to do or will he create more work for the other employees?
- Will this disability increase my company's health insurance costs?
- Will this person be a reliable worker?
- Can we adapt the work or the office to the disability?
- How much will these accommodations cost?
- Will the accommodation costs come out of my budget?
- If this person can do the job as it currently stands, what happens if things change or what if something happens that we haven't thought about or discussed yet? Will this person be able to adapt to these changes?
- How will this person get to work?
- What if this person doesn't work out? Can I fire her? Will I get sued?
- How will this person get along with the other employees?
- What if other employees become jealous of the person with a disability and the accommodations we provide? If the person is promoted would they think that I felt sorry for this person rather than see that he did a good job?
- How is this person going to communicate with the other employees?
- How will this employee avoid accidents on the job?
- Will this person have good attendance? Will she miss work because of doctor appointments?
- Will this person be productive on the job?
- If the person has a mental illness will he get violent on the job? Is he stable? Will he be a threat to other employees?
- How will this person handle emergencies on the job? What if we need to quickly evacuate the building?

How Do You Address These Concerns?

Even if your interviewer does not directly ask you these questions (and under the ADA, employers are forbidden by law to ask many of them), the interviewer is probably thinking about these issues, feeling the FUD Factor, and using heuristics to answer these questions. Unspoken or not, your disability is the proverbial elephant in the room. You will need to defuse these questions and address the concerns.

Here are some suggestions of how you can do this:

Raise the question yourself. Even if law prohibits the interviewer from asking these questions, you are permitted to raise the question yourself and then provide an answer to it that addresses the employer's fears and concerns. You might as well put it out there and give a positive answer to it.

Provide hard facts and details. Go beyond just naming your disability and explain what it is and give specifics of how it affects your life and what it prevents you from doing. But focus on the positives, including the tasks you can perform and what you can do if you have the right accommodations. Present the employer with some of the data and ideas from JAN about the costs of accommodations and the minimal impact that employees with disabilities have on company's insurance rates. You can also ask JAN for recommendations about your specific disability and share these with your interviewer. JAN and The Sierra Group can also provide you with information about some of the tax benefits that employers receive when they hire people with disabilities. If costs seem to be a concern, you can remind the employer that the ADA only covers "reasonable accommodations," which does not mean that the employer has to provide you with everything that you want. Under the law, an accommodation that creates "undue hardship" (defined as "significant difficulty or expense and focuses on the resources and circumstances of the particular employer in relationship to the cost or difficulty of providing a specific accommodation") is not considered reasonable and does not have to be provided by the employer. You can emphasize to a potential employer that by law the cost of any accommodations will not be unreasonable to them. Also, the law only applies to companies with fifteen or more employees so smaller companies are exempted from the requirements. For more on the ADA, check out the "Employers and the ADA: Myths and Facts" Web site at http://www.dol.gov/odep/pubs/fact/ada.htm.

Use positive examples from your past. Describe how you were able to get things done in your life, in your tasks, and in your previous jobs, and other activities (e.g., how you learned to do tasks with your prosthesis, how you were able to show up on time at your volunteer job, and how you interacted with other people without problems).

Break the job down into elements and address the elements. If you went through the *Parachute* exercises and did other work in self-assessment, you have a realistic idea of what you can do and where and how you will need help adjusting the task. Address the FUD by working with the interviewer to break the job down into discrete tasks and demonstrate how you are able to accomplish each task.

Emphasize your military experience. Unlike previous wars, almost every American says that they separate any feelings they may have about the current conflict from their opinions about the troops fighting the war. Almost everyone says that they respect, admire, and support the troops. Use this to your advantage in your job search and to overcome the fears that an interviewer may have about your disability. Talk about your leadership skills in tight situations, your ability to think "outside the box," how well you work with people of different backgrounds, your ability to learn material quickly, and your resourcefulness. Review the traits listed under the "What Advantages Do You Bring to An Employer" category in this chapter and emphasize those during the interview.

Work with a counselor. Utilize the advisors at RecruitMilitary, call the toll free line at JAN, contact The Sierra Group, or visit or call your local TAP office. Speak with other veterans with disabilities to see how they addressed employer concerns. All of these people have navigated these types of questions in the past and you can utilize their experience and knowledge to help you address them.

Practice. Write up your answers to the questions above and practice them with your friends and family members during a mock interview. Rehearse your answers so that you will be able to remember them and they will come smoothly when you need them.

Let them know that it is OK to fire people with disabilities. The ADA permits people with disabilities to be fired from jobs if they do not perform the requirements of the job. If the interviewer seems to be concerned about getting stuck with a bad employee, let her know that it's OK to fire you if you don't work out. In his book with Dale Brown, Richard Bolles suggests using the following phrase: "My injury has been a blessing in disguise, because it's forced me to choose a career that I can do well and stay in permanently. If you are willing to take a chance on me, I'll give it my very best shot. But, if things don't work out to our mutual satisfaction, I'd want you to tell me that straight out, and I'll pick up my tent peaceably and move on."

If You Were Interested, How Could You Start Your Own Business?

A number of people with drive and determination look to starting their own business as a way of avoiding the job search process. Self-employment is a particularly attractive option for people with disabilities since they do not have to worry about selling themselves to a hiring manager or an employer—the only people they need to impress are their clients and as long as the work gets done, most clients will not care what kind of disability you have. I know of one woman with limited use of her hands and legs who opened her own car washing business because she can run it from her desk with her specially adapted telephone and computer. (She hired people to do the actual washing of the cars.) Many of her clients do not even know about her disability.

Based on comments I have heard from people who have gone the self-employment route, self-employment is no escape from the difficulties of job searching. You do not have to sell yourself to an employer, but you do have to sell yourself to your clients each and every day. In addition, while you have more control over the possibility of your income, you also put yourself at risk of fluctuations in profits. Most founders of new businesses assume that they will lose money for their first few months of operation (or sometimes even their first year of business). You will need at least some source of income during this period. Also, do not expect that opening your own business will give you more time for your family or interests. Most entrepreneurs agree with the joke I once heard from a self-employed businessman: "I'm in business for myself so I get to work half days. And the best part is that I get to pick which twelve hours a day I work." But successful entrepreneurs note that if you thrive on the risk and the chance to control your own destiny through good and bad times, and if you can live with the potential for no income at times, nothing can compare with being your own boss and owning your own business.

The government has a number of programs available for veterans who would like to start their own business. The U.S. Small Business Administration's (SBA) Office of Veterans Business Development can provide you with useful information. Recently, the SBA introduced the "Patriot Express" loan program (http://www.sba.gov/patriotexpress/) for veterans. The SBA provides business counseling and training through 5 Veterans Business Outreach Centers, more than 1,000 Small Business Development Centers, nearly 400 SCORE chapters (groups of more than 11,000 volunteer small business owners who provide counseling to new small business owners and are listed on the Web at http://www.score.org), 100 Women's Business Centers, as well as business loans and loan guarantee programs. Veteran-owned businesses can receive priority in applying for federal contracts and other SBA federal procurement programs. The SBA supports veteran-owned businesses that want to expand into international trade.

Also, if you were a Reservist and your business was damaged by an extensive absence as a result of your military service, the SBA has a special Military Reservist Economic Injury Disaster Loan. A Veterans Business Development Officer is stationed at every SBA District Office. SBA's services can be found at http://www.sba.gov/vets/ (Reservists can find information at http://www.sba.gov/reservists/) or by calling 202-205-6773 or 1-800-U-ASK-SBA (1-800-827-5722).

Other resources are available to help you if you want to start your own business. The VA's Center for Veterans Enterprise is located at http://www.vetbiz.gov. Many states and some communities also have similar programs—the one in California, for example, is the Disabled Business Alliance (www.cadvbe.org). Check with your local VA for comparable groups in your state and local community. The National Veterans Business Development Corporation (www.veteranscorp.org) can provide you with the tools and resources to be successful in business, including access to capital, bonding, and educational opportunities to learn about being an entrepreneur. They also have information for Reserve and Guard members about rebuilding a business that may have been negatively impacted by overseas military service. They can be reached at (202) 449-9835 or (866) 283-8267 and online at info@veteranscorp.org.

Conclusion

A reoccurring theme throughout this chapter has been that with the right workplace accommodations and the right attitude from the employer, employment opportunities for people with almost any type of disability are virtually limitless. Because of your service to the nation, you have already demonstrated that you possess positive traits—as well as other abilities that employers say are in demand. The only other things you need now are the right opportunity, the right workplace accommodations, good leads, and an employer that understands what you can do for them in spite of—or because of—your injury. As I have tried to demonstrate in this chapter, a number of people and services out there are willing to help you achieve these goals. When you were in the military you never went into any battle alone. The same is true now: you have a squad of others who have your back and want to help you achieve your next mission—to find a great job that you will look forward to do every day.

I have mentioned how the ADA has helped people obtain accommodations in the workplace. But although the ADA is nearly twenty years old, the first recorded case of a workplace accommodation preceded this law—by about 3,000 years. The employee under consideration was Moses, and God was the employer offering the accommodation. In the book of Exodus (4:10–4:18), Moses appeared before the Burning Bush and was commanded to become God's emissary to free the Israelites. Moses tries to turn down this commission by highlighting his disability, saying that he is "slow of speech and slow of tongue." (An earlier part of the Bible explains that while he was a baby he burned his tongue as part of a test of his identity and had a speech impediment for the rest of his life.) God suggests that Moses' brother Aaron speak for him and serve as his voice. Both Aaron and Moses agree to this accommodation.

Thanks to this workplace accommodation, Moses was able to directly face and challenge the Pharaoh, (at that time the leader of the known universe); free more than a half million slaves and safely bring them across the desert; become one of the most successful military leaders in history; speak as a prophet for the Almighty; codify the system of laws that are still used around the world even to this day; and most importantly, be portrayed in the movies by both Mel Brooks and Charlton Heston.

Not a bad bit of work for a man that many would describe as "crippled."

Even if your plans are not to the scale of what Moses accomplished in his lifetime with his disability, I offer you my personal thanks for your service to our country and the best of luck and continual success with your own endeavors on the employment front.

Acknowledgments

This chapter pulls together a lot of information from disparate areas covering veterans, employment, and disabilities. The thoroughness, accuracy, and usefulness you may find in these pages are due to the assistance, advice, suggestions, and contacts I received from a number of great people who were ready and able to respond whenever I had questions. I could not have written this chapter without them and I offer my sincere gratitude to all of them. Maggie Roffee, the secretary of the Board of Independence Now, Inc., a center for independent living in Maryland, has been instrumental in my knowledge about disabilities, veterans, and employment not just for this book but also throughout all of my work in this area. Dale Brown, a published author and leader of the learning disability movement, also provided me with her insight and guidance (and gave me the idea for the first recorded workplace accommodation mentioned at the end of the chapter). Ron Drach, a Vietnam disabled veteran now with the Department of Labor's Office of Veteran Employment and Training Services, provided me with contacts and information. Carl S. Savino of *Corporate Gray* shared his information and insights. Drew Myers, Matt Murphy, and Joe Vroman of RecruitMilitary provided me with material on the transition process and the employer's perspective on the hiring of veterans with disabilities. Kendra Duckworth of JAN was always available with suggestions and ideas about accommodating all types of disabilities. And I would like to thank Richard Horne, Ed.D., of the Office of Disability Employment Policy, who—as he has done for so many people working in the areas of disability and employment—provided me with inspiration and guidance in my research to allow me to use the research and my writing to help those with disabilities achieve their dreams through employment. To all of you, a heartfelt thanks.

Bibliography

Benight, C. C. and Bandura, A. (2004). Social Cognitive Theory of Posttraumatic Recovery: The Role of Perceived Self-Efficacy. *Behavior Research and Therapy*, 42, 1129–1148.

Bolles, R. N. (2007). *What Color Is Your Parachute? 2008: A Practical Manual for Job-Hunters and Career-Changers*. Berkeley, CA: Ten Speed Press. (This book is revised and updated every year.)

Bolles, R.N. and Brown, D. S. (2001) *Job-Hunting for the So-Called Handicapped or People Who Have Disabilities*. Berkeley, CA: Ten Speed Press.

Brown, D. S. (2000). *Learning a Living: A Guide to Planning Your Career and Finding a Job for People with Learning Disabilities, Attention Deficit Disorder, and Dyslexia*. Bethesda, MD: Woodbine House.

Chapman, J. (2006). *Negotiating Your Salary: How to Make $1,000 a Minute* (5th ed.). Berkeley, CA: Ten Speed Press.

Dawson, R. (2006). *Secrets of Power Salary Negotiating: Inside Secrets from a Master Negotiator*. Franklin Lakes, NJ: Career Press.

Dixon, K., Kruse, D., and Van Horn, C. (2003). *Americans' Attitudes about Work, Employers and Government Work Trends: Restricted Access: A Survey of Employers about People with Disabilities and Lowering Barriers to Work.* New Brunswick, NJ: John J. Heldrich Center for Workforce Development, Rutgers University.

Job Accommodation Network (2007). *Workplace Accommodations: Low Cost, High Impact: New Research Findings Address the Costs and Benefits of Job Accommodations for People with Disabilities.* Morgantown, WV: Job Accommodation Network. http://www.jan.wvu.edu/media/LowCostHighImpact.doc (downloaded April 24, 2008)

Kador, J. (2002). *201 Best Questions to Ask on Your Interview.* Columbus, OH: McGraw-Hill.

Krannich, C. R. (2007). *Nail the Job Interview! 101 Dynamite Answers to Interview Questions* (6th ed.) Manassas Park, VA: Impact Publications.

Krannich, R. (2000). *Dynamite Salary Negotiations: Know What You're Worth and Get It* (4th ed.). Manassas Park, VA: Impact Publications.

Oliver, V. (2005). *301 Smart Answers to Tough Interview Questions.* Naperville, IL: Sourcebooks, Inc.

Ryan, R. (2004). *Job Search Handbook for People with Disabilities.* St. Paul, MN: Jist Publishing.

Savino, C. S. and Krannich, R. L. (2007). *From Air Force Blue to Corporate Grey.* Fairfax Station, VA: Competitive Edge Services.

———(2007). *From Army Green to Corporate Grey.* Fairfax Station, VA: Competitive Edge Services.

———(2007). *From Navy Blue to Corporate Grey.* Fairfax Station, VA: Competitive Edge Services.

Seligman, M. E. P. (1998). *Learned Optimism: How to Change Your Mind and Your Life.* New York: Pocket Books.

Yate, M. (2001). *Great Answers to Tough Interview Questions* (5th ed.). London: Kogan Page.

———(2007). *Knock 'em Dead 2008: The Ultimate Job Search Guide.* Cincinnati, OH: Adams Media Corporation.

———(2000). *Resumes That Knock 'em Dead.* Cincinnati, OH: Adams Media Corporation.

CHAPTER 7

Education Options

Charles J. Sabatier, Jr

Editors' Comments

Since the end of World War II, more than 21 million veterans, service members, and their family members have received more than $72 billion dollars from the government under the GI Bill to pursue their educational goals. We highly recommend that you be part of this group. Please give serious thought to obtaining additional education and utilizing the benefits that are due to you under this program. Research consistently demonstrates that people with more education earn more money so we encourage you to pursue these options and get the most that you can out of the government's veteran educational benefits programs.

Charles Sabatier, J.D., the author of this chapter, is a model of how education through the GI Bill can positively impact the life of a veteran. Shot and paralyzed by a bullet during the Tet Offensive in Vietnam, he learned about the GI Bill and used the program to get his undergraduate degree when he left the service. He later used other benefits to obtain his law degree and is now licensed to practice law in three states. He has been a practicing attorney and is now helping other veterans as a Senior Policy Advisor at the Office of Disability Employment Policy at the US Department of Labor in Washington DC. He is currently the lead policy person for the Heroes@Work initiative examining ways to improve the employment opportunities of veterans returning from the current conflict with post-traumatic stress disorder (PTSD) and traumatic brain injury (TBI). First describing his own life experiences to spur you to action, Mr. Sabatier then describes the educational benefits programs that are available to you under the GI Bill and subsequent programs and tells you how you can apply for them. In addition, information about how to accommodate your disability in the classroom is also included.

Introduction

As a 100 percent service-connected disabled veteran who took full advantage of the Veterans Administration (VA) education benefits, I feel confidant that my advice to this new generation of wounded and injured warriors is right on target: If you think you need time to "get it together" before going to work postdischarge, don't spend that time sitting in front of the television or engaging in behavior that is not productive—use your education benefits to maximize your potential future.

The information provided further in the chapter about the various education options available to veterans and their dependents might be the most important information you learn in this book about veterans' benefits. This is because education will allow you to reach your full potential—not just get a good job, but also kick off a new career. Education is the big equalizer. It is the thing that will catapult you into a new career path and allow you to pursue the career of your choice. There are so many options available to you in the information provided further in the chapter that (based on eligibility) if you have a genuine interest in pursuing something, the VA is likely to have a program that will help you reach your goal.

I offer my background as an example of the ways that the VA's education benefits allow you to pursue your goals. Although I was scheduled to do a regular tour in Vietnam, I returned home after seven months because I was shot and paralyzed by a bullet from an AK-47 during the 1968 Tet Offensive. My degree of paralysis requires me to use a wheelchair for mobility. After spending a year in the U.S. Army's Madigan General (WA) and Long Beach VA (CA) hospitals I did not have a clue as to what I was going to do with the rest of my life, but at the age of 23 I had a lot of life to live so I decided to occupy my first few postmilitary years by going to college on the GI Bill.

I first learned about my GI Bill and VA Vocational Rehabilitation benefits from a Paralyzed Veterans of America (PVA) service officer. PVA is a veteran's service organization (VSO) chartered by Congress to assist veterans. My PVA service worker who educated me about my education options had an office in the VA hospital near the spinal cord unit where I was being rehabilitated. Just after being discharged from the VA hospital I enrolled in college using my GI Bill benefits and earned my undergraduate degree. Years later, I used my VA Vocational Rehabilitation benefits to attend the University of San Diego School of Law. How this is possible is explained further in the chapter.

Today, I am married, have three kids, licensed to practice law in three states, and work full time at the U.S. Department of Labor (DOL). I am a Senior Policy Advisor helping the wounded and injured servicemen and women returning from Operation Enduring Freedom (OEF) and Operation Iraqi Freedom (OIF) obtain employment in the private sector. My triplets (born while I was in law school) are about to graduate from high school and will receive financial benefits for college as my dependents under The Survivor's and Dependents' Educational Assistance Program, described further in the chapter.

My utilization of the VA's educational benefits let me achieve these goals. If you use these benefits to obtain your own goals, you will be able to engage in something that is positive, therapeutic and something that will put you in the best position to maximize your full potential when the time comes. I compiled this chapter from pages of the VA's Web sites and from my own experiences to tell you what kinds of programs are available to you that can help you with your education.

As someone who engaged in combat, saw friends die in combat, and almost died myself, I know, first hand, how important time is and what a terrible thing it is to waste time. Most Americans know that more than 58,000 young Americans lost their lives in the Vietnam War. And today thousands more are dying in the War on Terror. For all those who have died, you will never hear a single complaint: No complaints about how hard college might be; no gripes about how hard it is to make ends meet; no complaints about the high cost of housing, etc. Why do I bring such thoughts up when I'm writing about VA education benefits? Because I truly feel that all disabled American veterans who suffered extreme trauma in combat and made it home have a duty to honor and respect the memories and sacrifices of our buddies who died on the battlefield.

The highest tribute we can pay to those who never returned is to use our time here on Earth in a way that maximizes our full potential. One way to do this is to take advantage of your VA education benefits. Knowledge is power and education is how we obtain knowledge. Look at http://www.USAjobs.com, the Web site for federal jobs and you will see almost all good jobs paying nice salaries with nice benefits have minimum education requirements. Although you may have veterans' preference, no one has to hire you because you are a veteran. Put yourself in the position to get the job, based on merit, because you meet the standards that apply, including the education requirements.

Reading this chapter is a good start but setting up a meeting with a VA counselor can provide you with even more information. One thing to remember is that you should not assume that all VA education benefits will only lead to four-year degree programs: VA education benefits are far more varied and interesting than you might think. Maximizing your education at this time in your life might be the most important thing you ever do, so get busy!

Who and What Does This Chapter Cover?

This chapter provides information about education options for veterans, veterans with disabilities, and eligible dependents of veterans who are permanently and totally disabled due to a service-related condition, or who died while on active duty or as a result of a service-related condition. The chapter covers following seven subjects:

1. The Montgomery GI Bill for Active Duty (MGIB-AD), Ch. 30 of Title 38
2. The Montgomery GI Bill for Selected Reserve (MGIB-SR), Ch. 1606 of Title 10
3. The Reserve Educational Assistance Program (REAP), Ch. 1607 of title 10
4. The Post-Vietnam Veterans' Educational Assistance Program (VEAP), Ch. 32 of Title 38

5. The Survivors' and Dependents' Educational Assistance Program (DEA/Chapter 35 of Title 38)
6. The Department of Veterans Affairs Veterans Benefits Administration's Vocational Rehabilitation and Employment (VR&E) Service for veterans with service-connected disabilities
7. State benefits

The Montgomery GI Bill—General Information

Information in the chapter concerning the GI Bill is divided into two parts: (1) The Montgomery GI Bill for Active Duty personnel (MGIB-AD/Chapter 30); and (2) The Montgomery GI Bill for Selected Reserve (MGIB-SR/Chapter 1606). The Montgomery GI Bill (MGIB) program, also known as "Chapter 30," is an education benefit earned by Active Duty, Selected Reserve and National Guard service members. The benefit is designed to help service members and eligible veterans cover the costs associated with getting an education or training. The GI Bill has several programs and each is administrated differently—depending on a person's eligibility and duty status.

The MGIB program provides up to thirty-six months of education benefits. This benefit may be used for degree and certificate programs, flight training, apprenticeship/on-the-job training, and correspondence courses. Remedial, deficiency, and refresher courses may be approved under certain circumstances. *Generally, benefits are payable for ten years following your release from active duty.*

The Montgomery GI Bill SR (Chapter 1606) is available to members of the Army, Navy, Air Force, Marine Corps, and Coast Guard Reserves, as well as the Army National Guard and the Air Guard. In addition to the MGIB SR, activated Reserve and Guard service members have two other GI Bill options. The first gives those who serve continuously for twenty-four or more months on active duty the option to pay into the GI Bill for active duty (Chapter 30). The second program is called the Reserve Education Assistance Program (REAP) which provides activated reserve and guard members up to 80 percent of the GI Bill for active duty (Chapter 30). The REAP program will be explained in more detail further in the chapter.

The MGIB SR Chapter 1606 benefit is worth more than $11,000. This amount is based on the 2007–2008 monthly full-time student payment rate of $317 multiplied by the thirty-six-month limit. This "payment rate" automatically increases on October 1 of each year. You get the increase no matter when you became eligible or start using it.

If you have access to the Internet, you can find most of the information presented in this chapter at http://www.gibill.va.gov. The http://www.military.com Web site is also a good source for information about the GI Bill.

The Montgomery GI Bill—Active Duty

The Montgomery GI Bill—Active Duty, called "MGIB" for short, provides up to thirty-six months of education benefits to eligible veterans for College, technical or vocational courses, correspondence courses, apprenticeship/job training, flight training, high-tech training, licensing & certification tests, entrepreneurship training, and certain entrance examinations.

Recent Developments in the GI Bill

As this book was going to press, changes were made to the GI Bill, affecting the benefits that veterans and their family members are eligible to receive. On June 30, 2008, President Bush signed the Post-9/11 Veterans Educational Assistance Act of 2008. As part of these new regulations, the amount of money available has been increased, calculation formulas for costs of living have been changed, entitlement will not be lost because of calls to duty, and benefits can now be transferred to family members. The changes will apply to training pursued on or after August 1, 2009 and payments will not be available to training obtained before that date. The web site of this book (http://www.warswounded.com) will track and provide updates on changes impacting the GI Bill, as some information in this chapter may now be out of date. See also http://www.gibill.va.gov.

The Veterans Administration has published a thirty-eight-page pamphlet titled *The Montgomery GI Bill—Active Duty* that summarizes the educational benefits under the Montgomery GI Bill—Active Duty Educational Assistance. The pamphlet is numbered "22-90-2 Revised" and can be found at http://www.gibill.va.gov/pamphlets/CH30/CH30_Pamphlet.pdf.

Who Is Eligible?

You may be an eligible veteran if you have an Honorable Discharge, you have a High School Diploma or GED or in some cases twelve hours of college credit, and you meet the requirements of one of the following categories:

Category I

- Entered active duty for the first time after June 30, 1985
- Had military pay reduced by $100 a month for first twelve months
- Continuously served for three years, *OR* two years (if that is what you first enlisted for), *OR* two years if you entered the Selected Reserve within a year of leaving active duty and served four years ("2 by 4" Program)

Category II

- Entered active duty before January 1, 1977
- Served at least one day between October 19, 1984, and June 30, 1985, and stayed on active duty through June 30, 1988, (or June 30, 1987, if you entered the Selected Reserve within one year of leaving active duty and served four years)
- On December 31, 1989, you had entitlement left from Vietnam-Era GI Bill

Category III

- Not eligible for *MGIB* under Category I or II
- On active duty on September 30, 1990, *AND* separated involuntarily after February 2, 1991

- *OR* involuntarily separated on or after November 30, 1993
- *OR* voluntarily separated under either the Voluntary Separation Incentive (VSI) or Special Separation Benefit (SSB) program
- Before separation, you had military pay reduced by $1200

Category IV

- On active duty on October 9, 1996, *AND* you had money remaining in a VEAP account on that date *AND* you elected MGIB by October 9, 1997
- *OR* entered full-time National Guard duty under title 32, USC, between July 1, 1985, and November 28, 1989, *AND* you elected MGIB during the period October 9, 1996, through July 8, 1997
- Had military pay reduced by $100 a month for twelve months or made a $1200 lump-sum contribution

If You Separate Early. If you did not complete the required period of service, you may still be eligible for MGIB if you were discharged early for one of the following reasons:

- Medical disability
- Hardship
- Preexisting medical condition
- A condition that interfered with performance of duty
- A reduction in force (RIF)—(Only certain RIFs qualify; check with your Education Service Officer.)
- Convenience of the government

If the "Reason for Discharge" on your DD Form 214 (Record of Separation) is for the "Convenience of the Government," you must have served at least thirty months if your enlistment contract was for three or more years, or at least twenty months if your enlistment contract was for less than three years. And if you were discharged early, your MGIB—AD benefit rates will be reduced accordingly. If you're separated for one of these reasons, you'll receive one month of entitlement for each month of active duty (up to 36 months) after June 30, 1985. For example, if you're discharged after nineteen months for hardship, and you meet the other eligibility requirements, you'll receive nineteen months of ADMGIB benefits.

What Will VA Pay?

The monthly benefit paid to you is based on the type of training you take, your length of service, your category, and if DoD put extra money in your MGIB (Montgomery GI Bill) Fund (called "kickers"). You usually have ten years to use your MGIB benefits, but the time can be less, and in some cases, longer under certain circumstances.

The following table shows the Montgomery GI Bill (Chapter 30 of Title 38) increased educational assistance allowance, effective October 1, 2007. For updated rates, go to: http://www.gibill.va.gov/GI_Bill_Info/rates.htm.

Montgomery GI Bill Assistance Allowance Rates

Institutional training	
Training time	Monthly Rate
Full time (12 hours or more)	$1,101.00
¾ time (9–11 hours)	$825.75
½ time (6–8 hours)	$550.50
Less than ½ time more than ¼ time	$550.50
¼ time or less	$275.25

Can You Be Eligible for More than One Benefit?

You may be eligible for more than one VA education benefit. If you are, you must elect which one to receive. But you cannot receive payment under more than one benefit at a time.

How Do I Apply?

Contact a Veterans Benefits Counselor by calling the toll-free number *1-888-GI-BILL-1 (1-888-442-4551; [1-800-829-4833(TTY)])*. You can also find information about your education benefits by contacting your nearest Veterans Affairs Regional Processing Office. You can find the office nearest you online at http://www.gibill.va.gov/contact/contact.htm.

The Montgomery GI Bill—Selected Reserve

The Montgomery GI bill—Selected Reserve (MGIB-SR/Ch.1606 of Title 10 U.S.C.) is the first education assistance program that does not require service in the active Armed Forces. The MGIB-SR program may be available to you if you are a member of the Selected Reserve. The Selected Reserve includes the Army Reserve, Navy Reserve, Air Force Reserve, Marine Corps Reserve and Coast Guard Reserve, and the Army National Guard, and the Air National Guard. If you are eligible, you can use the MGIB-SR toward any degree programs, certificate or correspondence courses, cooperative training, independent study programs, apprenticeship/on-the-job training, and vocational flight training programs. Even certain remedial, refresher, and deficiency training courses may be applicable. Under the MGIB-SR, you may receive up to thirty-six months of education benefits, with tuition payments sent directly from the VA to your learning institution.

Qualifying for the Montgomery GI Bill—Selected Reserve Program

The VA created the Montgomery GI Bill—Selected Reserve Program for Reserve personnel. If you are or were enrolled in the Reserves, you qualify for this VA benefit if:

- You have a six-year obligation to serve in the Selected Reserve signed after June 30, 1985. If you are an officer, you must have agreed to serve six years in addition to your original obligation. For some types of training, it is necessary to have a six-year commitment that begins after September 30, 1990;
- You have completed your initial active duty for training (IADT);
- You had a high school diploma or equivalency certificate before completing IADT. You may not use twelve college hours to meet this requirement; and
- You remained in good standing while serving in an active Selected Reserve unit.

If your Reserve or National Guard unit was deactivated during the period October 1, 1991, through September 30, 1995, or you were involuntarily separated (e.g., reduction in force) from Reserve or National Guard service during this same period, you are still eligible for MGIB – SR benefits for the full fourteen year eligibility period. You're also eligible if you were discharged from Selected Reserve service due to a disability that was not caused by misconduct. Your eligibility period may even be extended if you are ordered to active duty.

How Much Education Assistance Will You Receive?

You will receive the basic monthly rate increase October 1 each year based on the Consumer Price Index (CPI) increases. While you are in training, you will receive a letter with the current rates when the increase goes into effect each year.

Applying for Your Benefits

Your unit will give you a *Notice of Basic Eligibility* (DD Form 2384 or 2384-1) when you become eligible for Montgomery GI Bill—Selected Reserve. Your unit will code your eligibility into the Department of Defense (DoD) personnel system so that VA may verify your eligibility. If you're eligible, your Reserve or Guard component will code your eligibility into the DoD.

You will need to insure that your selected educational program is approved for VA training. If you are not sure, the VA can inform you and the school or company about the requirements to be approved for training. To do this, obtain and complete VA Form 22-1990, *Application for Education Benefits*. All VA education forms are located online at http://www.gibill.va.gov/GI_Bill_Info/education_forms.htm. Send it to the VA regional office with jurisdiction over the state where you will train. If you have already started training, take your application and your *Notice of Basic Eligibility* to your school or employer. Ask them to complete VA Form 22-1999, Enrollment Certification, and send all the forms to the VA. You can also apply online through the VA's Web site at http://vabenefits.vba.va.gov/vonapp.

The Clock Is Ticking

Your benefit entitlement from The Montgomery GI Bill—Selected Reserve ends fourteen years from the date of your eligibility, or on the day you leave the Selected Reserve. If your eligibility to this program began on or after October 1, 1992, your period of eligibility ends fourteen years later, or on the day you leave the Selected Reserve. If your eligibility to this program began prior to October 1, 1992, your period of eligibility ends ten years after, or on the day you leave the Selected Reserve.

Can a Veteran Be Eligible for Two or More VA Education Benefits?

Yes, you may be eligible for more than one VA education benefit program. However, you may only receive payments from one program at a time. You can receive a maximum of forty-eight months of benefits under any combination of VA education programs you qualify for. As an example, if you qualify for both MGIB-A (Chapter 30) and MGIB-SR (Chapter 1606), you can receive thirty-six months of entitlement at your MGIB-AD payment rate, and then an additional twelve months of entitlement at your MGIB-SR payment rate, up to the maximum total of forty-eight months entitlement.

If you are unsure about whether you qualify for more than one program, submit an application to http://www.gibill.va.gov/GI_Bill_Info/How_to_Apply.htm or to your local VA Regional Processing Office at http://www.gibill.va.gov/contact/contact.htm to determine eligibility. If you are eligible for more than one benefit program, you will need to notify the VA of which program you intend to use upon deciding to enroll in an approved education or training course. You can contact VA through its Web site or by calling 1 (888) GIBILL-1 (1-888-442-4551); [1-800-829-4833(TTY)].

If you need more information about a particular benefit program, information is available at http://www.gibill.va.gov/GI_Bill_Info/benefits.htm.

More Detailed Information about the Montgomery GI Bill—Selected Reserve

The Veterans Administration has published a thirty-page pamphlet titled *The Montgomery GI Bill—Selected Reserve* that summarizes the educational benefits under the Montgomery GI Bill—Selected Reserve (Educational Assistance Program). The pamphlet is numbered 22-90-3 and was revised January 2007. You can find the pamphlet online at http://www.gibill.va.gov/pamphlets/CH1606/CH1606_Pamphlet.pdf.

Accommodations in the Classroom

How will you get around the campus in a wheelchair? If you have problems remembering things because of TBI, how can you take tests or keep up with the lectures? As a veteran with a disability a number of resources are available to help with accommodations to insure that you will have the tools you will need to succeed in your education or training. By law, schools that receive federal financing have to provide accommodations for disabilities and will do whatever they can to accommodate yours. One war-disabled Vietnam veteran, for example, wanted to pursue a doctorate in the Washington DC area. Since the library was not accessible for a wheelchair, the VA purchased for him every research book that he would use in the library so he could use them at home. As you could imagine, he was quite popular with the other students in his program.

Most postsecondary schools have a disabled students' services office (DSS) so the first place to check is this office in your school. The national association for DSS offices is the Association on Higher Education and Disability (www.ahead.org) and they can provide information to you about which schools in your area have these offices. The AHEAD Web sit also has good information for students and their families about academic accommodations. Another good Web-based resource is the online clearinghouse on postsecondary education for individuals with disabilities located at http://www.heath.gwu.edu. The site contains information about educational support services, policies, procedures, adaptations, and accommodations, as well as financial assistance and scholarships.

The Job Accommodation Network (JAN) is referenced frequently in this book. A service funded by the U.S. Department of Labor's Office of Disability Employment Policy, in Washington DC, JAN has expert consultants who can advise you about assistive technology and other techniques and strategies that you can use to accommodate your disability both on the job and in the classroom. You can call or write JAN or visit their Web page, explain your disability and your educational goals and they will provide expert recommendations and ideas about how you can accommodate your disabilities in the classroom. JAN can be reached at http://www.jan.wvu.edu and by phone at (800) 526–7234; [877-781-9403 (TTY)].

Finally, we recommend that you connect with a service officer with one of the Veteran Service Organizations (VSOs) such as the Disabled American Veterans (www.dav.org), the Paralyzed Veterans of America (www.pva.org), or one of the other groups (contact information for these groups is located on this book's Web site at http://www.warswounded.com. Although the officers are sometimes located in VA offices across the country, they work for the VSOs and are there to represent your issues and advocate for your concerns. They are not VA employees.

The Reserve Educational Assistance Program (Reap/Ch. 1607 of Title 10, U.S.C.)

Detailed information about the Reserve Educational Assistance Program (REAP) can be found at http://www.gibill.va.gov/pamphlets/CH1607/REAP_FAQ. htm. Most of the information in this chapter comes from that site.

What Is REAP?

REAP was established as a part of the Ronald W. Reagan National Defense Authorization Act for fiscal year 2005. It is a new DoD education benefit program designed to provide educational assistance to members of the Reserve components called or ordered to active duty in response to a war or national emergency (contingency operation) as declared by the President or Congress. The DoD and the Department of Homeland Security will determine who is eligible for this program. The Department of Veterans Affairs administers the program and pays benefits from funds contributed by DoD.

Who Qualifies for REAP?

The Secretaries of each military service, DoD, and Department of Homeland Security (Coast Guard) will determine eligibility and establish the program to provide educational assistance to members of the Reserves of the armed forces who are called to duty for ninety days or more. Members may be eligible after serving ninety consecutive days on active duty after September 11, 2001.

How Much Does the REAP Benefit Pay Monthly?

The benefit payable under REAP is a percentage of the Chapter 30 three-year or more enlistment rate ($1,034 as of October 1, 2005).

- If you serve ninety days but less than one year, you will receive 40 percent of the three-year rate.
- A service period of one year but less than two years of active duty will pay 60 percent of the three-year rate.
- A service period of more than two years on active duty will result in an 80 percent payment of the three-year rate.

Note: Members on active duty are only entitled to be reimbursed for the actual cost of the tuition and fees of the courses taken (not to exceed the statutory rate).

This benefit is retroactive to September 11, 2001. A reservist attending school will be paid a percentage of the MGIB three-year rate in effect during the time in which the reservist was enrolled. For example: The three-year full time MGIB rate in June of 2002 was $800. Someone being paid the 40 percent rate for school enrollment in June 2002 would receive $320 for full-time monthly benefits.

How Much Entitlement Will I Get under REAP?

You will receive thirty-six months of full time entitlement at your given rate. A REAP participant may not use more than forty-eight months of entitlement under any combination of VA Educational programs. For example, if you have already used twenty months of Chapter 1606, you will only receive twenty-eight months of REAP.

What about Members Released Early for Disability?

Members released from service early because of disability incurred or aggravated in the line of duty receive REAP benefits at the rate they were qualified for when they were released. For example, if you served on active duty of one year and six months prior to being released, you are entitled to receive benefits at the 60 percent rate for as long as you were entitled to REAP benefits. Members released prior to completing ninety days of active duty service are entitled to benefits at the 40 percent rate. If you are released from service for a disability, you are entitled to REAP benefits for ten years from your date of eligibility.

Can I Receive REAP Benefits Concurrently with Another MGIB Benefit?

No, you cannot receive assistance under more than one VA Education program at one time. If you are eligible for MGIB-Active Duty (Chapter 30) because you served on duty for a minimum of twenty-four consecutive months you must make an irrevocable election as to which program you will apply your time on active duty. If you are eligible for a Chapter 1606 kicker, you can still be paid that kicker while receiving REAP.

What Education Programs Are Approved under REAP?

All education programs, with the exception of National Examination/Testing Reimbursement are payable under REAP.

Can I Apply for REAP Now?

Yes. VA Regional Processing Offices in Atlanta, St. Louis, Buffalo, and Muskogee are accepting applications and supporting documents for REAP claims. If you have never applied for benefits before, complete VA Form 1990 and write "REAP" in section one. If you are already eligible for VA Education benefits under another program, submit VA Form 1995 and note that you now wish to use REAP. Copies of these forms can be mailed to you or found at this site: http://www.gibill.va.gov/GI_Bill_Info/education_forms.htm. Submit copies of all DD 214s and copies of all orders for the period(s) you will use to claim eligibility.

Which Benefit Should I Use or Election Date Should I Choose?

Veterans eligible for REAP will most likely also be eligible for Chapter 1606. The REAP program pays a bit more than Chapter 1606. You must weigh the benefits of retroactively electing REAP with the benefits of using it for future training.

Example A. Bob is eligible for Chapter 1606 and REAP. He used four months of entitlement under Chapter 1606 in the spring of 2002. Bob could request retroactive payment under REAP for that period based on his active duty period in 2001. The full time rate under REAP for that period would be $320/month. For Chapter 1606, the full time rate was $272.00. Bob already received $1088.00 in Chapter 1606 benefits. Under REAP he would receive $1280.00. If Bob retroactively chooses REAP, he will receive an additional $192 for the difference between the two programs. Is it more advantageous for Bob to take the extra $192 for REAP, or to elect REAP from the current date forward? If Bob takes the retroactive benefit amount, he now has thirty-two months of REAP to use for any future school enrollment. If Bob doesn't request retroactive benefits, he now has thirty-six months of benefits at 40 percent of the current MGIB three-year rate ($401.60 for fiscal year 2005). Bob must determine what he has used in the past, how much schooling he needs to complete in the future, and determine which option will be most advantageous to him in the long run. In Bob's situation, it might be more advantageous for him not to retroactively elect REAP benefits.

Example B. Susie is eligible for Chapter 1606 and would be eligible for REAP based on active duty served in 2001–2002. She has been in school full time continuously since she returned from active duty. To date, she has used thirty-one months of Chapter 1606 benefits. For someone in Susie's situation, she might benefit more from retroactively selecting REAP benefits. She would receive the difference between the two programs, and would still have seventeen months of full time REAP benefits remaining.

More Detailed Information about the REAP Program

More information about the Reserve Educational Assistance Program (REAP) can be found at http://www.gibill.va.gov/pamphlets/CH1607/REAP_FAQ.htm. Most of the information presented in this chapter comes from that site.

Post-Vietnam Veterans' Educational Assistance Program (VEAP), Ch. 32 of Title 38

What Is VEAP?

The Post-Vietnam Veterans' Educational Assistance Program (VEAP) is an education benefit for veterans who paid into VEAP while they were in the service. Eligible veterans may be entitled to as much as thirty-six months of training. Eligibility usually ends in ten years after getting out of the service, but the time limit can be longer in certain cases.

What Programs Are Available?

The following types of training are available: college or university programs; business, technical or vocational training; on-the-job training and apprenticeship programs; remedial, deficiency, and refresher training, national tests; correspondence courses; flight training; work toward a high school diploma or its equivalent; and the cost of tests for licenses or certifications needed to get, keep, or advance in a job.

Who Is Eligible?

To be eligible for VEAP, you must have first entered active duty after December 31, 1976, and before July 1, 1985, contributed to VEAP before April 1, 1987, and completed your first period of service. You also must have been discharged under conditions other than dishonorable. You may be eligible while still on active duty; call 1-888-442-4551

What Does the VA Pay?

The total dollar amount of your benefits is the sum of your total contributions plus matching funds from VA equal to two times your contributions and any DoD contributions or "kickers."

How to Apply

When you find a program approved for VA training, you can apply for VEAP by completing VA Form 22-1990, *Application for Education Benefits*. You can also apply online at http://vabenefits.vba.va.gov/vonapp. For more information, call toll-free at 1-888-442-4551 (1-800-829-4833 [TTY]).

Survivors' and Dependents' Educational Assistance Program (Dea—Ch. 35 of Title 38 U.S.C.)

Benefit Description

The Survivors' and Dependents' Educational Assistance Program (DEA) provides education and training opportunities to eligible dependents of veterans who are permanently and totally disabled due to a service-related condition, or who died while on active duty or as a result of a service-related condition. The program offers up to forty-five months of education benefits. These benefits may be used for degree and certificate programs, apprenticeship, and on-the-job- training. If you are a spouse you may take a correspondence course. Remedial, deficiency, and refresher courses may be approved under certain circumstances.

Eligibility

You are eligible for this program if you are the son, daughter, or spouse of:

- A veteran who died or is permanently and totally disabled as the result of a service-connected disability. The disability must arise out of active service in the Armed Forces.
- A veteran who died from any cause while such service-connected disability was in existence

- A service member missing in action or captured in line of duty by a hostile force
- A service member forcibly detained or interned in line of duty by a foreign government or power
- A service member who is hospitalized or receiving outpatient treatment for a service-connected permanent and total disability and is likely to be discharged for that disability. This change became effective on December 23, 2006.

Period of Eligibility

If you are a *son or daughter* of a service member and wish to receive benefits for attending school or job training, you must be between the ages of 18 and 26. In certain instances, it is possible to begin before age 18 and to continue after age 26. Marriage is not a barrier to this benefit. If you are in the Armed Forces, you may not receive this benefit while on active duty. To pursue training after military service, your discharge must not be under dishonorable conditions. VA can extend your period of eligibility by the number of months and days equal to the time spent on active duty. This extension cannot generally go beyond your thirty-first birthday but there are some exceptions.

If you are a *spouse* of a service member, benefits end ten years from the date VA finds you eligible or from the date of death of the veteran. For surviving spouses (spouses of service members who died on active duty) benefits end twenty years from the date of death.

How to Apply

You should make sure that your selected program is approved for VA training. If you are not clear on this point, VA will inform you and the school or company about the requirements. Obtain and complete VA Form 22-5490 Application for Survivors' and Dependents' Educational Assistance ((located online at http://www.vba.va.gov/pubs/forms/22-5490.pdf). Send it to the VA regional office with jurisdiction over the state where you will train. If you are a son or daughter, under legal age, a parent or guardian must sign the application. If you have started training, take your application to your school or employer. Ask them to complete VA Form 22-1999, Enrollment Certification, and send both forms to VA. The 22-1999 forms are only available to school officials with the exception of VAF 22-1999c which is for correspondence courses. The school must contact their VA Representative to receive these forms.

How Much Will the VA Pay?

The following table shows the Survivors' & Dependents' Educational Assistance (DEA) Program (Chapter 35 of Title 38 U.S.C.) increased educational assistance allowance, effective October 1, 2007.

Institutional training	
Training time	Monthly rate
Full time	$881.00
¾ time	$661.00
½ time	$439.00
Less than ½ time more than ¼ time	$439.00*
¼ time or less	$220.25*

*Tuition and fees ONLY. Payment cannot exceed the listed amount.

To see tables showing rates for noninstitutional training, such as Apprenticeship and On-Job training, Special Cooperative, and Special Restoration training, go to http://www.gibill.va.gov/GI_Bill_Info/rates/CH35/ch35rates100107.htm.

Where to Find VA Regional Processing Offices

The location, addresses, and Internet site of U.S. Department of Veterans Affairs Regional Processing Offices can be found by going to http://www.gibill.va.gov/contact/contact.htm.

Phone Numbers

For assistance regarding your GI Bill and Survivors' & Dependents' Educational Assistance (DEA) Program benefits, call 1-888-442-4551. The TDD number is 1-800-829-4833.

The Department of Veterans Affair's Veterans Benefits Administration's Vocational Rehabilitation and Employment (VR&E) Service for Veterans with Service-Connected Disabilities

General Information

The VA's Veterans Benefits Administration's Vocational Rehabilitation and Employment (VR&E) service is vested with delivering timely, effective vocational rehabilitation services to veterans with service-connected disabilities. This program enables injured soldiers, sailors, airmen, and other veterans with disabilities to experience a seamless transition from military service to a successful rehabilitation and to suitable employment after service to the nation. For some severely disabled veterans, this success will be to live independently, achieving the highest quality of life possible with a realized hope for employment given future advances in medical science and technology. The VA's VR&E strives to exceed the service delivery expectations of veterans and their families.

The VA's VR&E's primary benefit program is to provide vocational rehabilitation services for veterans who have a service-connected disability. To receive access to these services a veteran must be found both eligible and entitled. The outcomes of these services lead to suitable employment that is consistent with their aptitudes and interests, or achieving independence in their daily living.

VR&E also provides educational and vocational counseling to eligible service members, veterans, and veterans' dependents. The outcome of this counseling is assistance in the selection of an educational or vocational goal and/or assistance in the selection of training institutions where this goal may be pursued.

Additionally the VR&E program provides educational and vocational counseling benefits for eligible dependent children of Vietnam veterans born with certain birth defects or children of Vietnam or Korean veterans born with Spina Bifida. In order to be considered for this benefit program, you must be the biological child of a veteran who served in Vietnam or on the Korean demilitarized zone during certain periods in the 1960s or 1970s. You must have been conceived after the veteran served some time in one of those two places.

What Is the Vocational Rehabilitation and Employment Program?

The Vocational Rehabilitation and Employment (VR&E) Program is authorized by Congress under Title 38, Code of Federal Regulations, Chapter 31. It is sometimes referred to as the Chapter 31 program. The mission of VR&E is to help veterans with service-connected disabilities (which are disabling conditions resulting from or aggravated by an injury or illness while the veteran was serving on active duty in the military) to prepare for, find, and keep suitable jobs. For veterans with service-connected disabilities so severe that they cannot immediately consider work, VR&E offers services to improve their ability to live as independently as possible.

Services that may be provided by VR&E include:

- Comprehensive rehabilitation evaluation to determine abilities, skills, interests, and needs
- Vocational counseling and rehabilitation planning
- Employment services such as job-seeking skills, resume development, and other work readiness assistance
- Assistance finding and keeping a job, including the use of special employer incentives
- Training, including On the Job Training (OJT), apprenticeships, and nonpaid work experiences (if needed)
- Postsecondary training at a college, vocational, technical, or business school (if needed)
- Supportive rehabilitation services including case management, counseling, and referral
- Independent living services

Who Is Eligible for VR&E Services?

To receive an evaluation for VR&E services, a veteran must have received, or will receive, a discharge that is other than dishonorable, have a service-connected disability rating of at least 10 percent, and submit a completed application for VR&E services.

The basic period of eligibility in which VR&E services may be used is twelve years from the latter of the following: the date of separation from active military service, or the date the veteran was first notified by VA of a service-connected disability rating.

The basic period of eligibility may be extended if a Vocational Rehabilitation Counselor (VRC) determines that a veteran has a Serious Employment Handicap (SEH) which is defined as a significant impairment of a veteran's ability to prepare for, obtain, or retain employment consistent with his or her abilities, aptitudes, and interests. The SEH must result in substantial part from a service-connected disability. For veterans rated at 10 percent and veterans beyond their twelve-year basic period of eligibility, the finding of an SEH is necessary to establish entitlement to VR&E services.

What Happens after Eligibility Is Established?

The veteran meets with a VRC for a comprehensive evaluation to determine whether the veteran is entitled to services. The comprehensive evaluation includes:

- An assessment of the veteran's interests, aptitudes, and abilities
- An assessment of whether service-connected disabilities impair the veteran's ability to find and/or hold a job using the occupational skills he has already developed
- Vocational exploration and goal development

What Is Entitlement Determination?

A VRC determines whether a veteran has an "employment handicap" (defined as an impairment of a veteran's ability to prepare for, obtain or retain employment consistent with her abilities, aptitudes, and interests). The impairment must result in substantial part from a service-connected disability. For veterans within the twelve year basic period of eligibility and rated at 20 percent or more, a finding of employment handicap results in entitlement to VR&E services) based on the results of the comprehensive evaluation. If the service-connected disability rating is less than 20 percent or if the veteran is beyond the twelve year basic period of eligibility, then a serious employment handicap must be found to establish entitlement to VR&E services.

What Happens after the Entitlement Determination Is Made?

The veteran and Vocational Rehabilitation Counselor (VRC) work together to:

- Select a VR&E program track leading to an employment or independent living goal
- Identify viable employment or independent living services options
- Determine transferable skills (reasonably developed skills, knowledge, and abilities attained through training and experience that relate to current employment opportunities in the labor market)
- Explore labor market and wage information
- Identify physical demands and other job characteristics
- Narrow vocational options to identify a suitable employment goal
- Investigate training requirements
- Identify resources needed to achieve rehabilitation
- Develop an individualized rehabilitation plan to achieve the identified employment or independent living goal

What Is a Rehabilitation Plan?

A rehabilitation plan is an individualized, written outline of the services, resources, and criteria that will be used to achieve successful rehabilitation. It is an agreement that is signed by the veteran and the VRC and is reviewed annually to determine whether any changes may be needed.

Depending on their circumstances, veterans will work with their VRC to select one of the following five tracks of services:

- Reemployment (with a former employer)
- Rapid employment services for new employment
- Self-employment
- Employment through long term services
- Independent living services

What Happens after the Rehabilitation Plan Is Developed?

After a plan is developed and signed, the VRC or a case manager will continue to work with the veteran to implement the plan to achieve suitable employment or independent living. The VRC or case manager may coordinate services such as tutorial assistance, training in job-seeking skills, medical and dental referrals, adjustment counseling, payment of training allowance, if applicable, and other services as required to achieve rehabilitation.

Summary of the Vocational Rehabilitation and Employment Program (Chapter 31) Process

A veteran who is eligible for an evaluation under Chapter 31 must complete an application and meet with a VRC. If the VRC determines that an employment handicap exists as a result of a service-connected disability, the veteran is found to be entitled to services. The VRC and the veteran will then continue counseling to select a track of services and jointly develop a plan to address the rehabilitation and employment needs of the veteran.

The rehabilitation plan will specify an employment or independent living goal, identify intermediate goals, and outline services and resources needed to achieve these goals. The VRC and the veteran will work together to implement the plan and achieve successful rehabilitation. If a veteran is found not to be entitled to services, the VRC will help the veteran locate other resources to address any rehabilitation and employment needs identified during the evaluation. Referral to other resources may include state vocational rehabilitation programs, Department of Labor employment programs for disabled veterans, state, federal, or local agencies providing services for employment or small business development, Internet-based resources for rehabilitation and employment, and information about applying for financial aid.

State Resources

State resources for education benefits can be found by visiting http://www.gibill.va.gov/links.htm and clicking on "State Veteran's Benefits." A list of State/Territory Veterans Affairs offices will pop up. You can click on the name of any State or Territory to visit the Web site for that location's Department of Veterans Affairs office.

For example, if you click on "Massachusetts" you will be at "The Official Web site of the Massachusetts Department of Veterans' Services." You will notice under the heading "Benefits" that there are five items to choose from. Three of them are "Annuities," "Bonuses," and "Education." If you click on "Annuities" or "Bonuses" you will discover details about financial benefits available for certain veterans. According to the site, the Massachusetts Annuity is "given in recognition of the service of our distinguished 100 percent service-connected disabled veterans and to the parents of distinguished veterans (Gold Star Parents) and the un-remarried spouses (Gold Star Wives or Husbands) of distinguished veterans who gave their lives in the service of their country during wartime."

Eligible applicants from Massachusetts need to meet the following criteria:

Veteran

- Meets one of the service time requirements set forth in 108 CMR 3.03
- Was discharged from military service other than a dishonorable discharge
- Is a resident of Massachusetts at the time of applying for the annuity and continues to be a resident of the Commonwealth as per M.G.L. ch. 115, s.6A
- Meets the requirements for blindness, paraplegia, double amputation or other disability set forth in M.G.L. ch. 115, s.6B and so certified by the Department of Veterans Affairs. Proof of service and disability shall be furnished to the Commissioner as per M.G.L. ch. 115, s.6C.

Parent or Spouse

- Death of veteran must be service-connected
- Parent/spouse must reside in the Commonwealth and must continue to reside in Massachusetts from the date of application and while in receipt of the annuity payments
- Spouses must not be remarried

Although the annuity is not an educational benefit, $2,000 a year, tax free, for as long as the veteran, parent, or spouse remains eligible, is certainly worth knowing about. Not every state pays veterans with severe disabilities an annuity, but if you happen to live in or move to one of the states that pays this annuity, it is certainly worth knowing about, so I recommend looking into it.

When you click on the Massachusetts "Education" button you will see, among other things, a "Financial Assistance" site. When you go there you will see a number of interesting items including "Tuition Waivers," "Tuition and Fee Waivers for Guard Members," "Grants," "Student Loans," "National Scholarships for Veterans," "Montgomery GI Bill," "Temporary Waivers on Student Loan Repayment," "Educational "Assistance for Family Members of Veterans," and something called the "Massachusetts Soldiers Legacy Fund." This fund provides education funds for children of Massachusetts military personnel killed in action during Operation Iraqi Freedom (OIF) and Operation Enduring Freedom (OEF).

As you can see, a lot of information about state resources for educational benefits is available at the state level. So, take the time to get on the Web site listed in this section and find your appropriate state or territory and see what is available to you and your family. You may find a tuition waiver or scholarship that you can combine with your GI Bill (or other VA educational benefits) and substantially reduce your costs of attending school.

Some Closing Advice

I believe education is a key ingredient in anyone's recipe for success. Unless you are one of those one-in-a-million people who has a great idea that can make you millions of dollars overnight without increasing the level of your education, I hope you take advantage of your well-earned education benefits. Pursuing your education is a "no brainer," the more education you have, the more money you are likely to make over the course of your life. Remember, most of the information here can be found online, so if you have access to the Internet, jump online and check out the sites, particularly http://www.va.gov and look at the information about veteran's education benefits. And, remember, the clock is ticking. Most of your benefits have a window of opportunity that opens the minute that you are discharged from the service and slowly closes over a period of years. Do not get so caught up in life's activities that you forget to pursue your education and you let your window of opportunity close. Use your VA educational benefits that you (or your spouse or parent) worked so hard to earn. Good luck!

CHAPTER 8

Disabilities and Injuries among the Members of the National Guard and Reserve Units

Jaine Darwin

Editors' Comment

An unprecedented number of "citizen soldiers" or members of the National Guard and Reserves have been deployed to fight overseas in numbers never before seen in our nation's history. The Guard and Reserve members are fighting alongside the active duty members in virtually all capacities and are thus receiving the same types of injuries and wounds. When they return home, they need to contend with the same reintegration and transition issues and the same symptoms of PTSD and other psychological issues created by their military service. But unlike active duty service members, these citizen soldiers are frequently unable to access the resources available to the other service members because many live in communities far removed from VA centers and military bases. Without community support, the recovery and reintegration process can be especially difficult for Reserve and Guard members.

This chapter was created for the returning members of the Reserve and National Guard and their families and friends. While most of the material throughout this book will be applicable and useful for you, your status as a citizen-soldier and the lack of the resources available to you will create additional issues that will need to be addressed. This chapter describes these potential issues and how you can face them. The author is Jaine Darwin, Psy.D., a psychologist and psychoanalyst and a founder and codirector of SOFAR (Strategic Outreach to Families of All Reservists), a pro bono mental health project that provides free psychological support, psychotherapy, psychoeducation, and prevention services to the extended families of National Guard and Reserve members. She draws upon her experiences counseling Guard and Reserve members and their families to offer advice on what issues you may be facing and how you can effectively face and address these concerns.

Introduction

The current conflicts in the global war on terrorism—Afghanistan, Operation Enduring Freedom (OEF), and Operation Iraqi Freedom (OIF)—are the first war zones in which citizen-soldiers (the category consisting of military reservists and National Guard) participated in multiple deployments. At some points in these conflicts, citizen-soldiers comprised almost 50 percent of the fighting forces. Currently, 556,000 of the 1.6 million soldiers who have deployed since the beginning of OEF are citizen-soldiers. When these citizen-soldiers (who were used to drilling one weekend a month and two weeks a year) became active duty soldiers for periods of one year to fifteen months, their families immediately became military families and had to contend with the same issues as the families of active duty service members. Blue star banners and yellow ribbons (indicating families awaiting the return of a soldier from the war) popped up in city and suburban windows where they had never hung before.

Because they immediately return to their civilian lives and previous homes and lack the social support and network that active duty soldiers have upon their return, soldiers in the Guard and Reserve—and especially soldiers who have received physical and psychological injuries as part of their service—face unique challenges upon their return. Only a citizen-soldier can return home after a deployment on a Saturday and return to a civilian job when the weekend ends. Only a wounded citizen-soldier can go from an all-military treatment center to a community with only a few wounded soldiers. These transitions are real challenges for the soldier and the soldier's family. The challenges for citizen-soldiers and their families include dealing with the highest rate of soldiers returning with a diagnosable mental health condition: 50 percent for citizen-soldiers compared to 40 percent for full-time military and 31 percent for Marines. They must cope with all those things that impact other soldiers but without a close-by peer group either for the soldier or for the family members. Being the only one coping with something is always harder than having a group with whom to share things as active duty soldiers do when they return to bases where everyone is familiar with what it means to go to war. This is the fate of citizen-soldiers and their families when they return to a civilian life that has continued unabated in their absences and even oblivious to the stresses of a war in which less than 2 percent of the population serves.

The Lead Up to War

When the alert for deployment was issued, a process began that still impacts family and returning soldiers once they return home. Soldiers and families had to be prepared for the separation. Soldiers made out wills, something most young people do not routinely do, and they had to consider and plan for their own deaths and their funerals. Soldiers in college delayed studies or refigured their educational plans. Sometimes wedding dates were moved up or postponed. If the soldier were the primary financial provider, families had to find ways to manage finances on what might be reduced levels of income. Household responsibilities also were redistributed. In some homes with children, the remaining parent had to learn to function as a single parent. Soldiers who were single parents had to find alternate living arrangements for their children. Soldiers with aging parents needed to arrange other care options in their absence. Some younger soldiers were leaving home for the first time, so they and their parents had to deal with normal issues of separation against the backdrop of coping with going off to war.

The first good-bye came when the troops mobilized and went to bases in the United States to prepare for combat in the war zone. The soldiers marched off with their comrades as the families went home to their own communities. This was the start of another important step. Soldiers have two families: the family of comrades who fight alongside them and the family who waits for them at home. Families usually only have one soldier and lack the comrades around them that the soldier uses to draw upon for support. While soldiers are preparing for duty in harm's way, other soldiers in the area share their experiences and surround them with support. But many families of Reserve and Guard members go back home to cope in isolation as the only people in their community with someone who is serving. The families of active duty soldiers, on the other hard, usually have a community of other military families to provide guidance and support.

The second good-bye comes when the outfit actually deploys. Sometimes, soldiers are issued passes and return home for several days. More frequently, family members go to the mobilization site to say goodbye. Even the decision about who goes to say good-bye is a complicated one for family members. One mother, seeing her husband off to a second deployment, chose to travel to the point of deployment by herself. She said, "My kids can't cope with one more good-bye." This marks the beginning of a period that changes the lives of all involved.

Soldiers in a 360-degree war zone (where the fighting goes on all around them without a designated front or a designated rear) are required to be in a state of constant alert. The may be exposed to sights, sounds, and smells that will remain with them throughout their lives. Families at home also serve with different strains. The family lives in a state of constant worry about the safety of their soldier. Families of citizen-soldiers often do this without the support of others who would surround them if they lived on a military base. Children with relatives who are serving may be the only children in the school impacted by a deployment, while children of the active soldiers are usually surrounded in school by the children of other soldiers. Since citizen-soldiers span the age range of 18 to 60 years and may even be older, the affected children may be siblings or even grandchildren of the soldiers.

Communications During Deployment

All soldiers, but especially the citizen-soldiers, worry about how the family will cope in their absence; they may feel guilty about not being there to help, and they could be worried about no longer being needed by their families. The family may fear burdening the soldier with problems at home and patterns of communication may start that will make the reintegration process easier or more difficult when the soldier returns. Does a soldier want to hear that a son or daughter was suspended from school moments before the soldier goes on a mission? Does a family want to hear about the IED (improvised explosive device) that exploded and injured the troops two cars ahead in the convoy? Each family has different norms and coping skills. The ability to understand the mutual distress of the deployment is the important factor in helping everyone cope with return. This takes on even more meaning when a soldier has been wounded. What was it like to be injured? What was it like for the family to get the call that the soldier is on the way to Germany or to Walter Reed for treatment? How resilient is the family, and how resilient can they become?

Families with good communications and good social networks tend to be better able to cope with the strain of an injured soldier. Families can learn resilience if they can be helped to understand and constructively express feelings. Feeling scared, angry, and grateful are common reactions that have to be shared for them to be bearable. Families can feel less helpless when they are trained to participate in the soldier's care and to advocate for the soldier. A soldier can help by being as clear as possible about his emotional needs. The soldier can be encouraged to let the family know when she feels ready to talk about the injury or any lasting incapacity. The family and the soldier both must learn to tolerate the emotional fluctuations each will endure and the potential problems that may emerge from some of the disconnects that may come when a family member and a soldier are not in harmony about what the other is experiencing.

The Homecoming

While a soldier's return is a joyous occasion, the homecoming begins the hard work of both the soldier and the family adjusting to the "new normal." After combat, separation, and the physical and psychological assaults, the reunited family cannot return to its old self. The family can grow and become better or fragment and function in a worse way, but staying the same is not an option. A number of factors contribute to the final result. One of them is how willing the returned soldier and the family members are to work on communicating as they go through the period of readjustment. Another is how resilient they have been as a family before the deployment. A resilient family is one that is integrated into the community and has a good social network. This might come out of membership in a church, synagogue, or mosque or participation in a group with people who share a special interest or strong ties among extended family members. While returning soldiers may not be ready to participate in many social events, connecting with others and not isolating themselves are important factors in reintegration and reunion.

No one can make the transition from a war in which they are completely surrounded by the war zone to a civilian community right away, and for the citizen-soldiers without the resources and community it can be even more diffi-cult. According to the Mental Health Task Force Report (2007) of the Department of Defense, "An Achievable Vision" (available online at http://handle.dtic.mil/100. 2/ADA469411), 50 percent of National Guard and Reserve members are return-ing with mental conditions. Many of these come under the category of "transient stress reactions" which is what may happen when someone has to make the read-justment from being in constant danger to the relative safety of civilian life.

Serving in a war zone calls for functioning in a continual state of alertness. In the community, this may be termed hypervigilance. At home every loud sound does not herald danger, but the mind and body of a returning soldier may take months to readjust to this standard. When survival depends on preparedness, the slower and less regimented pace of family life can be confusing and sometimes enraging. Family members do not understand the need to patrol the perimeter or obey a command without questioning. Nor do they understand the fear that may be generated in the returned soldier who may feel their "disobedience" endanger them all.

Family of active duty military who live on bases have been steeped in the idea of the chain of command and the idea of a military code at home. But families of citizen-soldiers have no exposure to these concepts and may regard the returning soldier as an alien from another planet. As an example one Major who had just returned from a twelve-month deployment in Iraq described walking around the downtown area where he lived and feeling like he was visiting a foreign country for the first time. He could not understand everyone's concerns with things he found inconsequential and the lack of concern with potential danger like people talking on cell phones while they drove or why no one was scanning the horizon for IEDs.

Transient stress reactions may cause a returned soldier to be sensitive to certain smells, sounds, and sights. The smell of gasoline or even starter fluid at a barbeque may fill the soldier with dread, because they trigger memories of the war zone. If these smells were associated with the soldier's wounding, the dread may escalate to panic. For the citizen-soldier, they may not have many other soldiers around them who understand the impact of this. Hitting the ground when a car backfires or wanting to zigzag down the road and driving defensively when something is spotted in the road may be greeted with ridicule or disregard instead of the knowing nod and the support that an active duty soldier will receive on return when many around them have shared the same experience.

Just as the families of citizen-soldiers cope with isolation during a deploy-ment, returning citizen-soldiers cope with isolation on retuning. Even if the sol-diers remain a member of the Guard and Reserve, they usually have a three-month break before they are required to return to monthly drill weekends. Un-derstanding the universal nature of an experience normalizes it for most peo-ple. Many of the veterans service organizations like the Veterans of Foreign Wars and the American Legion and other groups (listed on the book's Web site, http://www.warswounded.com) can provide returning Guard and Reserve soldiers with a place to discuss these worries with people who understand them because they too have felt these worries.

Family Relationships

Families are always in a state of change as they proceed through the stages of development as a unit. A young family begins as two partners choosing to make a life together. When a couple has a baby, the way the family operates changes. The couple must now organize around the needs of the baby. Each of them has to adjust to a changed level of intimacy, to more financial responsibility, and to long periods of little sleep. As the baby grows or as more children come along, the family continues to adapt. External stresses like job changes, moving to a bigger house, or an illness in the extended family may all impact the functioning of the family. A family with children in diapers has different challenges than a family with teenagers. Depending on the strengths and vulnerabilities of the family, different stages will be viewed as either hard or easy. Some people prefer the ages when the children need a great deal of supervision and are delighted to run after a crawling baby who puts everything in its mouth. Others do best when the kids are in Little League, on soccer teams, or attending scout meetings. Some breathe a sigh of relief when a teenager gets a driver's license because it frees them from chauffeur duty. For other families, this marks the return to sleepless nights until the car is safely in the garage and the teen is in the house.

The same holds true when a soldier deploys and returns. Soldiers return to a family that is different, while the family finds that the soldier is different too. During the deployment, children in the family have grown. A soldier may meet his baby for the first time. The toddler, the nursery school child, or the grade school child has moved on to new stages of growth and learning. The spouse who was running the home as a single parent during the deployment has now developed new skills and taken on jobs that used to be the soldier's domain. The extended family including relatives who are geographically separate is also impacted by the departure and return of a soldier. While all soldiers probably have extended family living far away from them, the extended families of citizen-soldiers may have less preparation for coping with a deployed family member. Families of regular military always knew that a deployment was part of the job. Families of citizen-soldiers have to change the mindset from "My relative is an electrician who belongs to the National Guard" to "My relative is an active duty soldier who is driving truck convoys in Iraq." This is a radical shift in the way the family views the soldier and now has to worry about the safety of their family member.

Spouses and Partners

For soldiers and their spouses or partners the readjustment takes place in every room in the house and in every area of the relationship. Couples require time to become reacquainted with each other. Each may have different expectations about sexual intimacy. One may long for passionate lovemaking immediately, while the other may feel strange even sharing a bed after the long separation. Couples in which one is a wounded soldier may worry about how the wounds will affect the ability to be sexually intimate. After almost a year of sleeping amidst sand and grime, a soldier may see the bedroom as a place to get a decent night's sleep, not as a site for passion. A soldier may return to discover children have been sleeping in the couple's bed with the spouse during the deployment, and relocation strategies may precede efforts at intimacy. What is important is that each member of the pair makes his or her needs known, tell the other what they hope for and what concerns them. Members of couples may talk in a personal shorthand and assume that the partner understands the meaning instead of speaking in whole sentences. As an example, the shorthand phrase "Billy is a crybaby" might actually mean "I am upset to find my son looking so vulnerable, and I feel guilty that my absence was so hard on him." The shorthand phrase "You never touch me anymore" might really mean "I was so scared while you were away, and I need to literally have you touch me to help me feel safer." So it is imperative for couples to speak out and insure that partners understand what is being communicated.

Couples may also have problems with communicating about PTSD and will need to make readjustments. As an example, the wife of a Reservist who returned from a year in Iraq said, "Tom has been having some problems with PTSD. It was very bad in the first few weeks that he came home in August/September. It got better in the fall, and then when we started all of the stress about our son's health, it got very bad. Anger . . . anxiety . . . isolation . . . then the lack of any feelings except for anger. . . . After our son recovered, he went through another bad period, until about a month ago, when he told me he should never have gotten married and that he should just divorce me and move to Colorado. He said that I could raise the children better without him. Well, enough was enough, and I told him that if I made him that miserable and he hated me that much, that he needed to go Monday morning and file for divorce. That kinda shocked him, I think, and he's been having some attitude adjustments ever since." This person's husband sought help for his problems but neither understood nor conveyed to his wife that she was both needed and eligible for services. He felt this was his problem to handle on his own. He was wrong.

A Family's Two Generational Trauma

An added incentive for seeking treatment is the impact that a parent with untreated PTSD can have on the children in the family. In *The Boston Globe,* on June 28, 2007, Charles Sennott wrote a story called "Father–Son War Trauma" in which he interviewed a father and son pair, George and Michael Burke, who were both being treated for PTSD. The father served during the Vietnam War and the son fought in the recent conflict. The reporter wrote that "for years after returning from Vietnam, he [the father] kept his distance and held his silence, a remote and angry presence for his family and, especially, his boy . . . They were feelings he had tried to suppress after his service tour by hard drinking in his town's string of Irish pubs. And then, when he became sober in 1975, he buried them even deeper into what he calls 'a numbness.' It was a state of mind that helped him, he believes, to survive, but also put a blank emotional space between himself and the world, and above all, his son . . . Michael finally signed up. He wanted to serve his country and also earn a measure of respect from his father. 'I guess I was hoping it might close the gap between us,' said Michael." To have a son serve is an honor for a family. To have a son serve because he is desperate to connect with a traumatized and unreachable father is a tragedy.

The person at home has spent a year running a household by themselves, even if the soldier was coaching or helping via phone and e-mail. Someone who did not know how to write a check or buy a money order may have learned to be the chief financial officer of the family. While a citizen-soldier's employer is required by law to keep a position available for the soldier when the soldier returns from deployment, a spouse is not. For the family unit to survive, the soldier's duties had to be redistributed in the soldier's absence. Everyone does not revert to their old roles when the soldier returns in the same way "Rosie the Riveter" happily returned to being a housewife at the end of World War II. Couples may have to learn to negotiate who does what tasks at home. Just as spouses respect the soldiers' service in the OEF and OIF, the spouses would like their service on the home front to be admired also. A female soldier who returns to find her husband has turned into a good cook is no less feminine. A male soldier who now has a wife who can fix a leaky faucet is no less masculine than before the deployment. Spouses would much rather hear the soldier say how proud they are of all that the spouse has learned than to hear the soldier ask what they think they are doing or barrage them with criticism.

A deployment is emotionally hard not just for the soldier but for the spouse as well. The wife of a Reservist says, "Maybe I am just in shock that he would tell me I played all year and did nothing! As I have said so many times they are fighting the war in Iraq and we [the families] have our war over here. However when we all get face-to-face we are all so proud of them, but yet they do not see what we did here. I am sure in time he will see how much strength it took to handle all the problems we had with the kids." She adds, "You get a soldier home first, a husband later." Another wife reflects almost one year after her soldier husband returned, "I think it's definitely true that it's even harder when the soldiers come home. No one really can prepare the families for what the soldiers will be like, since each soldier is different. But, for today, things are looking up. I've learned to live each day at a time (kind of like when Larry was overseas), and sometimes it's each minute at a time. Readjustment is a process.

Army Reserve couples may want to make use of the "Strong Bonds Program" (http://www.strongbonds.org). This is a free program run by the military's chaplains to help couples improve communication skills and learn ways of coping with the stresses of reunion. The program also allows Reserve Families to meet other couples that are undergoing the same transition.

Children of Returning Citizen-Soldiers

The returning citizen-soldier also has to become reacquainted with the children in the family. A year in the life of a child is filled with new developmental milestones. For those who left behind an infant, the pain of either not being recognized or the child being afraid of the soldier is very painful. At certain phases of normal development that occur at ages six months and nine months and from twelve to eighteen months, most children show some fear of strangers, and a stranger is anyone who is not the primary caretaker. It is hard (but necessary) not to take it personally when you return to a child in any of these age groups and the child starts to cry and shriek in your arms that have ached to hold the child during every day of the deployment. Sometimes toddlers and preschoolers will be sad or angry. They may be mad at having been left by someone so important to them. Duty and honor are too complicated for a small child to understand. Other children want the returning soldier's undivided attention and will be unaware of how the returning parent may need time to themselves. The preteen who was mom's or dad's sidekick may now be more interested in spending time with friends.

The spouse at home had the whole year to adjust to eye roll and look of scorn practiced by most adolescents, which conveys how adults are totally hopeless. A returning soldier may feel hurt and furious the first time this happens. Sometimes children who appeared to be unfazed by the parent's absence will develop problems after the soldier returns. For some children, they have to know the parent is safe before they dare let their guard down. When children or teenagers misbehave, they are not disrespecting or being ungrateful for their parents' military service. They are often begging for recognition of their sacrifice and the loss they endured during the soldiers' deployments. Children of full-time military parents have peers around them with whom they can share the experience of a deployed parent. Children of citizen-soldiers may have had no one who shared a similar separation. They may have assumed more responsibility at home because the lack of community support that exists on a military base that is equipped to help families with a deployed parent was not available to them.

Parents of Soldiers

Deployments and reunions are hard for parents of soldiers, especially younger soldiers who lived at home prior to deploying. For many young soldiers, the deployment was the first major separation from the family: the soldier may have been embarrassed by a mother's tears and worry. Sometimes, acting strong is the hardest to do in front of one's mother or father. Returning home and living by someone else's rules may feel impossible after having been in combat. In Iraq, the soldier who may have dodged IEDs or lobbed grenades may not want a curfew or someone saying, "clean up your room." Parents of soldiers may have felt left out and powerless during the deployment. One mother commented, "Even within my own community, which is a military town, everything is geared toward the families and spouses of married troops. We moms of unmarried military men seem pretty well kicked to the curb, as if raising a child and seeing him into a military career and then deployment magically ends our parental responsibilities up to and including any feelings of attachment, anxiety or affection. I really believe we single moms of Reservists are not even in the equation." Another mother of a son who lives in another state said, "I live in New Mexico, and my son was deployed from Georgia. What I hear from his family in Georgia is that 'I don't know why you are sad, you never see him anyway.' What a horrible thing to say to a mom."

The eagerness of parents, grandparents, and other relatives to see the soldier upon return and their attempts to help the soldier may feel like too much. Part of the returning process between the soldier and the family is to talk about what works and does not work for the soldier and the family. The soldier can ask that no more than one or two people visit the hospital at a time if having too many people at a time feels overwhelming. A soldier can also ask the family not to ask him to discuss his service or to ask questions like "Did you shoot anyone?" A wounded soldier has to teach people how she wants them to react and needs to tell her family members when they might be pushing too far. If the soldier feels better when people ask questions, then the soldier has to say that. The soldier knows life will not go back as it was before the deployment. It may be hard to hear such clichés as "You're as good as new" or "You'll be back to your old self in no time." Sometimes having a stock reply will enable the soldier to keep cool despite the many feelings going on inside. Sometimes saying something like "You always said someone should knock some sense in me and now they have" or "I hope I won't be back to my old self, my new self is so much better" may be what is needed at that point in the communication. A soldier may also ask someone else to send the message to the family, and that is okay too. What is not okay is for the returning soldier is to allow himself or herself to feel done in by well-meaning but inept family members. When Jeff returned from fifteen months in Iraq, for example, he was jumpy, irritable, and unable to sleep. He was humiliated when his Uncle Joe came up behind him, banging two pot covers, and Jeff dove for cover. Uncle Joe said, "I was just trying to help you get used to loud noises" and became very defensive when Jeff screamed at him. Someone needed to explain to Uncle Joe that Jeff would be helped more by gentle support and asking how he could be of help than deciding for himself how to intervene with his nephew.

Resources Available for Members of the Guard and Reserves

Citizen-soldiers may seek services from a number of sources. Couples who need help to improve their communication skills might talk with their clergy, commit to reading and discussing together a self-help book on couple's communication, or seek out couples' therapy sessions. Community mental health centers and social service agencies frequently offer workshops on couples' communication. For information on organizations and resources on improving communication, check out this book's Web site.

During the first six months after their return, citizen-soldiers are still covered by TriCare, the same insurance they carried while they were on active duty. Those who elect to continue with TriCare on a self-pay basis may obtain mental health referrals from them. Citizen-soldiers are eligible for services from the VA's as well. Many VAs will also provide mental health services to spouses, partners, or parents if they are the primary caregivers helping a veteran recover from PTSD or from physical wounds. Vet Centers (the free-standing clinics run by the VA) also provide free services to citizen-soldiers and their families. Staffs of Veteran Centers usually include other combat veterans who know what it's like to return home from battle. Many states have programs for returning veterans, including those from the Guard and Reserve. Ohio Cares (http://www.ohionationalGuard.com/ohiocares/), Beyond the Yellow Ribbon in Minnesota (http://www.minnesotanationalGuard.org/returning_troops/btyr_overview.php), the Citizen-Soldier Project in North Carolina (http://www.ribbonstoreality.org), and the Rhode Island Blueprint (http://www.riGuard.com) are some of them. Veterans should contact the offices in their states of the organizations that handle veterans' affairs to see if similar programs are in place. Many of the veterans service organizations—the Veterans of Foreign Wars, the American Legion, the Disabled Veterans of America, the Paralyzed Veterans Association, and others—provide resources and advocacy services for veterans seeking medical and mental health services. These organizations and their contact information are listed on the Web site http://www.woundedwarrior.com. Many volunteer groups have also started to offer free mental health services to returning veterans and their families. They include:

- SOFAR (Strategic Outreach to Families of All Reservists at http://www.sofarusa.org): It was founded in New England and became national. SOFAR provides free individual and family therapy to extended family members of deployed citizen-soldiers from alerts through reunion and reintegration. SOFAR prefers that soldiers with PTSD receive services at the VA or Vet Centers but is committed to supporting the rest of the family members, because dealing with a soldier who suffers from PTSD is hard for everyone
- Give an Hour (http://www.giveanhour.org): With 600 registered therapists nationally, it is a Web-based referral network that provides free therapy services to veterans who have returned from war. Give an Hour operates on a "pay it forward" system. The idea behind it is that all those who receive services will utilize whatever skills they possess to help someone else after they receive the services.
- The Soldier's Project (http://www.thesoldiersproject.org): It is based in Los Angeles and provides free therapy services to veterans returning home.

- The Coming Home Project (http://www.cominghomeproject.net): Based in San Francisco it offers daylong workshops for returning veterans and their families. These workshops teach yoga and relaxation techniques and provide safe places for veterans and families to share their experiences with others who have also served.
- The Returning Veterans Resource Project Northwest (http://www.returningveterans. com/): It is based in Portland, Oregon, and is a Web-based referral program that provides free therapy services for veterans and their families.

Return to Work or School

Citizen-soldiers held civilian jobs before they deployed. Some will return to their old civilian job, and others may seek new employment because they wish to or because the wounds from their service leave them unable to perform their former jobs. As stated earlier, the transition from soldier to civilian worker may take place within a week of return from deployment. Returning Guard and Reserve members have certain legal rights. The Uniformed Services Employment and Reemployment Rights Act (USERRA) of 1994 is supposed to protect the employment rights of the returning Guard and Reserve members. The purpose of USERRA is "to minimize the disruption to the lives of persons performing service in the uniformed services as well as to their employers, their fellow employees, and their communities, by providing for the prompt reemployment of such persons upon their completion of such service; and to prohibit discrimination against persons because of their service in the uniformed services." Under the terms of USERRA, a "person who is a member of, applies to be a member of, performs, has performed, applies to perform, or has an obligation to perform service in a uniformed service shall not be denied initial employment, reemployment, retention in employment, promotion, or any benefit of employment by an employer on the basis of that membership, application for membership, performance of service, application for service, or obligation."

Under the law, the returning worker has certain obligations in exchange for these rights. They include how soon returning soldiers have to submit an application for reemployment (fourteen days after deactivation in most cases), the need to document that the time away from work was for active military service, and other proofs of fitness to perform the job. Employer Support of the Guard and Reserve (ESGR, http://www.esgr.org) is the organization within the Department of Defense, which is available to inform returning soldiers about their rights and to provide advocacy services when necessary. Under USERRA, a grievance may be filed with the U.S. government if a soldier faces unfair denial for reemployment. ESGR will provide technical assistance to file these grievances. When a soldier who returned wounded is unable to return to a civilian job because the wounds have left the soldier unable to perform the job, the soldier is entitled to job training from the Veterans Administration. For more information, please see the chapter of this book that deals with employment and the resources at http://www.warswounded.com.

Citizen-soldiers are eligible to continue their education under the provisions of the Montgomery GI Bill-Selected Reserve (MGIB-SR). These benefits are available for thrity-six months of educational training for soldiers who remain in good standing while serving in an active selected Reserve unit. They may be used for degree and certificate programs, flight training, apprenticeship/on-the-job training, and correspondence courses. These benefits are also available for soldiers discharged from a select Reserve unit because of a disability. Information on the educational benefits can be obtained at the GI Bill Web site (http://www.gibill.va.gov/GI_Bill_info/benefits.htm) and the chapter of this book on educational benefits. The citizen-soldier must continue to be a member of the Guard and Reserve to collect benefits as opposed to those in the regular military who may collect benefits after being discharged.

Conclusion

Citizen-Soldiers, members of the National Guard and Reserves, have been disproportionately represented in OEF and OIF. For the first time, they have participated in multiple deployments. Since the members of the Guard and Reserve live in communities without major military installations, they and their families face special challenges. They are isolated from other military families, so they are alone with the stresses of deployment and reunion. When Guard and Reserve are cross-leveled or assigned to a unit other than the unit with which they train, they often return without a peer group to offer support and with whom they can process the experience. Families have been isolated during the deployment as well and while coping with the reunion and reintegration. Many do not learn that many other spouses share the problems of reunion and reintegration. Children, alone in their schools, do not receive sufficient support because teachers do not learn about the pressures specific to deployment and return. In the course of multiple deployments, citizen-soldiers may oscillate between civilian employee and active duty soldier several times. Employers, fellow employees, friends, and relatives may not identify with or understand the task of reentry the citizen-soldier must negotiate. Starting out as a weekend warrior and ending up as a wounded warrior is a task that requires courage, fortitude, and the right to be proud. Now is the time for families and veterans to draw strength from each other as they move forward. The families have honed their skills at coping in the absence of their soldier. The soldiers have sharpened their skills, as they have dealt with the rigors of war. The synergy of the families' resilience and the veterans' perseverance to heal and to survive can form a cohesive team that allows growth in the absence of the support available on a military base.

CHAPTER 9

Impact on Family and Friends

Shirley M. Glynn

Editors' Comment

For every service member stationed in the military, the individual's family and friends back home are also deeply affected and must endure their own form of separation, deprivation, and emotional costs. The nature of the current conflict can make it even more difficult for families and friends of service members, since the military is now more diverse (and has more women and older members with established families back home), with more Guard and Reserve members serving and all members called upon to serve longer terms overseas With better medical care, service members are surviving more extensive injuries. Each of these injuries can create additional stress and hardships for their family members and friends. While the rest of this book is directed at the veterans, this chapter is written for the family members and friends of injured veterans to describe what is happening to the veteran, how they can communicate with him, and how they can best help her on to full recovery and reintegration.

This chapter was written by Shirley M. Glynn, Ph.D., a clinical research psychologist at the VA Greater Los Angeles Healthcare System, who provides training and consultation to improve family services nationally throughout the VA. She is also a research psychologist at the Semel Institute for Neuroscience and Human Behavior at the University of California, Los Angeles. She has been conducting clinical research in family interventions for persons with serious psychiatric illnesses and combat-related PTSD for over twenty years. Providing the perspective of a caregiver is Colleen Saffron, an Army spouse for the past eighteen years from Harker Heights, Texas. Since her husband's injury in Iraq in 2004 she has managed to care for him and their three children while also returning to school to graduate with honors. She is one of the founders and creators of the group Operation

Life Transformed (http://lifetransformed.org/), which works to fill the gaps in veteran care related to the family's economic recovery by providing training and job placement opportunities to family member caregivers.

Introduction

Participation in combat can elicit strength and other positive character traits that warfighters never even knew they possessed. However, the combat experience can also lead to physical injuries and psychological distress that can be chronic and pervasive. Furthermore, the very act of trying to intentionally maim or kill other individuals (or being the target of such actions) can profoundly impact on the core way warfighters think about and experience human relationships. These new understandings may then color their relationships with their families and friends back home.

Life brings people challenges, but the challenge of caring for a wounded veteran can seem almost overwhelming. So many things can become uncertain—finances, living arrangements, careers, the future, even life itself. Keeping one foot in front of the other and doing what can be done each day to help the person with the injury and still take care of oneself can be a mind-boggling task. While supports may be available to help, it is easy for the family member or friend of the person who has been injured to feel alone.

Caring for someone who is injured or sick or troubled provides "carers" (that is, family, friends, and coworkers of the ill or wounded person) with the opportunity to learn the best and worst about themselves. It can be a time of despair and growth, grief and wisdom. Ties can be broken, or they can be solidified for life. Caring can help bring out one's best self, but it can often be difficult, and how to put the caring into action may not even be clear. The goal of this chapter is to provide those who care about the wounded veteran—family, friends, and coworkers—with ways to put caring into action while making sure they take good care of themselves. First, we begin by outlining some unique aspects of the Operation Iraqi Freedom (OIF) and Operation Enduring Freedom (OEF) conflicts that make it challenging for families and friends to provide care, then we discuss the types of injuries that are common in these conflicts. We next talk about ways carers can help the injured veteran and conclude with how carers can also care for themselves. There is no one right way to approach this challenge, and over time carers learn what works well for them. However, there are shared challenges and creative solutions that may help all of the individuals out there who are taking care of the returning service members.

Unique Features of the OIF/OEF Conflicts that Challenge Carers

There are unique features of the OIF and OEF campaigns that are especially likely to harm family and other close relationships and thus complicate recovery from injury. First of all, more women are opting for military service, which means that more children have limited access to their mothers, and more husbands have less access to their wives. Notably, the divorce rate for female enlisted persons is twice as high as for males (Karney and Crown 2007). Despite the growing effort to equalize gender roles in the society to reduce some of the effects of the loss of a wife and/or mother on the family, most studies in fact indicate women still assume primary responsibility for child and household care. Family life is often seriously disrupted when wives and mother are deployed. More than when a man is injured, when a woman is injured, her family often loses its "glue."

Little information exists now on the special needs of female warfighters and their carers, and the research field is in its infancy. One study has reported that women are more likely to be evacuated from the war zone for psychological difficulties than men, but these evacuations appear more related to general environmental stress (including sexual and physical abuse) than combat exposure (Rundell, 2006). In contrast, a recent report found no difference in the kinds and frequency of mental health problems seen in male and female OIF/OEF veterans who have enrolled at the Veterans Administration for treatment (Seal, Bertenthal, Miner, Sen, and Marmar, 2007). Whatever future research may reveal, the carers of both male and female veterans can still find the advice in this chapter to be useful.

Second, the nature of deployments has changed in OIF/OEF. In World War II, once individuals entered the service, they remained until the war was over (unless they were wounded or had an urgent need to go home). In Vietnam, individuals had set single tours of duty in the conflict zone of twelve or thirteen months, unless they reenlisted or opted for multiple tours. From the time of entry into the service in the combat zone, service members had clear predictability of length of service, and for most individuals it would involve at the most two or three years of active service time at risk.

The parameters of service time in the OIF/OEF conflict are different. The durations of the conflict and the overall "global war on terrorism" are expected to be lengthy, and the transition to an all-volunteer military has yielded significantly fewer individuals available for service during this extended period. This set of circumstances had necessitated multiple troop rotations. While the benefit of this plan is that families have the opportunity for more face-to-face time between deployments, it also means that everyone must accommodate an uncertain future and extended time away from home. Individuals serving three or four deployments in Iraq or Afghanistan may end up spending the better part of four years away from home in a five-year period. Naturally, both the overall time away from the family as well as the "on again–off again" nature of time spent at home creates more uncertainty and strain for all involved. Furthermore, longer and repeated deployments are associated with heightened risk of adverse psychological outcomes for the warfighter—more depression, anxiety, and acute stress, similar to post-traumatic stress disorder (PTSD) according to the Office of the Surgeon General Multinational Force Iraq & Command (2006).

Third, the reduction of the size of active Army, Navy, and Marine services means that there is greater reliance on the National Guard and the Reservists to bolster troop strength. While the active duty forces are typically primarily comprised of young single combatants in their late teens and twenties, many who opt for the National Guard and Reserve do this later in life, often after serving in the active services. They are more likely to have partners and children at home and will need to take a temporary break from their jobs in their prime working years. Even if the law protects their return to specific jobs, they often lose critical time needed to refine work skills. Also, their time in Iraq and Afghanistan is likely to be particularly disruptive for their families and their employers.

As discussed in Chapter 8 of this book, Guard members and Reservists and their families usually have less connection with available military services (as they do not live on the base and do not define themselves as "military families"), and thus they can be particularly isolated and bereft during the time of deployment. It may take them a while to access needed supports, and these supports may not be as available to the families in their communities. After deployment, Guard and Reserve members and their families may have little contact with other warfighters and their families. There may be no other warfighters in their neighborhoods or in their jobs, and they may not come into any contact with individuals who have shared their experiences. They may live hundreds of miles from a Department of Defense or Veterans Administration facility. The fact that more Reservists and National Guard members have dependent families and are not tightly woven into the fabric of military life can greatly complicate recovery from injury.

Injuries Come in Different Varieties

Many war injuries are obvious. For example, in the current OIF and OEF conflicts, the most common types of physical injuries result from blasts and improvised explosive devices (IEDs)—essentially homemade bombs, often placed in cars on the side of the road, that are detonated as warfighters drive by. Because most warfighters wear armored flack jackets, their trunks are protected—even with a blast, their chests, abdomens, and backs are safe. However, their limbs and neck and head are not protected, which means many of the physical injuries in the current conflict occur to the arms, legs, neck, and head. This has resulted in a higher proportion of amputees than in many other conflicts and a higher proportion of individuals with damage to their heads and faces.

The development and skill of military medicine has been evolving at an astounding pace. In the OIF and OEF conflicts, the medical treatment system was designed to assure almost immediate medical evacuation of warfighters at risk of loss of life, limb, or eyesight. The advantage of this program is that fewer individuals have died in this conflict, in proportion to those who are actually fighting, compared to any other war the United States has fought. The OIF/OEF rate of injury to death had been reduced to 9:1 by 2004; in World War II the ratio was 7:3, and in the Vietnam conflict it was 3:1 (Gawande, 2004). The complication of this strategy, of course, is that many persons are surviving with massive injures that would have killed them in previous wars. Thus, while there are a relatively small number of physically wounded warfighters returning from war, compared to the number of overall combatants, their wounds are often very severe.

While physical wounds can be devastating to both the veteran and the carers, it is important to note that there are two other kinds of injuries that are thought to be especially common in warfighters returning from OIF and OEF, both of which can be equally challenging: traumatic brain injury (TBI) and psychological disorders such as post-traumatic stress disorder (PTSD), depression, and other anxiety problems; and substance abuse. Adding to the physical injury, there are special circumstances of the OIF and OEF conflicts that render individuals who fight them at higher risk for either TBI or psychological disorders (or both).

In terms of TBI, exposure to blasts and IEDs means that many warfighters are knocked off their feet and blown a distance or take hard hits to their heads. Their heads may rock back and forth in their helmets, causing their brains to swish back and forth in their cerebral fluid and repeatedly hit the skull from the inside. These are called concussive injuries, and they can be deceptive. The person with the injury may not lose consciousness and may have no apparent wound. However, the individual may still have developed some level of brain damage, especially to the frontal lobe (right behind the forehead). This is the part of the brain responsible for the "executive processing" of activities that are used in planning for the future, reasoning, weighing options, and holding back from acting on impulses. Memory and attention may also be affected. Caring for a person with a traumatic brain injury can be challenging. When the problems are subtle and are not associated with any obvious wounding, these are often called "mild" TBI. Importantly, the onset of these problems may not be apparent for days or weeks after the injury, which can further complicate diagnosis and treatment. Furthermore, without a physical wound, it can be easy not to recognize or to forget the person's limitations and not notice that the person has a brain injury.

Being involved in war also raises the risk of exposure to a traumatic event, which increases the likelihood of psychological harm and PTSD. In its early stages, PTSD is understood as a stress reaction that is a "normal" response to an "abnormal" event. That is, humans are "hard wired" to become extra watchful and to have reduced emotions during the height of battle; this is a way they protect themselves and focus completely on staying alive. The problem arises when stress symptoms continue, or even worsen, when there is no longer obvious danger.

There are three symptoms clusters that comprise the disorder of PTSD—reexperiencing symptoms (nightmares, flashbacks, and the like), numbing/avoidance symptoms (feeling numb and/or avoiding reminders of the trauma), and hyperarousal (irritability, sleep difficulties, being overly watchful, and being easily startled). A table listing the symptoms of PTSD and the way carers can help the service member is included in Chapter 3 of this book. When these symptoms last at least one month after the trauma and make it difficult for the person to function well at work and at home, a diagnosis of PTSD is made. PTSD rates are the highest in the persons who have had the most exposure to trauma, which means they tend to be higher in warfighters who have had multiple deployments, been involved in a lot of actual fighting, or been injured.

It is important to note that PTSD is *not* the only psychological disorder associated with returning home from war. The second most common psychological difficulty found in returning war fighters is depression. A table listing the symptoms of depression and the way carers can help the service member is included in Chapter 3 of this book. Depression is diagnosed when, for a period of at least two weeks, an individual experiences depressed mood, inability to enjoy activities, problems concentrating, changes in eating habits or appetite, weight gain or weight loss, changes in sleeping habits, difficulty going to work or taking care of daily responsibilities because of a lack of energy, feelings of guilt and hopelessness, wondering if life is worth living, slowed thoughts and speech, preoccupation with thoughts of death or suicide, and bodily complaints that have no apparent physical cause such as headache and stomachache.

It is not surprising, in light of the high rates of PTSD and depression found in returning warfighters, that substance use often increases. Many veterans use alcohol and street drugs to either improve their mood or help them calm down. While alcohol and street drugs may do this for a brief period, it is important to recognize that most people need to use more and more of these drugs to achieve these effects, and then the drugs often loose their ability to provide the benefits the person first desired when he started using them. Depression and substance use are especially common in veterans who have been injured.

Issues in the Readjustment Period

Coming home from a war and reentering civilian life usually relieves the veteran and those who love him or her, but it can still often be a stressful experience for all involved. The warfighter has developed a "battlemind"—a particular way of looking at the world and reacting that is useful in war but may cause problems at home. Being watchful all the time and very sensitive to sounds may save the warfighter's life in a combat zone but may not be helpful if the veteran returns to live on a busy city street. He or she is likely to get tired, anxious, and irritable over time as a result, and those who love him or her are likely to be confused and frustrated by this new behavior. As one wife said of her recently returned husband, "It's like he's home, but he isn't really here".

The veteran is likely to picture returning to the same family he or she left for the war, but both the veteran and his or her loved ones and friends are likely to have changed during the deployment. This is especially true for the veteran's immediate family. Husbands who have been off at war are now faced with families who have had to survive without their presence and have learned to handle all the things the husbands may have done—everything from getting the car repaired to paying the bills. Mothers returning from the war may have to watch their children playing more comfortably with their caregivers than with the mothers.

With longer and multiple deployments, the family members become even more self-sufficient, leaving the veteran feeling "outside the loop" and requiring the family to readjust to including the veteran as part of the home experience again. Many families have successfully made this readjustment for centuries, but it can be stressful on both sides and it takes time, effort, and patience.

If the veteran has experienced a physical wounding, a psychological problem, or both, as a result of the war, this readjustment period can be even more complicated. The veteran is home, and even though both he and the family have to make the necessary readjustments, he may also need extra support to thrive. This can be taxing on all involved—the veteran may now feel like he has new problems that may be hard to live with and require care and attention from others, and the carers may have to provide extra support to compensate for the veteran's new deficits. Veterans with physical injuries may feel especially ashamed, as their once strong bodies now need special attention and care. Both the veteran and those who care about him or her are likely to be strained during this adjustment, but it can also be a period of growth and recommitment. For example, one veteran with severe PTSD and facial disfigurement from shrapnel was reluctant to discuss combat or the traumatic events with his wife. Nevertheless, he knew he was now too troubled to work and felt embarrassed to go outside because of his scars and facial injuries. After much hesitation, he finally decided to enter a family therapy program with his wife and daughter, and, as part of that program, he began to share a little of his war experiences and why he did not feel able to work just then. While he anticipated his wife would be critical of his current frailty, she was, in fact, very appreciative of his willingness to talk about what he had experienced and his openness about his shame about how he looked now. She said to him, "I don't know what you see when you look in the mirror, but when I look at you, I see a hero." Her acceptance and kindness helped him gain more courage in interacting with others and strengthened his resolve to get on with his life.

Helping the Veteran

As has been described above and in the other chapters in this book, veterans may experience a wide range of injuries during the war, everything from severe brain injury to amputation to PTSD and depression. No one set of tools or advice would be able to fit the needs of every veteran, but there are some general guidelines that will be useful for most carers.

Remember the Veteran's Positive Qualities, Even when They Might Be Hard to See

If it seems like the veteran has changed, actively recalling his or her earlier positive qualities that may not seem so apparent right now can be useful. Readjustments do not occur overnight, and individuals who have undergone traumatic stress often take time to right themselves. They may feel ashamed of their new problems and their need to be dependent on others after having been strong and self-sufficient in battle. Actively remembering the veteran's good qualities every day and the positive history together with the carer can help provide some solace to smooth over the rough spots. As one wife said of her husband with combat-related PTSD, "Sure I get frustrated. I remember how active my husband was and how much he wanted to do and all his dreams, and I see him now, and he can barely spend any time with the kids; it is just so hard to handle. But, then I think, at least he is trying to be with the kids; at least he is trying to stay here with us; he is not throwing in the towel. Even if he does need to stand on the side and pace at the kids' sporting events since he feels too agitated to sit down, at least he is going. And that is better than some of the other parents in our neighborhood."

Strengthen the Relationship; Strengthen the Recovery

Physical injuries, PTSD, and depression all make individuals feel isolated. Veterans are likely behaving in ways that feel unfamiliar to them, and, if they also have severe wounds, many might have experiences that are strange and difficult. As they look around, many of these veterans feel alone and scared and cut off from those who care for them. They are likely worried about the future. They may feel unlovable, either because of their wounds or for what they did during the war or both.

The encouragement and assistance of those who care about another individual is termed that person's "social support". Social support can take many forms—everything from listening and offering a positive word of encouragement to actually providing physical assistance with errands or appointments to supplying money when funds are low. Research shows that the availability of social support helps with the recovery process for both physical injury (Burger and Marincek, 2007; Rauch and Ferry, 2001) and PTSD (Brewin, Andrews, and Valentine, 2000). Furthermore, greater support is related to better recoveries. Many family members might understandably try to provide encouragement for positive change through nagging and prompting, but research shows that individuals with PTSD (Tarrier, Sommerfield, and Pilgrim, 1999), depression (Hooley and Teasdale, 1989), and substance abuse problems (Fichter, Glynn, Weyer, Liberman, and Frick, 1997) are especially sensitive to criticism and negative feedback. A lot of prompting and constructive input, even if offered in a loving spirit, can have the unintended consequence of making symptoms worse instead of better or leading to treatment dropout. To avoid this problem, those who care for persons with physical or psychological war wounds usually benefit from trying to find positive things to praise rather than negative things to criticize. For example, if the veteran is supposed to be exercising to strengthen muscles or reduce stress, rather than commenting negatively on the days he does not do this, provide praise on the days on which he does exercise.

When thinking about providing constructive feedback, carers need to choose their priorities and the ones on which they want to focus. The ones that are most important are those that involve the assurance of a safe home and those who support recovery. It is critical to protect physical safety and address any behaviors or attitudes in the injured person that interfere with recovery, including substance abuse, missing medical appointments, and not following through with the treatment plan. On the other hand, fighting about household chores or little details (like the toilet seat being left up and running a little late) may not be worth the effort. Some issues are worth fighting over, but many are not worth the fight when viewed in perspective.

Help the Veteran Enroll for Services

This chapter is primarily written for those who care about veterans who have been injured physically and/or mentally in the OIF and OEF conflicts. Many of these individuals will benefit from professional help to recover, and most often these services are provided at Department of Defense and Department of Veterans Affairs facilities, although sometimes they may also receive care in the private sector. Whatever the venue of care, it is important to help the veteran access the care he or she needs. For a list of the types of services available to the veteran, refer to this book's Web site, http://www.warswounded. com.

Make sure the veteran enrolls at the VA, even if she does not plan to initially use VA services. Once veterans have returned from deployment, they are eligible to receive cost-free health care and readjustment services through the VA for any conditions related to combat service for a minimum of five years following active duty, and Congress may extend this eligibility in the future. After five years, services are typically still available for a co-pay fee based on the individual's income. If a person served in the National Guard and Reserves and was deployed to a war zone, that service member is also eligible for the same benefits, but the person must also enroll first in order to qualify.

The VA's big agencies can be daunting, and the red tape in the VA has a reputation for being notorious. Nevertheless, it is important to enroll in care systems even if the veteran does not feel ready to use them now so that she can qualify for services at a later date. The carers can offer to go to the facility and wait with their family member during appointments to provide encouragement and to help lighten the load.

Assist the Veteran in Organizing Paperwork

Systems like the DoD and VA rely on documentation to access services and obtain benefits. It is critical that the individual seeking services be able to present all requested paperwork, such as a social security cards and DD 214 discharge papers, when enrolling for services. Once medical treatment begins, there are usually important lab and medical reports. Furthermore, when applying for benefits such as a service-connected disability, there are even more forms including application forms, responses from the DoD and VA, possible appeals, and responses to appeals. It is a sea of paperwork, and getting and staying organized is critical. Even though DoD and VA are trying to institute a plan for "seamless transition" and "continuous care," materials do get lost, and being able to produce paperwork when needed can greatly facilitate medical care and access to benefits. Carers can be of great help in setting up an organizational system early and helping keep it current and updated. Chapter 3 in this book has examples of systems that can help with organizing this paperwork.

Support Involvement in Prescribed Treatment Plans

There are now many established recovery programs that lead to improvements in PTSD (Nemeroff et al., 2006; Solomon and Johnson, 2002), depression (Hollon, Stewart, and Strunk, 2006), and substance abuse (Moos, 2003, 2007a, 2007b). There are also tremendous strides being made in tissue and nerve regeneration and in the development of prosthetics to replace missing limbs. If the veteran does choose to receive medical or psychological treatment, carers can support these efforts in many ways that will be beneficial toward faster recovery.

First, praise the veteran for attending treatment, whether it involves going to a PTSD psychotherapy session, going to a cognitive remediation program for mild TBI, or going to physical therapy for an injured arm or leg. Admitting one needs help is often hard, and both psychotherapy sessions and physical rehabilitation sessions can be grueling. Knowing that others appreciate the efforts can make a big difference when it seems like treatment will be too hard to continue, which often happens at some point during an extended recovery. As one veteran said, "I kept thinking I would stop the therapy; it hurt and I felt so hopeless and tired. But then my wife would tell me she was proud of how I was making it to the VA everyday, and I thought of how much I want to be a good father and strong for my kids, and I thought, well, I can bear this for at least one more day. I can decide tomorrow to quit. And I just kept stringing days of recovery together."

Second, carers can educate themselves about the rehabilitation program in which the veteran is participating. They can learn what the difficult aspects might be and when a bit more encouragement or a brief lightening of responsibilities around the house might be helpful. Some treatments can seem a little scary and demanding. For example, prolonged exposure is the one form of psychotherapy that has the strongest scientific support for the treatment of PTSD (see the review *Treatment of Posttraumatic Stress Disorder: An Assessment of the Evidence* published by the National Academy of Sciences, available at http://www.nap.edu/catalog/11955.html). This treatment involves a repeated retelling of the traumatic combat events during the therapy sessions. This retelling is done so the trauma survivor becomes less aroused and agitated by the memory of the event as well as assured that he or she has a chance to examine all his or her beliefs about the event in great detail in the cold, clear light of day, when his or her life is not in jeopardy. Under careful examination in a therapy session, a veteran may come to understand, for example, that even though she feels responsible for a buddy's death, there is nothing more she could have done to protect the buddy.

While prolonged exposure is an effective treatment, participation in the treatment is like starting a new exercise program—things often hurt more after one starts the program, and one has to work through the temporary pain to achieve the long-term benefits. Carers who understand this can be a bit more relaxed when the veteran seems to be a little more stressed when he or she starts the therapy. They can also provide encouragement when the veteran seems a bit down or discouraged or talks about quitting treatment prematurely.

Third, if there are tools the veteran can use at home to speed recovery, encourage their usage. For example, many persons with mild TBI find that they can compensate for poor memories by preparing lists to remind them to complete tasks. Similarly, they do better when they write down important new information that they are supposed to commit to memory. Encouraging the use of these compensatory devices can be another way to support improved functioning and recovery.

Fourth, if there are opportunities for carers to become involved in the treatment, they should carefully consider taking advantage of them. In most DoD and VA settings, wounded individuals are assigned a "care manager" or "case manager" who is typically most knowledgeable about the veteran's situation and is the gatekeeper for the carer to join the system. As the DoD and VA increasingly recognize the role of families in recovery, they are developing special programs for carers and encouraging more open communication between the family and the care team. New VA privacy policies allow family members who are involved in the day-to-day care of the veteran to have greater access to the treatment team to ask questions or express their concerns. Patients can agree to a "limited disclosure of information" which permits the team to talk with family members about specific issues which could include medical treatment, side effects, participation in treatment programs, and other recommended treatments. Carers can ask the veteran to speak with the treatment team about signing a limited disclosure of information agreement, so the carer can then talk with members of the team. Carers can also ask for a conjoint session with a member of the treatment team, the veteran, and themselves. Just getting to know the treatment staff and having a name and number to call in an emergency can help coordinate care and relieve anxiety when a loved one is recovering from an injury.

Many of the most effective treatments, especially for substance abuse (O'Farrell, Chouquette, Cutter, Brown, and McCourt, 1993) and depression (Jacobson, Dobson, Fruzzetti, Schmaling, and Salusky, 1991; O'Leary and Beach, 1990), often involve couples or family counseling, so exploring whether this is an option at the veteran's treatment facility may be useful. Even with PTSD, there are newer studies indicating that couples counseling help improve symptoms (Monson, Schnurr, Stevens, and Guthrie, 2004).

Finally, be prepared to advocate for the care the veteran needs. It is easy to get lost in large service systems run by the DoD and VA. New programs are being developed for injured veterans everyday, but sometimes there are waiting lists, or it can be hard to find the programs. The Web site for this book (http://www.woundedwarrior.com) will list updated information about these programs. Keep in touch with the veteran's care team and bring up the option of other potentially useful programs often if the veteran is unable reluctant to do so. It is the squeaky wheel that gets the grease.

Veterans service organizations, such as the Disabled American Veterans, Veterans of Foreign Wars of the United States, Military Order of the Purple Heart, and the American Legion often provide support and guidance in overcoming the bureaucracy that sometimes interferes with getting treatment or benefits. A full directory of veterans service organizations can be found at http://www1.va.gov/vso/index.cfm?template=view. Support groups for active duty and veterans of the OIF/OEF conflicts include the Wounded Warriors, the Military OneSource, and the Iraq and Afghanistan Veterans of America. Information on some of these groups and others are available on this book's Web site http://www.warswounded.com. These groups are invaluable sources of support and information.

Be Flexible about Talking about War Events

Many warfighters saw horrible things or did things for which they have a hard time forgiving themselves. Some veterans want to talk with their families and friends about their experiences but many are reluctant to do this. They may feel ashamed about what they did, are afraid of "contaminating" their families with the events and memories that trouble them, or may believe their loved ones could never understand their choices and behavior and might judge them harshly. Warfighters who have been wounded or have mild TBI may not even remember some of the traumas to which they were exposed.

There are no data to suggest that veterans have to tell their families and friends the specifics of their war experiences to heal. Rather, carers can be open and flexible in responding to how the veteran wants to handle the situation. If the veteran wants to talk, the carer can listen carefully and actively—which means sitting down close to the person, looking him or her in the eye, offering reassuring touch and comments. Even if the veteran does not want to share the specifics of traumatic events, conversations about what the traumatic events mean to the veteran and how he feels the war changed him can still be a way to reestablish intimacy and connection. Here again, active listening is key.

Supporting the Caregiver

Up to this point, we have used the term carers to indicate the broad range of family, friend, and coworkers who care about the veteran. Here, we use the term caregiver, and we mean more specifically the person or persons assuming primary responsibility for caring for the veteran if and when she requires more intense support and supervision. Caregiving is a complicated task—and it can provide wonderful opportunities for personal growth, but it can also be extremely draining. Family members involved in caregiving for an ill relative are at higher risk of anxiety, depression, and health problems (Magliano, Fiorillo, De Rosa, Malangone, and Maj, 2005; Manguno-Mire et al., 2007; Zarit, Reever, and Bach-Peterson, 1980). While data regarding OIF/OEF veterans on this point are lacking at this time, partners of Vietnam veterans with PTSD reported high levels of caregiver burden and stress even twenty-five years after the war (Calhoun, Beckham, and Bosworth, 2002; Manguno-Mire et al., 2007), and rates of domestic violence are higher in families of Vietnam veterans with PTSD than those without PTSD (Beckham, Feldman, Kirby, Hertzberg, and Moore, 1997).

Some have referred to the traumatization of the loved ones by exposure to the veteran and her difficulties as "secondary traumatization." That is, the carer also becomes traumatized by the events of the war that were experienced by the veteran and the trouble that accompanied the events. Family members may find themselves with some of the symptoms of PTSD including nightmares, feeling cutoff from others, irritability, and sleep difficulties. PTSD symptoms of numbing and avoidance have shown to be particularly harmful to marital functioning (Evans, McHugh, Hopwood, and Watt, 2003; Riggs, Byrne, Weathers, and Litz, 1998). Taken together, these data suggest that caregivers must work hard to take care of themselves as well as the recovering veteran to avoid "compassion fatigue." Compassion fatigue describes a phenomenon where the caregivers feel less compassion, empathy, or caring for the ill individuals over time, typically because they are overwhelmed with the caretaking obligations. Here are some of the ways that caregivers take care of themselves and avoid secondary traumatization and compassion fatigue:

Remember to Live Your Values

While caring for an injured loved one can be very demanding, it is also a way to live a life of value. Caregivers demonstrate everyday what is important to them and for what they are willing to work. They are not caught up in the trivial such as continually trying to impress friends and acquaintances, engaging in pointless gossip, or shopping just to pass the time. Their lives now have a higher purpose. Caregiving is not easy, but there is a true comfort and clarity that comes from focusing on some of the most important things in life, like honoring a commitment to love and care for a family member or spouse. The caring can give life meaning in a way that few things can.

Find Effective Ways to Deal with Uncertainty

One of the most difficult aspects of caregiving is the uncertainty that surrounds the veteran: Will he get better? Will this treatment help her? What are we going to do it if we run out of money? How are we going to go on? None of these questions are easily answered, and carers often live in the realm of uncertainty. They know what to do today, but they have no idea how the picture will turn out in the long run. While some planning for the future is always called for, caregivers often benefit from learning to live "in the now" and realizing that they just have this moment to manage. The past is gone, and the future is not here yet. Once a person had done what he or she can to manage a situation, more worry will not make anything in the future better. Many caregivers find it helpful to use relaxation, mindfulness, prayer, or other forms of spirituality to stay in the moment. Books such as *Full Catastrophe Living* or CDs such as *Mindfulness for Beginners* (both created by Jon Kabit-Zinn) are tools that some caregivers have found helpful in dealing with the anxiety and depression that often accompany the caregiving role.

Be Mindful of Your Own Development

As many women have entered the work force, there are fewer caregivers who are not employed outside the home. The competing needs of an ill spouse or adult child and a job can wreak havoc on peace of mind. Caregivers can be pulled in many directions, so that they are not giving 100 percent to either their families or their jobs. This can be an extremely difficult position, and there is no one right or wrong way to handle it. Some caregivers negotiate time off from work under the auspices of the Family Medical Leave Act, which allows for twelve weeks of unpaid leave per year to care for an ill family member in businesses employing more than fifty individuals (see http://www.dol.gov/esa/whd/fmla/ for more information). Some caregivers schedule treatment appointments for the veteran around their own work schedules, and there is now a new VA national directive prompting the availability of more evening appointments and services at VA facilities. Caregivers can advocate for more compliance with this policy and request evening appointments as they become available. Some caregivers opt to work at home or reduce their hours to part-time until the veteran is more self-sufficient in his/her recovery. Regardless of the strategy chosen, it is important to remember that the vast majority of wounded individuals do improve and that they are usually able to take on more responsibility for their own care over time, so most adjustments in the caregiver's schedule usually only need to be temporary.

Take Care of Your Own Physical Health

Caregivers are at heightened risk for serious health risks as their immune systems get worn down. It is easy for caregivers to lose sight of their own needs when a loved one is sick or injured. Nevertheless, caregivers are "running a marathon and not a sprint," and they will be unable to support the injured veteran if they develop illnesses too. Most of the times, they should be following the same guidelines given to the veteran for his/her recovery—eat healthily, avoid excessive alcohol, get enough sleep, get regular exercise, and spend time with people they care about. While this can be daunting advice, especially if one's loved one requires a great deal of physical care and one has small children. It can be hard to fit in all the tasks that must be managed each day, let alone fitting in time for exercise or mindfulness. Nevertheless, caregivers have an obligation to both themselves and those how love them to take as good care of themselves as they possibly can, and to search for opportunities to have time for themselves to recharge their batteries and take care of their bodies and spirits.

Ask for Help When You Need It

The most effective caregivers ask for help when they need it and use the resources offered to them. Loving a physically or psychologically wounded veteran requires a community, not just one or two people. There is a list of resources on this book's web site that can provide support and encouragement for caregivers, including educational Web sites and blogs for wives and other family members. Many VA hospitals are now developing support and educational programs for family members, such as the SAFE program. Many of these programs also provide information on respite care or family retreats, which can be a way for family members to make sure that their needs are met. Social workers or case managers on the veteran's treatment team are usually an excellent resource for other programs available to support caregivers. Some caregivers decide to enter their own therapy, so they can find a way to get some nonjudgmental, objective supports. Whatever the venue, caregivers need to find ways to strengthen themselves.

Summary

Individuals who go to war to protect our values and safety are meeting their highest calling, and those who are wounded in this effort deserve our best attention and care. Warfighters can develop both physical and psychological injuries as a result of war trauma, and though there are effective treatments to help most veterans return to a high level of functioning, the recovery road can be long and the support of family members and friends is needed. There are many ways that family and friends can be helpful, but it is equally important that they take care of their own needs during the recovery effort.

One Carer's Perspective

Colleen Saffron is one of the founders of Operation Life Transformed, a group that was formed to provide education and resources to the carers of the war wounded and military spouses through private and corporate entities. The group's members work to increase awareness of the long term needs of these families and support them as they reenter the civilian sector. The members work to fill the gaps in veteran care related to family economic recovery and help the carers who struggle every day to make ends meet as they transform shattered lives into productive family units again by providing training and job placement opportunities to family member caregivers of our war wounded. Saffron's husband, an Army soldier, was seriously wounded in Operation Iraqi Freedom in 2004.

Saffron notes that nearly a quarter of all wounded surveyed by the President's Commission on Care for America's Returning Wounded Warriors said that a family member gave up a job to be with them or act as caregiver. She adds, "Many of the remaining families must now develop alternative or additional income sources to replace those lost through injury or permanent disability of our wounded heroes. War Wounded caregivers must find employment in fields that readily fit around medical and rehabilitation schedules, disabilities, and transition requirements for their affected military family."

She describes her experiences working with the carers of the wounded veterans and the needs of the needs of these family members: "Families where a soldier is severely wounded need to first and foremost develop a support system, something that they can fall back on. The people willing to step in should be prepared to watch children for extended periods of time and to hear long lists of depressing events from the family members—this is the family's reality on many occasions. However the families also tend to inspire others around them since they usually are not focused on the negative things in life but the positive."

"A number of groups, companies, and programs have focused on retraining and giving jobs to wounded soldiers, and this is great. However, the VA already does that and thus these programs are reinventing the wheel. What we need to begin to look at is the carer situation. The spouse or carer (who can often be a parent or sibling) can lose their job or find themselves in a situation here they are thrust into the main breadwinner's position and they need to be trained and then employed in a position that allows the flexibility necessary to deal with the appointment schedule, surgery schedule and rehab schedule of the wounded service member."

"Providing employment does more than give a job; it provides stability and hope to a family already in crisis. To yank from the family all they know to be normal and then to also put them into a financial crisis is to devastate them. The carers need to receive rapid training in a viable career field to remove added financial burden, provide a respite for caregivers, and help the family to transition with less stress."

"Another issue seldom addressed is the children of the wounded. Often times [sic] the soldier's injuries are life changing and altering. It is something that hits to the very core of their "safe" worlds and impacts them greatly. Currently we have NO system in place for the children of these families. Although there is a huge emphasis on the families of the deployed and the fallen, little if nothing seems to be directed at the wounded. These children themselves often suffer from PTSD type depressions."

"Once these issues are addressed the family can begin to transition and they need to be aware these things even exist. Through mentoring by other families and programs that connect them to community resources we can see our families successfully face this tragedy and grow through it instead of be destroyed by it."

Bibliography

Beckham, J. C., Feldman, M. E., Kirby, A. C., Hertzberg, M. A. and Moore, S. D. (1997). Interpersonal Violence and Its Correlates in Vietnam Veterans with Chronic Posttraumatic Stress Disorder. *Journal of Clinical Psychology*, 53(8), 859–869.

Brewin, C. R., Andrews, B., and Valentine, J. D. (2000). Meta-Analysis of Risk Factors for Posttraumatic Stress Disorder in Trauma-Exposed Adults. *Journal of Consulting and Clinical Psychology*, 68, 748–766.

Burger, H., and Marincek, C. (2007). Return to Work after Lower Limb Amputation. *Disability Rehabilitation*, 29(17), 1323–1329.

Calhoun, P. S., Beckham, J. C., and Bosworth, H. B. (2002). Caregiver Burden and Psychological Distress in Partners of Veterans with Chronic Posttraumatic Stress Disorder. *Journal of Traumatic Stress*, 15(3), 205–212.

Evans, L., McHugh, T., Hopwood, M., and Watt, C. (2003). Chronic Posttraumatic Stress Disorder and Family Functioning of Vietnam Veterans and Their Partners. *Australian and New Zealand Journal of Psychiatry*, 37(6), 765–772.

Fichter, M. M., Glynn, S. M., Weyer, S, Liberman, R. P., and Frick, U. (1997). Family Climate and Expressed Emotion in the Course of Alcoholism. *Family Process*, 36, 203–221.

Gawande, A. (2004). Casualties of War—Military Care for the Wounded from Iraq and Afghanistan. *The New England Journal of Medicine*, 351(24), 2471–2475.

Hollon, S. D., Stewart, M. O., and Strunk, D. (2006). Enduring Effects for Cognitive Behavior Therapy in the Treatment of Depression and Anxiety. *Annual Review of Psychology*, 57, 285–315.

Hooley, J. M., and Teasdale, J. D. (1989). Predictors of Relapse in Unipolar Depressives: Expressed Emotion, Marital Distress, and Perceived Criticism. *Journal of Abnormal Psychology*, 98(3), 229–235.

Jacobson, N. E., Dobson, K., Fruzzetti, A. E., Schmaling, K. B., and Salusky, S. (1991). Marital Therapy as a Treatment for Depression. *Journal of Consulting and Clinical Psychology*, 59, 547–557.

Karney, B. R., and Crown, J. S. (2007). *Families under Stress: An Assessment of Data, Theory, and Research on Marriage and Divorce in the Military*. Retrieved November 19, 2007 from http://rand.org/pubs/monographs/2007/RAND_MG599.pdf.

Magliano, L., Fiorillo, A., De Rosa, C., Malangone, C., and Maj, M. (2005). Family Burden in Long-Term Diseases: A Comparative Study in Schizophrenia vs. Physical Disorders. *Social Science and Medicine*, 61(2), 313–322.

Manguno-Mire, G., Sautter, F., Lyons, J., Myers, L., Perry, D., Sherman, M., Glynn, S., and Sullivan, G.(2007). Psychological Distress and Burden among Female Partners of Combat Veterans with PTSD. *Journal of Nervous and Mental Disease*, 195(2), 144–151.

Monson, C. M., Schnurr, P., Stevens, S. P., and Guthrie, K. A. (2004). Cognitive-Behavioral Couple's Treatment for Posttraumatic Stress Disorder: Initial Findings. *Journal of Traumatic Stress*, 17(4), 341–344.

Moos, R. H. (2003). Addictive Disorders in Context: Principles and Puzzles of Effective Treatment and Recovery. *Psychology of Addictive Behaviors*, 17(1), 3–12.

Moos, R. H. (2007a). Theory-Based Active Ingredients of Effective Treatments for Substance Use Disorders. *Drug and Alcohol Dependence*, 88(2–3), 109–121.

——— (2007b). Theory-Based Processes That Promote the Remission of Substance Use Disorders. *Clinical Psychology Review*, 27(5), 537–551.

Nemeroff, C. B., Bremner, J. D., Foa, E. B., Mayberg, H, North, C. S., and Stein, M. B. (2006). Posttraumatic Stress Disorder: A State-of-the-Science Review. *Journal of Psychiatric Research*, 40(1), 1–21.

O'Farrell, T. J., Chouquette, K. A., Cutter, H. S. G., Brown, E. D., and McCourt, W. (1993). Behavioral Marital Therapy with and without Additional Couples Relapse

Prevention Session for Alcoholics and Their Wives. *Journal of Studies on Alcohol*, 54, 652–666.

O'Leary, K. D., and Beach, S. R. H. (1990). Marital Therapy: A Viable Treatment for Depression and Marital Discord. *American Journal of Psychiatry*, 147, 183–186.

Office of the Surgeon General Multinational Force Iraq and Office of the Surgeon General United States Army Medical Command (2006). *Mental Health Advisory Team (MHAT) IV Final Report—Operation Iraqi Freedom*. Retrieved November 28, 2007 from http://www.armymedicine.army.mil/news/mhat/mhat_iv/MHAT_IV_Report_17NOV06.pdf.

Rauch, R. J., and Ferry, S. M. (2001). Social Networks as Support Interventions Following Traumatic Brain Injury. *NeuroRehabilitation*, 16(1), 11–16.

Riggs, D. S., Byrne, C. A., Weathers, F. W., and Litz, B. T. (1998). The Quality of the Intimate Relationships of Male Vietnam Veterans: Problems Associated with Posttraumatic Stress Disorder. *Journal of Traumatic Stress*, 11(1), 87–101.

Rundell, J. R. (2006). Demographics of and Diagnoses in Operation Enduring Freedom and Operation Iraqi Freedom Personnel Who Were Psychiatrically Evacuated from the Theater of Operations. *General Hospital Psychiatry*, 28(4), 352–356.

Seal, K. H., Bertenthal, D., Miner, C. R., Sen, S., and Marmar, C. (2007). Bringing the War Back Home: Mental Health Disorders among 103,788 US Veterans Returning from Iraq and Afghanistan Seen at Department of Veterans Affairs Facilities. *Archives of Internal Medicine*, 167(5), 476–482.

Solomon, S. D., and Johnson, D. M. (2002). Psychosocial Treatment of Posttraumatic Stress Disorder: A Practice-Friendly Review of Outcome Research. *Journal of Clinical Psychology*, 58(8), 947–959.

Tarrier, N., Sommerfield, C., and Pilgrim, H. (1999). Relatives' Expressed Emotion (EE) and PTSD Treatment Outcome. *Psychological Medicine*, 29(4), 801–811.

Zarit, S., Reever, K., and Bach-Peterson, J. (1980). Relatives of the Impaired Elderly: Correlates of Feelings of Burden. *The Gerontologist*, 20(6), 649–655.

CHAPTER 10

Peer Support Services

Wayne Gregory

Editors' Comment

Veterans and their families need 24/7 services that address the problems of both body and mind across all the hours of their daily lives. But many of these services cannot be carried out only by medical and mental health personnel. So to meet these needs, many consumers of medical and mental health services have organized themselves into peer support groups to provide these types of services to each other and to lend support and provide guidance to each other. In the process of assisting others, many veterans and family members gain strength and knowledge to assist their own recovery process. From Alcoholic Anonymous (AA) to the National Alliance for the Mentally Ill (NAMI) examples are plentiful of consumers working together in peer networks to help others just like them through recovery and reintegration. To give an example, estimates suggest that there are more than 8,000 groups in the United States alone organized by mental health consumers and families to provide peer support, which far exceeds the estimated 5,000 formalized agencies in the United States to the same population of people with medical and mental disorders.

Combat veterans, with their history of insuring that no soldier is left behind on the field, are doing the same with their fellow veterans by forming and creating volunteer-based organizations to insure that those who risked their lives can return to communities that provide support long after war has ended. And where formal services do not exist, they have created their own groups and organizations to provide their own support.

Peer Support consists of groups of consumers providing training and experiences for: mutual acceptance; empowerment in solving problems; information about and advocacy for mental/medical health services; skills training in reducing social withdrawal and increasing interpersonal interactions;

education to increase work skills and find better jobs; and training to reintegrate into families, work, and one's community of choice. The guiding notion of these groups is that those who have been treated are well qualified to help those who are entering treatment. Those who have learned skills of recovery are now qualified to teach those who begin to master the skills of providing for their care and rehabilitation.

As "all politics are local" (as Massachusetts Congressman "Tip" O'Neill taught us), all mental and medical treatment also has to be local. All individuals need to draw upon the resources of their home communities to supplement their strength and the support of their families. To draw upon your community's resources, we recommend that you locate and become involved with the peer support groups in your area. In this chapter, Wayne Gregory, Ph.D., of the Central Texas Veterans Health Care System draws upon the local groups in which he has worked to offer one example of the specific steps that need to be taken to create and to carry out peer counseling. His work demonstrates that all such programs must be specific to the community and must reach out to other volunteers and need to be implemented where combat veterans live and interact. Dr. Gregory's approach centers primarily upon veterans with serious mental illness. As a consequence, his intervention may be more place-centered when compared with other approaches that, for example, center only on increasing work and vocational benefits.

While this chapter looks at the groups in central Texas, similar groups are available throughout the nation and thus in your community as well. Because of their localized and informal approach (and the fact that there are thousands of them across the country with more starting up regularly) a centralized list of these groups is not available, and we are unable to provide you with a directory or listing of these groups. If you and your family are interested in receiving or becoming involved with peer counseling we recommend that you check with your local VA facilities, speak with other veterans and their families, and contact the local Veterans of Foreign Wars chapters, the Disabled American Veterans, and the other groups mentioned on our Web site, http://www.warswounded.com. And if you do not find a group in your community, you can start one by following the model presented in this chapter. As Dr. Gregory demonstates below, the benefits received from the participants in these groups are immeasurable, as they supplement the care received from physicians, counselors and other treatment providers.

Introduction

This chapter describes an array of veteran-developed peer support services. This array of services is only one sample of a great variety of possible service implementations based on the concept that people who are successful in recovery have something to teach all of us. The array of implementations in central Texas described here is just one in a great number of possible implementations. The central Texas plan is not the only plan, and it serves as just one example of what is possible in the realm of peer support services. Hopefully, by example, it will help broaden the scope of possible contributions coming from those who have gone through the process of recovery and have returned to share with us their discoveries.

Peer Support

Have you ever wanted to know the following?

1. Where do I go to know which VA services are available?
2. How do I get the available services?
3. How do I get through all the steps to receiving services?
4. Am I the only one who is experiencing these things?
5. Am I the only spouse dealing with these things?
6. Are there any "lessons learned?" Are there people out there who have been through the treatment program and can advise me on this program?
7. Is there hope for me?
8. Is there hope for my family?
9. Who has answered these questions successfully, and how can I reach them?
10. Who cares about my concerns?

Peer support and peer support teams can provide you with answers to these questions. Peer support can provide these answers because with enough people in recovery organized into a group chances are that someone has already found solutions to some of the challenges you are facing. Peers are people who have been through experiences similar to yours. Peer support provides support, information, and encouragement—in other words, help—from people who have been through experiences similar to those you are going through.

Background

It has been recognized for a long time and especially within the VA that veterans want to help other veterans. From service organizations such as Disabled American Veterans and Veterans of Foreign Wars to local grassroots organizations such as the Veterans Helping Veterans in Central Texas, veterans have demonstrated the wish to help fellow veterans. Within VA itself, veterans have found opportunities to coalesce and to gather around formal existing structure to provide highly valued assistance to their peers. This veteran-initiated activity can be observed in every program, especially the VA's mental health programs. Veterans are constantly extending themselves to be helpful and provide service and support to other veterans who need them. The peer support project in central Texas was constructed on the belief that good things could happen if VA observed the naturally occurring tendency and wish of veterans to help other veterans and proactively created opportunities for veterans to help each other in a planned and purposeful way. The planned and purposeful way does not eliminate the natural and spontaneous way veterans will help each other. Moreover, the peer support services are designed to complement and enrich existing professional services, not to replace them. While peer-generated services may range from information sharing to skill development as described below, none of the peer support services would be described as psychotherapy: psychotherapy is only conducted by professionals who are trained and certified as qualified to provide such services. However, a relatively similar training process is followed for the provision of peer services.

What Are the Services?

Vic Felts, an original peer support volunteer, once said to me, "Doc, I have PTSD, but there's a lot I know how to do. What if we asked our vets, 'What do you know how to do and would be willing to teach another veteran?' And what if we asked them, "What would you like to learn from another veteran?' And then what if we linked up veterans wishing to learn with veterans willing to teach?"

Vic proposed to categorize, inventory, publish, and share strengths currently in existence in our veteran community. Our veteran community is an extremely rich source of knowledge, skills, and abilities, and our effort has been to make this richness known and accessible to other veterans. Vic's proposal was based on a way of viewing each other that involves much more emphasis on what we do right and well and much less on what is wrong with us mentally or physically.

Our belief is that our peer support effort has tapped that part of the human spirit that wishes to help and make constructive contributions to community. Our belief is that this part of the human experience is refined and focused by the veteran experience. It has recognized that *everyone* has something good to offer. It has recognized that making constructive contributions to family, peers, and community is itself an activity that improves the quality of life for both the recipient and the maker of contributions. A large focus of our efforts in central Texas has been to create opportunities for veterans to engage in the activities that provide increases in knowledge, skills, and abilities for other vets, using existing strengths within individuals and communities, knowing that those providing these services will themselves receive enhancements through the giving of themselves. Out of this giving a situation is created in which everyone is a winner. Our experience is that the veteran community is very rich in knowledge, skills, and abilities and wants to share these things with others and in the process is itself enriched.

The Vets' ASK Inventory

The following is one tool developed to link veterans with different experiences with other veterans with questions of general concerns. It is called the Veterans' Abilities, Skills, Knowledge Inventory, or the Vets' ASK Inventory. This form is not rocket science, but it has shown that it has the powerful ability to tap strengths and develop relationships of support and caring, producing possibilities so rich that we cannot yet fully describe its effect. If you find it useful, please feel free to use the form in your own community to create these kinds of connections.

Veterans' Abilities, Skills, and Knowledge

Veterans who have abilities, skills, and knowledge in special areas have offered to teach these to veterans who want to learn them. These veterans have suggested an inventory of these abilities, skills, and knowledge be built, so that the inventory could be made available to veterans who wish to learn in a special area.

Please take a moment to look over this sheet and see if there is something you would like to teach another vet or learn from another vet. The information you provide will be placed in a book and be available to other vets.

I know the area(s) below and would be willing to teach another vet		I would like to learn more about
_____	Computers	_____
_____	English	_____
_____	Budgeting	_____
_____	Financial Plans	_____
_____	How to Shop in a Crowd	_____
_____	How to File a VA Claim	_____
_____	Travel	_____
_____	Fishing	_____
_____	Boating	_____
_____	Stop Drinking or Using Drugs	_____
_____	Get Started in School	_____
_____	Look for Work	_____
_____	Other (*please specify*)	_____
_____		_____
_____		_____

Name/phone number/date:_____

More Specific Recovery Focus Support

Extending this concept of veteran knowledge a bit further, there is a special knowledge base possessed by veterans and family members who have successfully faced and negotiated special challenges, including recovery from mental illnesses. While computer skills, independent living skills, social skills, etc., can be obtained in a variety of venues, veteran knowledge of what facilitates recovery from stress and mental illnesses is a body of knowledge that is available in no venue other than the one that involves a person undergoing the experiences of recovery. What a veteran needs to recover and what it takes for veteran families to survive mental illness and to survive through the process is a special source of knowledge that can only be obtained through those who have successfully lived through these challenges, survived them, and even thrived in the difficult times. The veterans and their family members who survive these challenges possess a special source of information and knowledge that can be obtained in no other venue. Therapists and other practitioners who have not been through the process cannot provide this guidance—the only ones who can really connect and help are the veterans and family members who have faced the issues and come through to the other side.

What does all this mean for veterans and families seeking information and services? First—and foremost—it means that there are individuals, couples, and families who have experienced challenges and have successfully responded to them. The message is, "Have hope."

Examples of Peer Support Services

Services provided by peers can be separated into several kinds of activities depending upon the amount of skill and training required to deliver the services. One end of this continuum is the group of services consisting of veterans sharing with other veterans the knowledge and abilities they have acquired in the natural course of their lives. An example might be a retired computer analyst teaching basic computer skills to a veteran who wants to learn how to operate a computer and search the Internet. A more sophisticated peer support offering would be what is referred to as "mutual support groups." These are groups that require no training agenda but may be led by those who have attended the groups and have volunteered to take a leading role. Some of these groups include Alcoholics Anonymous groups, Narcotics Anonymous groups, and others.

Even more sophisticated service offerings are those that require specialized training in order to deliver the services. Most of these peer support services have a special focus and are rarely implemented without a guiding agenda and specific training in the use of that agenda. Modules on helping veterans to improve problem solving skills and skill development in setting goals for living are also important examples of peer-supported skill development. Veterans telling their own stories of challenge and recovery, moving from victimization to survival and on to creating a life of thriving, are a source of great hope for veterans and family members not so far along in the recovery process. Training in telling one's recovery journey is a special module unlike any other known in traditional treatment settings. Organizations such as the Texas Mental Health Consumers, Depression and BiPolar Support Alliance, and National Alliance on Mental Illness each provide trainings in these types of peer supported services.

Settings Offering Peer Support Services

Peer support services may be delivered in a variety of settings. Venues for service delivery may be complex and involve embedding the peer provider in voluntary service or teaching skills/knowledge learned in life experiences. The venue may extend to participation as part of a treatment team as a function of full-time employment. Research is beginning to show that peer support services tend to thrive best in rehabilitation and recovery settings in which consumer empowerment and consumer self-determination are values implemented in the environment. Accumulating research appears to indicate that peer support services are most effective when offered in an environment that is operated by consumers themselves. One example of this kind of environment is the Independence Center, described later.

Some peer support services include:

• Warm Line
• PTSD Solutions for Families and Friends
• Dual Recovery Anonymous
• Independence Center
• Goals Setting
• Problem Solving
• Outreach

Warm Line

A warm line is a step down from a "hot line" or a phone number that people call when facing a crisis. A warm line is a phone service designed to solve relatively minor problems or to prevent those problems from becoming serious. Essentially, the warm line is an opportunity for veterans to seek and give information, support and fellowship to other vets and family members using a telephone line. A warm line is typically manned during published hours during the day or evening in order for regular and consistent contact opportunity. Such a warm line was created and is operated by veterans in the PTSD residential program at the Central Texas Veterans Health Care System, Waco Campus. The vets use the warm line to stay in touch with and support veterans who have been in the residential program and have transitioned to their community.

Since veterans from all over the United States, particularly Texas, access care in the PTSD residential program, it is helpful for them to have a way to stay in touch and receive continued support from each other. The warm line provides such an opportunity. Veterans entering the residential program can contact veterans currently in the program and speak with them before they check into the residential program. The vets currently in the program are aware of the difficulty experienced in leaving one's family and community to access residential care in an unfamiliar location and can advise the veterans entering about these difficulties. They are aware of how important it can be to obtain support before they leave home and how this support will help the veteran follow-through on their requests for residential services. This awareness comes from having been through the very same circumstances, so they can convey (from their experience) what the transition to the residential program is like—and what incoming vets can expect. Callers to the warm line can build a bond prior to arrival at the center and continue that bond after a veteran leaves. This it is a unique opportunity that can only be communicated from one concerned veteran to another. During the calls, anxieties can be addressed and dispelled; misconceptions and misinformation can be corrected; and foundational bounds can be created and passed along through work on the warm line.

PTSD Solutions for Families and Friends

This peer support offering is the extension of the module created by Patience Mason (the wife of a Vietnam helicopter pilot and a writer and activist) for families, friends of and also for those with PTSD. Ms. Mason has provided an agenda-driven resource, along the lines of a twelve-step group. Such a group is implemented not by professionals but by people with PTSD and their families and friends. John Robertson originally created this group when he realized he had seen more PTSD groups than he could count. One day John said, "We need to create a 'solutions' group because we have spent far too much time living in and describing 'the problem.'" So John searched about and found Ms. Mason's agenda and began offering it to veterans and their family members and friends. Wives, children, and interested friends have been welcomed into the group to discover information about PTSD from the curriculum guide and (most importantly) from the people with PTSD themselves. At these meetings, attendees share solutions that have worked for them in coping with, surviving, and thriving in PTSD. Wives and the children share their experiences with others to complete the picture of what it looks like to live through and thrive in the face of PTSD. This picture is invaluable to an individual or family member still in the darkness of initial recovery. The PTSD Solutions group is a peer-run "point of contact group" where any veteran may attend without needing a referral. No membership in any program is required nor is any form of eligibility needed to attend this group. The only thing that the veteran or family member has to do is walk in and take part in the group.

Dual Recovery Anonymous

Like PTSD Solutions, Dual Recovery Anonymous (DRA) is an agenda driven group based on twelve-step principles seen in groups such as Alcoholics Anonymous (AA). Since it is now recognized that mental illnesses and substance abuse disorders are commonly co-occurring disorders, it is now recognized that the treatment of both disorders at the same time is a more effective procedure than treating each disorder separately. Along these lines, the DRA agenda was developed as an educational and supportive approach for individuals having both a mental illness and a substance abuse disorder. Much like the PTSD Solutions group, DRA groups are point of contact—anyone is welcome. Each meeting of the group is run by a member with the leadership of the group often rotated among the members.

Outreach

The central Texas VA recently hired its first peer support technicians as full-time regular VA employees. It was anticipated that they would be a valuable addition to our treatment teams. But no one saw just how valuable they could be in outreach, especially street outreach, to veterans either not in treatment or only marginally involved with treatment programs. Their presence as a first point of contact, the immediate authenticity their presence conveys to veterans whose trust of the "system" is not what it might be, and the peer support's dedication and determination to engage fellow veterans in improving the quality of living all make the peer support an excellent resource for this work. Who better to orient a veteran to a complex system of care than a veteran who has been through it? And who better to serve as a "travel companion" to a veteran new to VA services as the person begins to access the care at the VA?

Independence Center

It is the opinion of some mental health professionals that most change happens in people without professional intervention and that change interventions would be best if they were based on the natural change processes experienced by people. Peer support services are based on the recognition that people in recovery have discovered significant and effective change processes to help themselves. The idea that fellow veterans are "good" for each other, especially when some are further along in recovery than others, has led to the idea that it could be helpful to provide consumers of mental health services opportunities to be with and help each other in an atmosphere *controlled* by consumers themselves. Such an environment is called a "consumer-operated drop-in center." A consumer-operated drop-in center is an environment that is run by the consumers and one in which consumers are welcome to be involved as little or as much as they choose. In 2005, peer supports, in a partnership between the Central Texas Veterans Health Care

System (CTVHCS) and the Heart of Texas Region Mental Health Mental Retarda-
tions Center (HOTRMHMR), opened the Independence Center. Modeled after the
Paradise Center in Fort Worth, Texas, the Independence Center in Waco is operated by a member advisory board (MAB) consisting of sixteen consumers. All
decisions about operations and services in the Independence Center are made by
the MAB. Activities offered range from social opportunities and outings to friendly
sports and weight loss competitions to personal wellness and recovery planning to
Spanish/English classes to birthday celebrations and holiday events. Recently, the
MAB has asked for some professional services to be offered through the Center.
Now, consumers can attend services by professionally prepared clinical staff. Consumers are welcome to sleep during their time at the Center if that is what they
desire or to wash clothes if they want. They can also attend professionally delivered services. The Center's Web site is at www.independencecenteronline.org.
The Web site, by the way, was built and is maintained by one of the consumers
at the Independence Center.

The Independence Center, like most consumer-operated drop-in centers, seeks
to provide a "safe place" for people with mental illnesses—a place that offers the
consumer a welcoming opportunity to do what he or she feels the need to do at
whatever stage of recovery. It is not uncommon for consumers to blossom in this
atmosphere from very quiet, shy people who come and sit quietly several hours
a day watching television to very social, outgoing members who volunteer their
time and skills to make the Center better.

In the beginning of planning the Independence Center, a number of concerns
were expressed about the ability of peer supports' ability to manage such a
project. These were double-edged fears about possible negative mental health
consequences for peers doing this work combined with concerns about the
safety and security of vulnerable people with mental illnesses. While the effects
of increased stress on overall functioning must be successfully addressed, there
is little doubt that the thrills of contributing constructively to a project like this
can itself be a sustaining, creative emotion resulting in resilience and increased
strength. And while it is true that people with mental illnesses can be vulnerable
to abuse from their helpers, the data will demonstrate that the contributions
received from peer providers are of considerable value to the consumers of these
services. When consumers may express their feelings about services by choosing
to attend and stay at a place, their very choices can become goals for mental
health providers and services and become part of the treatment program.

The Independence Center is a destination for about sixty consumers a day. It
is a place and a collection of services that consumers *choose*. It is a place where
there is a place for everyone at any point in the process of recovery. It is a place
that invites continued recovery and expanded recovery and accepts times when
their hopes and dreams are further away than anyone could dare hope to achieve.

In the future, the Independence Center will support the development of a
community resilience center. A significant grant from a local foundation will provide the springboard that will allow the Independence Center that extra spring

to launch it into community resilience from the community resilience center. We expect that the community resilience center will offer quality of life coaching for any member of the community who might wish to improve life satisfaction. A significant portion of this program's coaching will be provided by peers—by the people who have been through it and can share their experiences with others. A lot of research has been conducted on the issues underlining the important complexities of contributions to recovery made by peer support persons, but none is more important than the idea that the best way to propose hope is by someone who can demonstrate a living example of success.

Special Focus Peer Modules

Most psychiatric rehabilitation centers and formal peer support organizations have developed modules for teaching consumers to set goals and to solve their own problems. Self-determination in recovery is a key concept in many mental health service plans. Self-determination has a distinct civil rights root, since self-determination in mental health service provision means that the consumer, with informed choice, determines the course of service provision and utilization of his own recovery.

Other than rekindling hope for recovery, there may be no more important self-empowering skill sets that we can convey to consumers than teaching someone how to set goals and how to solve problems. These tools enable consumers to become independent of their teachers. Because the techniques are fairly common and straightforward, the modules, regardless of origin, have more in common with each other than differences between themselves. However, the problem solving and goal setting modules developed by Larry Fricks, Ike Powell, and Lisa Goodale with the peer-to-peer resource center at the Depression and Bipolar Support Alliance (DBSA) were developed for use by consumers for consumers. This group came to the Waco VA in 2005 to train thirty peer supports and clinical staff partners from communities across Texas in these and other techniques. As a result, veterans and nonveterans from around Texas are receiving training on creating the lives they want (goal setting) and negotiating barriers (problem solving) they encounter along the way.

Is Peer Support Safe and Effective?

The question about vulnerabilities for people with mental illnesses was raised in an earlier section. What safeguards are in place to ensure that peer-provided services do what they say and no more and no less? And what about their quality? In customary services, treatment modalities that have been shown by research to be effective are called "evidence-based" practices. That is, there is an "evidence base" to support the effectiveness of the services provided. Peer support services have been acknowledged to be a set of services with an evidence base.

Our own survey research with recipients of peer support services in CTVHCS shows that the services are highly valued by recipients and that the services are delivered in a way that is highly consistent with the training model (that is, peer supports provide services in the manner in which they were trained).

In one study, we asked 129 recipients of peer support services a series of questions about peer support services. Here are their responses:

	Yes	No
• Maintains confidentiality as a peer counselor	113	0
• Maintains confidentiality as a participant in group	124	0
• Acts a referral source to veterans (gives direction, not advice)	120	4
• Is flexible in all areas of peer support	129	1
• Has demonstrated the ability to cope with own illness	122	1
• Participates and gives feedback in peer support/consumers meetings	125	2
• Demonstrates ability to resolve conflicts with others	113	3
• Is empathic to the problems and feelings of all veterans	122	1
• Demonstrates good interaction with peers, fellow vets, and VA employees	122	2
• Uses coping skills and tools of interaction with peer support groups	116	1
• How would you rate the contribution of this peer support specialist to those of regular VA staff?		

Less than staff	Equal to Staff	More than Staff
19 (15%)	47 (36%)	63 (48%)

Venues of Peer Support Service Provision

The value of peer-provided services requires that we promote provision of services in the most extensive of continuum. This continuum would range from the volunteer to the employed peer support technician. It is to be expected that viable forms of peer support will take spontaneous shape between veterans. And it is to be expected that this shape will extend to local veterans organizations willing to be involved in both spontaneous opportunities and those with a more or less planned design for services.

Vets Helping Vets may be just such a venue. Vets Helping Vets (VHV) is a private not-for-profit organization created to promote veteran involvement and self-determination in a range of activities extending from clinical services to advocacy and self-help services. Originally, VHV was a consumer-operated organization that eventually brought about the existence of a consumer council in VISN 17 (the Heart of Texas Health Care Network) that promoted the development of peer services and consumer-oriented service determination.

As in all consumer-based services, expectations for VHV depended on those who saw such enterprises as potentially rewarding—namely those with the most to lose! VHV, as described in this current chapter, is a snapshot. The program is a once in an afternoon or a morning or an evening episode or an opportunity to express and experience a piece of life that is constantly changing, constantly evolving and developing. The organization and activity of VHV is just a snapshot in the continuum of the evolving possibilities produced by empowerment, self-determination, and the values of recovery and hope in an individual's life journey. Even now, peer support activities have evolved away from VHV as a center of support and activity and toward community-based/community-oriented venues such as the Independence Center. Another direction for peer support has been toward employment of people in recovery as full-time VA employees. Movement in this direction has the effect of permanently changing VA structure to provide a valued and respected place for the consumer voice in the array of services offered to veterans in recovery.

For the Future

Michael Frisch, Ph.D., of Baylor University, has published a quality of life therapy/coaching manual that is built around concepts in positive psychology. Positive psychology is about developing wellness, strengths, and talents rather than focusing on illness. Dr. Frisch has proposed a strategy of helping people increase their quality of life by helping them focus on the degree to which they are satisfied with various aspects of living. He does this through the use of his quality of life instrument (QOLI), which measures both priority and level of satisfaction in sixteen different areas of living. Areas of high priority and low satisfaction can be identified for "coaching." Who better to be a coach than someone who has made his or her own adjustments and adaptations to improve an area of living?

The hope is that peer support services can move away from problem-based services to those that involve coaching for people with and without mental health concerns. They should have an important role in the community resilience center.

Summary

It may be that the veteran experience has brought special focus and refinement to that part of the human spirit that wishes to help and contribute constructively to peers, family, and community. Veterans have always demonstrated this wish to help each other. In central Texas, the staff has recognized this wish of veterans to help and have set out to provide multiple opportunities for veterans to act on their wishes. Many of these opportunities involve the simple sharing of what individual veterans have come to learn over a lifetime of experience. Other opportunities are based on existing mutual support processes and technologies adapted for use with veterans. Still other opportunities involve specialized techniques specifically developed for use by peer for peers. Without doubt, such a variety of new offerings of services significantly enriches the choices available to veterans. And in addition, these offerings are not available from any other methods or sources. As veterans are increasingly involved in the planning and delivery of services and in the provision of services such as peer support services, we can expect the creation of new services that are currently unimaginable. This is the promise quickened by creative involvement of veterans in their own recoveries and by recognizing what a gift they can be to each other.

Acknowledgments

Humberto Rodriguez, Marvin Hooper, Victor Felts, Joe Bartlett, and John Robertson, are all coauthors of this chapter. Their lived contributions made everything in this chapter a concrete reality. Their spirit is the essence of this chapter.

CHAPTER 11

The Psychological Impact of Disabilities

Walter E. Penk and Ralph Robinowitz

Editors' Comment

The last chapter of this book focuses upon psychosocial impacts of war that persist into times of peace as warriors return home. The chapter is structured around three themes: 1) the new goals that warriors must develop for themselves as they transition home; 2) the maladies impacting their transitions to home life; and 3) the means that they can use to overcome these maladies, so that they can achieve their goals at home.

Unlike past wars, service members in the current conflict are no longer taught to cope with memories of war by burying the memories and are now encouraged to learn new skills for coping with the symptoms of war that persist into the times of peace. Also, clinicians now provide services in the war zones, marking a massive change from previous wars when few such services were available at scenes of battle and even later, after warriors returned home.

This chapter covers new ways of coping. These new ways of coping share in common the ingredient of learning new ways to reduce the fears and anxieties that are invoked by the memories. Just as soldiers were trained to become warriors to fight in war zones, they must now be trained to overcome the memories of war in order to live successfully in peace at home and at work. This chapter is structured around learning three sets of new skills: 1) new skills for coping with the problems that often arise in the aftermath of war; 2) learning the motivations that are needed to apply these new skills in coping; and 3) learning how to overcome negative feelings and attitudes that impede motivations to learn new ways of coping. And to apply these new sets of coping skills, the chapter is organized around the structure that new goals for living need to be developed to overcome the maladies of war based upon learning new means to cope—especially the means of self-control, taking control of one's own life, and organizing one's life around the goals that one will want to achieve.

This chapter is written by Walter Penk, Ph.D., and Ralph Robinowitz, Ph.D., J.D. They began their work together as colleagues in 1963 at the Veterans Administration Medical Center in Dallas, Texas. They published their first study on post-traumatic stress disorder (PTSD) in 1981, based upon their experiences in identifying differences in psychosocial adjustment of substance-abusing veterans and those without exposure to combat. Their contributions to this chapter arise from their learning about the importance of education and work to treat trauma-related disorders as alternatives to addictive use of illicit drugs. Dr. Penk and Dr. Robinowitz are now entering their forty-fifth year of collaboration, conducting research on vocational rehabilitation as key psychosocial interventions for warriors who continue to be distressed by war.

Dr. Penk retired from the VA after serving forty-five years at the VA Medical Center in Bedford, Massachusetts. He is currently a professor in psychiatry and behavioral sciences at Texas A&M University College of Medicine and a consultant for the Central Texas Veterans Health Care System. Dr. Robinowitz is both a clinical psychologist and an attorney and served as a commissioned officer during the Korean War era, completing his military service in the Reserves and retiring as a major. He was a clinical psychologist in Veterans Health Administration medical centers in Texas and retired from the VA as director of the drug dependence treatment center at the VAMC Dallas. After leaving the VA, Dr. Robinowitz obtained a law degree and now pursues his legal interest in disabilities and the law.

Introduction

Wars, and rumors of war, have always been with us. And those who fought have learned, and always will learn, how to cope with war and what happens after war. How to cope with the aftermaths of war have been recorded since histories have been written. Typical is the mission statement of the Benedictine Order—*Ora et Labora*—written 1,300 years ago in the sixth century. In a time of terror and war, St. Benedict designed and built a religious order as one way to protect and to rehabilitate those ravaged by conflicts. *Ora et Labora* is Latin for "Pray and Labor." It is chiseled on the gateway of Monte Casino in Italy, a place where thousands across the centuries have come to learn ways to cope with war by seeking peace and safety. *Ora et Labora* is one of the earliest lessons learned about how to cope with war and its aftermaths.

In this chapter, we will emphasize how worshipping and working are the keys to recovery from war. We will examine how today's warriors learn to cope with war and be at peace and safe once wars are temporarily suspended. We introduce the *goals* that warriors need to generate when they return home from war zones; then we present the *maladies* many warriors experience once the fighting stops; and then we list the *means* that can be used by warriors to tap into their strengths and their resiliencies to assuage the maladies that can prevent them from reaching their own personal goals. Central among means are learning new skills of which there are two forms: 1) adapting actions for surviving in war zones for adjustment to new demands and new rules for adjusting as a civilian; and 2) learning new skills for life as a civilian in a world of competition that not only is different but, like the military, is also always changing.

Goals

Leaping forward thirteen centuries from *Ora et Labora* (Pray and Labor) to find more modern statements about how to cope with war and its aftermaths, we look at the fourth inaugural address of President Franklin Delano Roosevelt (FDR) to the nation shortly before he died in 1945. Looking back upon the economic disaster of the Great Depression and the five years of fighting in the Second World War, he believed that maladies of wars would be assuaged if citizens were assured certain rights. To the Bill of Rights and the Constitution warriors were still fighting to protect, FDR added new rights as the cure for the ills of war such as the right to a useful and remunerative job, the right to earn enough to provide adequate food and clothing and recreation, the right for farmers to raise and sell their products to earn them decent wages, the right of every family to a decent home, the right to a good education, and the right to adequate protection from the economic fears of old age, sickness, accident, and unemployment. It is noteworthy that these rights are strikingly familiar to what scientists today have found in their research to be the benchmarks for determining the well-being of most people. They are also the goals that most veterans, as individuals, aspire to reach today as they transition from life in war zones to living in peace and safety as civilians. These are the rights so many warriors have fought to defend.

We suggest that these rights and benchmarks of well-being also are the goals by which you can decide whether you are overcoming the maladies most often associated with war and its aftermath. To know whether you are recovering from war, you need to acknowledge your goals and be able to measure the progress you make toward achieving these goals.

Transitioning from a war zone to home is the most important of all transitions that warriors make in their lifetime. One of the first challenges to be faced and resolved is the task of reconceptualizing and redefining your goals. Returning home from war comes to this: You're back. Now what? The first step to answering this question is to decide and reset the goals for your life and, if you are living with others, to reset the goals for your family as well.

Among the many advantages of having served in the military is that you have learned many skills, and one of these is "Re-set Training." This training means that warriors, upon return to base, can assess what they have lost, what they still have, and based on this assessment can start to repair equipment and plan for the next battle. Re-set Training not only is valuable in planning for battles in war zones but can also provide the blueprints for building the structures needed to achieve individual and personal goals for returning home. Returning home involves the equivalent of Re-set Training in which you can now reassess what you lost and what remains, and you can now prepare to fight the new battles of becoming a civilian.

So, now, you are back. What are your *goals*? What are the *maladies* that keep you from achieving your goals? And, finally, what are the *means* by which you can overcome your maladies to get to your goals?

War happens within the person. You left the war zone, but now you are home. Now is the time to face, to fight, and to defeat the maladies that keep you from your goals to achieve safety and peace as a civilian. What will keep you from achieving your new goals as you return home from war? What are the risks you face as you transition home?

Maladies

War takes place within the person. And, further, as Bessel van der Kolk (a recognized researcher on trauma) once so eloquently phrased it, "the body keeps score," and so does the mind, and so do the emotions.

Difficulties in returning home from combat are well known throughout recorded history. Homer's *Iliad* and *Odyssey* are among earliest writings, remembered by warriors in ancient times to help warriors in future generations. In *Achilles in Vietnam*, author Jonathan Shay, M.D., reminds us that war zone experiences in ancient texts are quite similar to reactions and readjustments experienced by warriors across the ages and still seen today. We can learn today by reading how past generations of warriors fought in battle and fought in returning home. And Dr. Shay has found maladies and ways to recover listed in the ancient texts similar to what health researchers continue to discover about warriors of today and how they recover.

Resources and Resiliencies among the Maladies

But to understand maladies associated with war, we must understand the resources and resiliencies of the warrior. What does it take to become and to be a warrior? It begins with deciding to put one's life at risk for others, to protect and to defend. The fights against terrorism and terrorists take warriors away from home to foreign lands. And being away from home means that one has lost direct touch with family and with friends. It also means going into circumstances in which your military income will be far less than what you earned in a civilian job, suspending control over your finances, and confronting challenges as to whether you can really live up to your ideal and function effectively in your unit to support and to protect your fellow warriors. Going to war not only increases the likelihood that enemies can wound or kill, but one also learns that, while there are positive experiences in being part of a unit, the risks are increased for the negatives of being together: for example, being around those who may drink and use drugs; encountering predators in the military who prey upon vulnerabilities of their comrades; experiencing bad leadership that does not protect the unit; finding that anger and aggression within yourself and/or among others is like letting a genie of destructive forces out of the body, a genie of madness difficult once again to bottle up, even when fears and threats have subsided, and the environment is at peace; as well as returning home where support may not be as strong as what you wish or need, and where others may not have sacrificed, while you gave your all.

Being in the military means that you must constantly develop and improve the balance in your style of living—for example, assessing the resources that you have as well as continuing to evaluate your personal strengths and weaknesses. And embedded in the balance of your lifestyle are the resiliencies that you bring to the military, into war, and into the return from war to home.

The task for the warrior in returning home is to reduce weaknesses and increase strengths, and to prevent weaknesses from prevailing while nurturing resiliencies to thrive.

Risks for Maladies

Surveys show that of the 1.5 million warriors who fought in Afghanistan and Iraq since 2002, already nearly 4,000 have died, 30,000 have sustained physical wounds, and, at least 200,000 self-report problems arising from war zone stresses and traumas. Of the 500,000 veterans of combat in Afghanistan and Iraq (OIF/OEF era veterans) now eligible for VA services through fiscal year 2006, already 30 percent (about 150,000) have applied for and are receiving VA care. Nearly a third (about 50,000) of OIF/OEF era veterans now enrolled in VA care are diagnosed as meeting criteria for mental disorders. Post-traumatic stress disorder (PTSD) is the leading problem (affecting about 22,000 people), closely followed by abuse of drugs (21,000), depression disorders (14,000), and neurotic disorders (11,000). These numbers do not include healthcare-seeking behaviors either in the military or in the private sector. And these numbers are increasing as Operation Enduring Freedom (OEF) continues in Afghanistan and Operation Iraqi Freedom (OIF) goes on in Iraq.

But at the same time that surveys show upwards of 40 percent of warriors are troubled in some serious way, medically and/or psychologically, many more warriors report growth in personal character, developing maturity and becoming more capable of coping as a civilian than they were before they went to war. And certainly warriors have mastered one characteristic that distinguishes them from some of their fellow citizens: many have learned how to deny their personal needs and place their very own lives at risk to protect and to defend the lives and properties of their fellow citizens. For some, hopefully for many, the experience of war can produce strengths in character and in spirit. In discussing maladies, we must consider not only risks but also the possibilities of resiliencies that produce growth.

Prevention and Recovery as the Approach to the Maladies

Maladies must also be considered as opportunities to develop skills to prevent other maladies and to promote recovery. As war happens within the person, war also changes the person; the person who went to war was not the same person who came back, as more than 90 percent of warriors report in surveys. But such changes are likely true of everyone, not just those who went to war but also for those who did not fight. While everyone changes, warriors appear to change faster. All the persons who return from war are likely to be wounded in some way. And not all the wounds are physical—most are psychological. The numbers of those with psychological and social "wounds" far exceed those with physical wounds (Tanielian & Jaycox, 2008). In one sense, all warriors are in some ways wounded; Nearly all will have suffered, even those who only trained and never fought. Anyone who feared the loss of life is likely to have been transformed in some way. No person who killed or feared being killed remains the same.

Given these experiences, maladies can be approached as risks that need to be prevented, risks to be managed before they worsen. And so, transitioning from war zone to home is the time to prevent maladies. Taking action to prevent maladies does not mean the warrior is crazy or has a mental disorder. Killing and nearly being killed means that, in a time of peace, such an individual must now work to overcome the negatives associated with having fought in war, overcoming changes in looking at life by developing new goals. Those who cope best are those who admit and talk about what they have experienced and then engage in Re-set Training by creating new goals to which they strive in times of peace. Re-set Training becomes a search for new meanings in life once war is over. Re-set Trainings are the ordinary steps warriors take to prevent maladies that sometimes arise when one has nearly died been killed.

Re-set Training includes some of the following behaviors designed to prevent maladies: 1) developing clear and certain goals to achieve as a civilian, now that you have survived death and destruction; 2) restoring connections to family and friends; 3) learning not to avoid reminders of war but facing and reducing anxieties associated with horrifying memories; 4) finding someone with whom you can talk about the good, the bad, and the ugly of war; 5) restoring skills to control your feelings, especially of anger and aggression; 6) developing a better sense of self as a person; 7) relearning how to sleep and sleep well without nightmares; 8) restoring physical health and fitness, the way you became physically fit to be a warrior; 9) managing the pains of wounds and pains of losses; and 10) and, having discovered that life is not the same, you are liberated to discover new meanings for living and new objectives to achieve.

These are just a few of the many skills to combat maladies that you can re-master in returning home to the battlefield within, the battlefield of mind and emotions, the battle to reinvent one's self as a new person in a new world.

The key factor in being at higher risk for psychological and social "wounds," or maladies, is the extent to which you perceived emotionally and cognitively that you were at risk to die. If you experienced a situation in which you concluded that you were going to be killed, then you are at risk, at some time later, for psychological and/or emotional difficulties. But being at higher risk does not mean that each and every person at risk will develop a psychological and/or emotional disorder; it only means some will. How many? Again, surveys are not precise. Health care researchers estimate that perhaps as many as 25 percent will at some time in their life develop a mental disorder, while the number who seek advice and counsel may be higher. That's the bad news.

The good news is that upwards of 75 percent of those at high risk will not develop a certifiable disorder. Most find ways to successfully treat themselves and get support from family and friends to survive emotional crises. Further, we also know from surveys that symptoms within the person do subside with time (Dohrenwend, 2006). Again, the good news: disorders resulting from fighting in war can be treated. But Dohrenwend's findings warn us that interferences in social and occupational functionings that persist are greater and last longer than do symptoms of mind and emotions. Sometimes emotional crises of war are hidden, appearing only through avoiding contacts with people, which, in turn, then reduces effectiveness at work and in the home. The "cures" for the diseases of war remain in setting your goals and then learning the skills to achieve what you need and want.

Maladies we focus on in this chapter are thoughts, emotions, and behaviors; problems from physical wounds and medical problems associated with traumas are discussed in other chapters in this book. The most common emotional and behavioral disorder associated with combat is post-traumatic stress disorder (PTSD). But other kinds of psychological, emotional, behavioral, and social disorders may persist long after the warrior returns home, like depression. Sometimes excessive drinking and drug use will be used to "self-medicate" the psychological and social "wounds".

Maladies: Post-Traumatic Stress Disorder (PTSD)

Post-traumatic stress disorder (PTSD) is one of the more widely known mental disorders associated with combat. As noted above, risks for developing PTSD vary from warrior to warrior, depending upon precombat personal and social strengths and weaknesses of the individual, intensity and frequency of exposure to life-threatening situations, unit cohesiveness of groups that fought together, preparation for combat, and support once combat has concluded—just to cite a few of the exposure and resiliency factors that influence risk.

As noted earlier, symptoms of PTSD start off as normal reactions to stress and trauma. PTSD is not classified until these normal reactions persist over months and develop into ways of coping that reduce productivity and social satisfactions. Only when symptoms last do clinicians speak of mental disorders that require professional treatment. But for those who meet the criteria for PTSD, research empirically validates that treatment works for PTSD. Since 1980, based upon what was learned about mental disorders from the Vietnam War, it is customary to describe PTSD as consisting of three sets of symptoms.

The first set of symptoms consists of feelings, emotions, and thoughts about *reexperiencing the life-threatening episode(s)*. Reexperiencing consists of "flashbacks"—intense and frightening reminders of combat and nightmares about actual previous episodes in combat that bring about physiological responses within the body and disturb your sleep, even though now the fighting has stopped and you are now at home.

The second set is of behavioral symptoms, or *actions taken as a civilian to avoid reminders of life-threatening situations in combat from your past*. Examples of such behaviors include reducing activities in places that remind you of events in combat, isolating yourself from people in order to reduce the reminders that bring back feelings of rage that in combat were expressed in aggression, protecting yourself by actually restricting emotions so that reminders of war are avoided, losing interest in things or people because you do not want to be reminded of or feel an attachment to others that might again be lost, and stultifying numbing in which you strive not to feel any emotions.

The third of set of symptoms consists of *physiological arousal associated with life-threatening experiences in war zones*. Physiological arousal includes difficulties in sleeping, hypervigilance (constantly fearing attack), irritability and difficulties in controlling anger and aggressive outbursts, startled responses (like overreacting to loud noises), and interferences in concentration.

All the "symptoms" listed above are, for a time, normal emotions, behaviors, and reactions, that any one may feel or act upon immediately after being traumatized. These "symptoms" are normal for anyone who goes through an event in which they conclude that they are going to die. The symptoms listed above are within the range of normal reactions to a life-threatening event—as long as "symptoms" do not persist for more than a month. It's only when these reactions continue for longer periods of time and when the symptoms drastically change your way of producing and interacting with others that they become symptoms of PTSD. The same is true of reacting to memories of combat. When reactions persist over long periods of time and result in drastic differences in how you go about living, then they become "symptoms" indicative of PTSD.

The major set of criteria that clinicians look for when classifying PTSD are avoidance behaviors. That is, a warrior is said to have PTSD when after a month the person is still socially withdrawn; inaccurately focused upon pain and bodily symptoms that are imagined but cannot be diagnosed; indulges in "binge'" drinking; experiencing "dissociative" reactions (blocking out memories of trauma by suddenly not being in touch with reality); abusing substances as ways of blocking out memories of trauma; or hurting one's self as a way of forgetting trauma.

Since the year 2000, studies have suggested that another set of symptoms need to be added as criteria for classifying PTSD—the reductions in social and occupational functioning. Many who have been traumatized in combat can socially withdraw from interacting with friends and family and give up being productive and no longer be able to or want to work. In recent research, Dohrenwend and colleagues re-interviewed many combat veterans forty years after military service in Vietnam and found that whereas the symptoms of intrusive imagery, avoidance, and emotional arousal listed above were still strong for many, the primary problems for Vietnam combat veterans (upwards of some 40 percent) were failure to be socially active and productive in work.

Means

Central to the American character is self-reliance. This is what our Declaration of Independence, our Constitution with its Bill of Rights, our laws, and our Democracy are all about—promoting self-reliance. Self-reliance is what warriors fight to protect. So the answer to the "Now what?" question is that warriors must develop the means to overcome their risks for maladies in order to achieve personal goals of life, liberty, and the pursuit of happiness that promote self-reliance.

In the final section of this chapter on psychological wounds of war, we present some examples of the means by which warriors in transition can access their resiliencies and resources to cure themselves and insure their self-reliance. Some means are found in the VA, while others are available as interactive, "manualized" treatment on Web sites that teach warriors in transition how to cure themselves. (By "manualized," we mean that training materials have been developed consisting of lessons and homework guiding individuals in techniques to learn skills to reduce symptoms of PTSD and other aspect of trauma-related disorders.) So this chapter lists some means that others have found to be effective in fostering their self-reliance. We can learn from those who have gone before what they discovered to be beneficial, as we learn from written histories about those who recovered from war. We can learn from DoD and the VA and from the books that have been published on self-help.

But only you can develop the means to overcome the risks brought about by your experiences in war. No one but you knows what you experienced, what you perceived as experiencing, and what you think about your experiences. And no one but you can learn from other war fighters who found means for problems they discovered as wars stopped and the search for peace at home started. But relying upon just yourself does not mean that you are alone. There are many who experienced events similar to what you went through, others who are available to be with you as you develop your goals to continue your life, as you learn skills to avoid risks for maladies, as you master means to defeat the war within you. You march in the tradition of "Leave No One Behind," based upon your willingness and your mastery of your skills to rely upon yourself.

DoD and the VA

The Department of Defense (DoD) and the Veterans Administration (VA) continue to develop their traditional partnership for facilitating transitions of warriors from the military to civilian living. Both DoD and the VA offer many resources that warriors can choose to access as they develop their goals in living as civilians. Below are some, but not all, of the opportunities to access means to resolve the maladies that interfere with you achieving your goals.

The Army Medical Action Plan. DoD links to the VA in many ways, including the Warrior in Transition program. When it is determined that a warrior in transition is being released from active duty, DoD will send soldiers (some on temporary duty status) to an initial clinic appointment at a VA medical facility before discharge from the military. The VA has hired hundreds of OIF/OEF program managers to insure that the first VA appointment while on active duty becomes a reality. Goals of DoD's Warrior in Transition program are to insure that active duty personnel separating from the military know firsthand about benefits to which they are entitled and know how the VA provides means to achieve goals that veterans seek. VA benefits are guaranteed by the gratitude of your fellow citizens through a contract with warriors for their service given to the nation. VA benefits are not entitlements; rather, VA benefits are what you have earned by placing your life at risk.

The VA. Structurally, the VA is comprised of two parts—the Veterans Benefits Administration (VBA), which oversees education and job training, and the Veterans Health Administration (VHA), which delivers medical and mental health services. The VA's mission is, as Abraham Lincoln stated in his second inaugural address, "[T]o care for him who shall have borne the battle, his widow and his orphan." Nearly one-third of VA employees are themselves veterans: more veterans work in the VA than in any other federal agency. This means that the VA not only is *for* veterans, but also, to a significant degree, the VA is *by* veterans. No other health-providing agency, public or private, employs as many veterans as does the VA. The VA is the federal agency most experienced in providing means for veterans to overcome their maladies from wars.

The VA has 7.6 million enrollees and provides health care benefits to more than 5.1 million veterans each year. At more than 1,300 sites of care across the nation, the VA employs nearly 200,000 specialists skilled in providing care and rehabilitation for and by veterans. The VA consists of 157 medical centers, linked to 862 ambulatory care and community-based outpatient clinics, with 142 nursing homes, forty-two residential rehabilitation programs, 207 Vet Centers, eighty-eight comprehensive home care programs, administered by twenty-one regional veterans integrated services networks (VISNs) that represent unique needs of veterans close to home. In addition, the VA has more volunteers (greater than 125,000 each year) than any other health care agency, public or private, in the United States. Many of these volunteers are veterans or relatives and friends of veterans. The VA trains more medical professionals than any other medical facility in the United States: 80,000 health care professionals are trained in the VA each year; and a total of 25,000 faculty members of medical schools and universities are affiliated with the VA. Nearly one-half of the nation's physicians will at some time during their career train in the VA or be affiliated with the VA.

DoD formed a partnership with this large VA health care system to make sure warriors are transitioned as they leave the military. As soon as warriors in transition start the medical examination board (MEB) process (see chapter five of this book), DoD will refer each soldier to the nearest veterans benefits counselor to conduct the Benefits Delivery at Discharge (BDD) services. DoD strives to insure that each person separating from the military has at least one direct contact with the VA *before discharge*. Similarly, for warriors in transition, soldiers in exiting the service (ETS) or being released from active duty (REFRAD) status are referred to the nearest veterans benefits counselor and to the VA health care facility nearest to the veteran's residence upon release. Service members who qualify for the global war on terrorism (GWOT) ribbon are assigned to coordinate with a VA OIF/OEF case manager. Comparable linkages are also arranged with TRICARE (the military's health care program) prime referrals.

And now that acronyms have been introduced into the text, the reader familiar with the military can expect the listing of federal form numbers. But we will only cite one: VA Fom 10-10EZ, the application for health benefits, available online at https://www.1010ez.med.gov/sec/vha/1010ez/, or you can call the following number to request the form: 1 (877) 222 VETS. Or you can obtain the form via mail or fax by contacting state or county veterans services officer (VSOs). You can find their numbers by looking up the local number in local phone book under "United States Offices" and the subtitle "Veterans Affairs."

Examples of VA Services: Means to Reach Goals by Resolving Maladies. The VA determines eligibility for services. For those eligible, experts are available to determine services that are needed. The VA, like DoD, invests heavily in health services research to determine which forms of treatment and rehabilitation are most effective as means to help veterans in their recovery. Examples of VA services are provided in considerable detail at the VA Web site, http://www.va.gov. Further guides to learning means to reach goals by resolving maladies can be found at the Web site for the National PTSD Center (http://www.ncptsd.org), and for research outcomes emerging from the VA's Mental Illness Research, Education, and Clinical Centers (MIRECCs) one can visit http://www.mirecc.va.gov.

The VA also has developed the means for self-help by which veterans can, in privacy, measure the extent of progressing in goals and objectives that can foster adjustment as a civilian. One is the Web-based program "My HealtheVet" and another is "My Recovery Plan". Both build upon measurement and feedback essential to determine progress in achieving one's goals for physical, psychological, and social well-being. Both My HealtheVet and My Recovery Plan are available to veterans eligible for care at http://www.myhealth.va.gov/. My HealtheVet and My Recovery Plan were both developed by VA staff in collaboration with the nation's veterans who use the VA's services. The My HealtheVet Web site measures and provides feedback about progress of actions taken to improve physical health. My Recovery Plan enables veterans to learn new skills that improve the quality of living for one's self, one's family, at work, and in the community.

Through the My HealtheVet and My Recovery Plan, theVA's specialists—working alongside the veterans who use these programs—have designed these services along lines of a recovery model that guides warriors and their families to learn how to cope with wounds of war. The VA's recovery model is based upon the President's New Freedom Commission on Mental Health in which work restoration is central (see http://www.mentalhealthcommission.gov), which mandates that the VA treat veterans with severe emotional disturbances, so that they learn "to live, work, learn, and participate fully in their communities."

As is happening throughout medical and mental health services, the VA is increasing work restoration, integrating employment rehabilitation into medical care. This idea was begun many years ago and was first inspired by Edith Nourse Rogers and the GI Bill legislation that she coauthored in 1944 and then actualized by the leadership of many psychologists who contributed to establishing mental health services in the VA. (See Dr. Baker's chapter in this book, summarizing the history of services for veterans, as well as two books by Dr. Baker listed in the selected references.) Likewise, military psychologists who moved into the private sector have continued to develop means by which those at risk for maladies can learn to overcome difficulties and achieve their goals.

As an example, more than a decade ago, Robert Drake, M.D., and his associates in New Hampshire stopped asking those with mental disorders what was wrong with them and what their disorder was. Instead, Dr. Drake turned the diagnostic process upside down, asking his patients if they were working. If the answer was no, then treatment plans were written with the primary objective to return those with mental disorders back to work. Mental health services in every state and the Veterans Health Administration are attempting to replicate this "New Hampshire model" (Drake, 1996).

This concentration upon work restoration as a central part in the treatment and rehabilitation of veterans now aligns with the latest work in the classification system used by psychiatrists—the *Diagnostic and Statistical Manual of Mental Disorders* of the American Psychiatric Association, DSM-IV-TR (2000). The latest version of the DSM now includes occupational dysfunctioning (or inability to hold down a job) as one of its criteria for all mental disorders—including PTSD. By making occupational dysfunctioning a diagnostic criterion, the DSM thereby renders unemployment and underemployment and mismatches in employment as criteria by which the success of any and all mental disorders can be assessed.

The U.S. Congress funds both DoD and the VA, and they are investing resources into determining which means work best to assure that warriors avoid the maladies and achieve their goals. They sponsor rehabilitation research, where scientists design and empirically demonstrate which rehabilitation procedures work best for veterans. These demonstrations take place by use of what are called clinical trials. Clinical trials involve randomly assigning volunteers to one of two conditions and then determining best practices based upon the identification of which treatments work best over long periods of time. (For a list of current trials, visit the Web site at http://www.Clinicaltrials.gov.) Such clinical trials would not take place unless veterans volunteer to participate in randomized clinical trials. But driven by their duty to service and to help each other, veterans distinguish themselves by the high rates at which they volunteer to participate in clinical trials. As drugs have been tested and shown to be effective, work restoration interventions have been empirically validated as effective means to reduce maladies and achieve goals to improve adjustment and quality of life in living.

Supported education is likewise important as a means to overcome maladies, an approach central to the enormous positive impact of the GI Bill after the Second World War. Returning to college and/or training is a vital means, in particular learning and upgrading skills, to increase marketability in an ever-changing job market. The U.S. military is one of the best educated workforces as a group, but, like all workforces, workforce demands are always changing and changing quickly. As a consequence, the Veteran Health Administration, with the Veterans Benefits Administration (VBA) are joining forces with DoD to improve training to upgrade the existing skills of warriors as they transition into the civilian sector and recover from the wounds of war.

Means Beyond the VA to Assuage Maladies of Wars Within

Many warriors, however, choose not to fight the war within by seeking help from those outside. This is a reality: for each soldier who signs up for services in the VA, another goes alone to other places. Those who go alone can access resources for recovery and self-improvement from many resources, some of which are outlined below and on the Web site accompanying this book at http://www.warswounded.com.

Some of the most recent means developed through research to assuage the maladies of the wars within are listed below. But we must sound a cautionary note: this chapter contains no information about medication as a treatment for the symptoms of PTSD. Without question, medication can be beneficial, as Foa, Keane, and Friedman (2000) summarize in their book. But like all methods of treatment and rehabilitation, medication is limited in the range of its benefits. The best approaches are those that combine ways to change the body, body chemistry, the mind, and behaviors, particularly behaviors that increase one's skills and investments in living. But whereas medications may produce undesirable side effects after prolonged and/or overuse, methods described here are not associated with negative outcomes when used too much and/or in large "doses."

Flannery and Lifestyle. Fifteen years ago, Raymond Benedict Flannery, Jr., Ph.D. published one of the first "self-help" books about PTSD. Dr. Flannery, an associate professor in psychiatry at Harvard Medical School, was venturing into an area new for scientist-practitioners who were developing interventions for those who had been traumatized; that is, he initiated the exploration of a new realm in treatment and rehabilitation—the willingness and capacities of people to treat themselves.

Dr. Flannery studied the lifestyles of students he was teaching in "night school," those who worked by day and took courses at night to upgrade their skills and get better jobs. Those who succeeded differed notably from those who struggled to tolerate stresses of adding the complications of schooling to their lives. Successful students were found to take more personal control over their lives; were more task focused; made wise life-style choices by reducing intake of stimulants, engaging in aerobic exercises, and learning relaxation exercises; sought and engaged in more social supports; had much better senses of humor; and opened themselves to religious experiences through which they expressed higher degrees of concerns for others and their communities. These were the main characteristics Dr. Flannery learned that differentiated those who coped with stresses of college as they worked from those who could not cope as successfully as the others. Dr. Flannery called his project for becoming stress resistant "Project SMART".

Dr. Flannery pioneered many of the methods that others now have developed and are available at numerous Web sites for self-management of symptoms associated with trauma, some or which are cited in the Web site for this book (http://www.warswounded.com).

Brett Litz and Internet-Based Interactions Addressing PTSD Symptoms. In addition to self-help books such as those written by Flannery and others, veterans proficient in the use of computers can now interact with manualized treatment interventions for PTSD at selected Web sites. Only a few of these interactive manualized approaches have been tested to determine whether the traumatized can actually learn by the Internet to reduce symptoms of PTSD. But one approach has already shown to yield positive results, and it is an Internet-based self-tutoring adaptation of cognitive behavioral therapy called DE-STRESS developed by Brett Litz and his associates at the National Center for PTSD in Boston. Dr. Litz found that Internet-based tutorials produce skills to self-manage symptoms associated with trauma-related disorders, as well as reduce symptoms. Dr. Litz's work is innovative and pioneering. He has demonstrated that Web-based approaches can be helpful to many of those traumatized who would prefer to resolve their problems on their own, particularly those who prefer privacy in struggling with their symptoms (for such reasons as believing that admitting PTSD would interfere with promotions in the military and/or those who fear stigma of being classified as mentally ill).

Central to the discoveries that Dr. Litz and his associates have made is the conclusion that interventions for PTSD and other trauma-related disorders need to be started as soon as possible. Treatment for PTSD is frequently delayed or is not started until a different kind of crisis occurs long after the original trauma. But just as Re-Set Training emphasizes the need to repair and retool as quickly as possible upon return from the hot spots in the war zone, it is likewise essential that the Re-Set Training of the body and mind begin as soon as it safe. And one of the underrated advantages of Web-based interactive treatment is that you can access such resources any time you want—no waiting in clinic offices or for an appointment three months down the road, and the Internet is there at a time of time crisis and you have privacy and confidentiality.

Martin E. P. Seligman and Positive Psychology: Growing in Character and Authentic Happiness. The techniques of positive psychology go well beyond symptom reduction associated with PTSD. The positive psychology movement concentrates on the resiliencies and the resources of warrior and not on the symptoms. The basic approach of positive psychology is for individuals to build up strengths by learning what comprises the character of a person.

Seligman and his associates at the University of Pennsylvania have developed Web sites—free for all—where they transfer technologies to strengthen aspects of character as a means to overcome maladies. Seligman recommends first self-administering by the Internet through his VIA Classification of Strengths Survey. It takes about twenty to thirty minutes to complete, and those who take the test get a printout of top character strengths as well as those used less frequently. After taking the test, you can use the results, in the form of individual profile of character strengths, as a blueprint to guide development of skills to solve problems. The Web site for the test is that of the University of Pennsylvania Positive Psychology Center at http://www.ppc.sas.upenn.edu, and the Web site for the training is the Authentic Happiness Web site, http://www.authentichappiness.com.

The Gratitude of Christopher Krebs. Proceeding with gratitude—accentuating the positives while eliminating the negatives—is how the health services research group at the Edith Nourse Rogers Veterans Memorial Hospital in Bedford, Massachusetts, proceeds in its search to discover how to recover after war. One team, led by Christopher Krebs, is experimenting with a manualized approach in which combat veterans learn how to focus, and keep their attention in daily living concentrated, upon the positives in their lives. Dr. Krebs has developed a fifteen-step program, briefly described here.

Training in accentuating the positive is built upon the ideas that the negatives of trauma are defeated by the positives of measuring on a daily basis what has gone right in life, praising the pleasures, prohibiting the pains. Measuring is at the heart of the fifteen steps: keeping a journal of events for which one is grateful, rating specific events over time and then consciously increasing activities rated as good; reminding yourself daily about your goals and keeping your priorities consciously in mind; speaking positively and optimistically to yourself, axing the negative self-speak; practicing your strengths while anticipating the troubles ahead; concentrating on doing more with others and stopping to try to get more things; taking brief vacations every day; and training oneself to see the positives and increase the pleasures in living.

Summary

These are some of the more recently developed means that can defeat the maladies of the war within yourself. Each approach capitalizes on your capacities to develop reliance upon yourself and requires practice, practice, practice essential for mastering any skills in living. Flannery shows how the traumatized can take control of their lives by starting with diet, exercises, and learning relaxation to counter anxieties while, at the same time, strengthening social interactions based upon concern for others. Litz emphasizes that memories of trauma cannot be reduced by running away; the symptoms of PTSD must be addressed by developing specific skills to reduce emotional numbness, intrusive images, and hyperarousal, constant fears that one once again will act to destroy when challenged. Seligman finds the helplessness induced by trauma can be counteracted by strengthening one's character. And Krebs says we must let go of what is negative in lives and stay focused upon the goals that bring us the most that is good about what we want and what we need.

By combining what can be learned from Flannery, Litz, Seligman, and Krebs, warriors can help themselves transition from war zones to home. Wars happen within. Peace follows when the wars within are defeated.

Bibliography

Baker, R. R. (ed.) (2007). *Stories from VA Psychology*. Bloomington, IN: Author House.

Baker, R. R., & Pickren, W. E. (2007). *Psychology and the Department of Veterans Affairs*. Washington, DC: APA Books.

Diener, E., & Seligman, M. E. P. (2004). Beyond Money: Toward an Economy of Well-Being. *Psychological Science in the Public Interest*, 5, 1–31.

Dohrenwend, B. P., Turner, J. B., Turse, N. A., Adams, B. G., Koenen, K. C., &. Marshall, R. (2006). The Psychological Risks of Vietnam for U.S. Veterans: A Revisit with New Data and Methods. *Science*, 313, 979–982.

Drake, R. E. (1996). The New Hampshire Study of Supported Employment for People with Severe Mental Illness. *Journal of Consulting and Clinical Psychology*, 64, 390–398.

Flannery, R. B. (1990). *Becoming Stress Resistant through the Project SMART*. New York: Continuum.

———. (1992). *Post-Traumatic Stress Disorder: The Victim's Guide to Healing and Recovery*. New York: Crossroad.

Foa, E., Keane, T., & Friedman, M. (eds.) (2000). *Effective Treatments for PTSD: Practice Guidelines from the International Society for Traumatic Stress Studies*. New York: Guilford Press.

Krebs, C. (2007). Starting at the Source: Fifteen Key Ways to Use Positive Psychology to Improve Your Personal and Professional Life. Paper presented at the conference on integrating positive psychology and clinical services in the Veterans Health Administration. Edith Nourse Rogers Memorial Veterans Hospital, Bedford, Massachusetts, May 9, 2007. Available at http://www.warswounded.com.

Litz, B. (ed.) (2004). *Early Intervention for Trauma and Traumatic Loss*. New York: Guilford Press.

Peterson, S., & Seligman, M. E. P. (2004). *Character Strengths and Virtues: A Handbook and Classification*. New York: Oxford University Press.

Seligman, M. E. P. (2002). *Authentic Happiness: Using the New Positive Psychology to Realize Your Potential for Lasting Fulfillment*. New York: Free Press.

Shay, Jonathan (1994). *Achilles in Vietnam: Combat Trauma and the Undoing of Character*. New York: Simon & Schuster.

Shay, Jonathan (2002). *Odysseus in America: Combat Trauma and the Trials of Homecoming*. New York: Charles Scribner's Sons.

Tanielian, T., & Jaycox, L. H. (Editors) (2008). Invisible wounds of war: Psychological and cognitive injuries, their consequences, and services to assist recovery. Santa Monica, California: RAND (MG-720-CCP).

Van der Kolk, B. A. (1994). The Body Keeps Score: Memory and the Evolving Psychobiology of Posttraumatic Stress. *Harvard Review of Psychiatry*, 1, 253–265.

Chronology

Editors' Comment

The way our nation treats service members and veterans with disabilities has evolved over time. Social factors, people's attitudes, legislative decisions, changes in the government's leadership, reevaluations of the definition of disability, and even actions and lobbying by veterans themselves have all contributed to the way that our nation thinks about and provides services to returning service members.

This chronology presents some of the important events through the centuries that have impacted veterans and service members with disabilities and shows the changes in ways that society thinks about and cares for people with disabilities. As with the first two chapters of our book, this chronology may provide you with some perspective on your own situation. It can also demonstrate how veterans and individuals with disabilities can organize themselves, protest, and influence systems of recovery in order to receive better care and improve their benefits. Finally, it demonstrates how perceptions of disabilities (and how we treat people with disabilities) have changed over time, from such extreme ideas like the euthanasia movement recommending forced sterilization (or even execution) of anyone with a physical difference sixty years ago to the rehabilitation and recovery movements of today that promote the benefits of restoration into one's community of choice.

This chronology tracks events and changes in a number of areas:

- The definition of disability has changed over time from a medical model (where the individual is "afflicted" with a physical condition) to a social model that focuses on the barriers and prejudices raised by others as the primary "disabling" variables.
- Concern for veterans has expanded to encompass the lifespan of the soldier, from the time of entry into the military to old age and death.

- Our nation's military force has become more diverse by admitting members of minority groups and women into full participation—thus also increasing the number and types of people in the groups who return home with disabilities.
- Medical understanding of psychiatric disorders (including PTSD) has changed over time and treatment for patients has improved with this understanding.
- To respond to demand, the government has created and altered agencies to serve the military's members and veterans.
- Society's understanding of the treatment of people with disabilities has changed over time, from ancient times when people with disabilities were locked away or pitied to modern times, when we emphasize the importance of restoring functioning and providing services, so that those with disabilities can again become active in their homes and communities.
- Because of changes in accessible technologies and the way we think about disabilities and work, employment has become an option for more people with more types of disabilities.
- Improvements in field medicine and protective devices have increased the percentage age of people who are able to survive after injuries in battles. With higher rates of service members returning home alive, even more are coming back with disabilities. According to data provided by the Department of Defense and summarized in Chapter 2, the casualty to death ratio was 1:1 during the Civil War (for every person injured in the war, another person died), but now during the current conflict the ratio is 9:1 (which means only one person is killed, but nine people return home and many more return home with serious injuries, some of which would have killed the individual in previous conflicts).
- Veterans of past wars (and family members) have created organizations to serve veterans of current wars. At the same time, people with disabilities have formed organizations and have been able to lobby and protest for better conditions.
- Psychiatric conditions are losing their stigma over time, and treatment for psychiatric patients in hospitals has improved as the movement to deinstitutionalize individuals with psychiatric disabilities has intensified. Individuals with these conditions organize to make their voices heard to alert the public to their situation and to lobby for better treatment and conditions.
- A number of laws have been passed to improve the situation of people with disabilities in this nation.

Chronology of Veterans and Disabilities

3500–1800 BC

The first written account of a prosthesis for a war injury appears in the *Rig-Veda*, a collection of sacred hymns of India. In it, Queen Vishpla loses a leg in battle but returns to fight after she is fitted with an iron replacement. Such stories from long ago underscore for us today the tradition of preserving the functioning of those who take part in battles.

1210 BC

The first recorded workplace accommodation of a disability is offered, as Aaron is selected by the burning bush to speak on behalf of Moses (who has a speech disability), to approach Pharaoh and lead the Israelites out of Egypt.

400 BC

Greek physician Hippocrates begins to treat mental disorders as diseases of physiology rather than as reflections of the displeasure of the gods or as if the person were possessed by a demon (which is how the disorders were previously seen).

218 BC

After sustaining twenty-three injuries and losing his right arm in battle, Roman General Marcus Sergius has an iron hand made so he can hold up his shield and return to the fight. Although he was honored for his success in battle with his prosthesis, he was denied the chance to participate in the religious sacrifices because one needed to have two normal hands to take part in the ceremonies.

1592–1593

The English Parliament passes "An Acte for the Reliefe of Souldiours" to provide benefits to the soldiers and sailors who helped the British defeat the Spanish Armada.

1636

In what will become the state of Massachusetts, the Pilgrims of Plymouth Colony pass a law stating that soldiers maimed in the course of battle will be maintained by the colony for the rest of their lives.

1670

King Louis XIV establishes the Hôtel des Invalides to care for aged and disabled soldiers of the French Army.

1696

Dutch surgeon Pieter Andriannszoon Verduyn introduces the first nonlocking below-the-knee prosthesis that resembles those that are still used today.

1749

In America, a hospital for sick soldiers is founded in Charlestown, South Carolina.

1752

Pennsylvania Hospital is established in Philadelphia to provide care for all veterans.

1775–1783

Almost 217,000 American service members fight in the War for Indepedence. A total of 4,435 are killed in battle, and 6,188 are wounded in the fighting.

1776

To encourage people to serve in the War for Independence, the Continental Congress creates America's first pension law by granting half-pay for a disability. But because the Congress did not have the authority or money, the actual payments were left to the states. Few veterans received the pensions.

1798

President Adams signs an act for the relief of sick and disabled seamen.

With the ratification of the Constitution, the first Congress assumes the burden of paying benefits to veterans.

1801

Dr. Philippe Pinel of France (the man considered to be the father of modern psychiatry) publishes his book *Traité médico-philosophique sur l'aleniation mentale; ou la manie (Medical-Philosophical Treatise on Mental Alienation or Mania)*, beginning the modern understanding and treatment of mental illness. Based on his theories, he advocates for the humane treatment of people with mental illness.

1812

Dr. Benjamin Rush publishes *Medical Inquiries and Observations upon the Diseases of the Mind* and becomes one of the first American physicians to classify mental illness through the medical model and suggest appropriate treatments based on this analysis.

1812–1815

Almost 286,730 American service members fight in the War of 1812, out of which 2,260 are killed in battle, and 4,505 are wounded in the fighting.

1817–1898 (approximately)

The Indian Wars see 106,000 American service members fight, and 1,000 (estimated) are killed in battle.

1818

The Service Pension Law now provides pensions to any veteran needing assistance and not just those with disabilities. (The pension rates are $20 per month for officers and $8 per month for enlisted service members.)

1833

The Bureau of Pensions is established to oversee payments to veterans and is the first administrative unit of the national government dedicated solely to providing assistance to veterans.

1846–1848

Approximately 78,718 American service members fight in the Mexican War, out of which 1,733 are killed in battle, 11,550 are killed in theater but not in battle, and 4,152 are wounded in the fighting.

1848–1854

Social reformer Dorothea Dix lobbies for a plan for a federal land grant of 12,500,000 acres to be set aside as a public endowment to support the deaf, mute, and mentally ill. Congress passes the legislation and President Millard Fillmore favors the idea. But because the bill does not reach Fillmore's desk before the end of his term, in 1854 President Franklin Pierce vetoes it.

1851

The U.S. Soldiers' Home is established in the Washington, DC, area to provide care for veterans. This facility is funded by contributions from the military.

1855

St. Elizabeth's Hospital opens in Washington, DC, as the first major medical care system for veterans with mental disorders.

1858

Congress authorizes half-pay pensions to the widows and orphans of veterans.

1861–1865

The American Civil War is fought, and 2,213,363 service members serve in the Union forces, of which 140,414 are killed in battle, 224,097 die in theater of other causes, and 281,881 are wounded. On the Confederate side (and these numbers are approximate), 1,050,000 service members serve in uniform, 74,524 are killed in battle, 59,297 are killed in theater of other causes, around 30,000 die in Union prisons, and the number wounded is unknown.

1862

The Veterans Reserve Corps is created by the U.S. Army to allow disabled and infirm soldiers the chance to serve and perform light duty, so that other soldiers can fight on the front lines.

The General Pension Act provides for payments based on rank and the degree of disability and also covers military service in times of peace as well as war. For the first time diseases (such as tuberculosis), incurred while in service are covered by pensions.

Union Army veterans are assigned a special priority in the Homestead Act and are given western lands at the cost of $1.25 per acre.

1865

In his second inaugural address, President Lincoln calls upon Congress "to care for him who shall have borne the battle and for his widow, and his orphan." This phrase later becomes the mission statement of Veterans Administration.

Following the Civil War, 1.9 million Union Army soldiers are now veterans. Confederate soldiers are not included in these numbers and are not able to receive federal veterans benefits for more than a hundred years. (In 1958 Congress pardons Confederate service members and extends benefits to the last living Confederate veteran.) State governments, however, create facilities to serve needs of Confederate soldiers.

Union veterans of the war organize the Grand Army of the Republic, the largest veterans organization at the time, to represent their concerns.

To care for the large number of returning Civil War soldiers with disabilities, Congress establishes the National Asylum for Disabled Volunteer Soldiers. (The name is changed to the National Home for Disabled Volunteer Soldiers in 1873).

1873

The Consolidation Act revises pension legislation, so that veterans are now paid based on the degree of their disability rather than their service rank. The

Act also allows disabled veterans to hire nurses and housekeepers to help them at home.

1881

In the novel *A Study in Scarlet* by Sir Arthur Conan Doyle, Dr. John H. Watson is injured in Afghanistan fighting with the British Army. He returns to London with a medical disability pension to look for affordable housing. A friend introduces him to the detective Sherlock Holmes (who is looking for a roommate to share his apartment and housing costs) and thus begins a lifelong friendship and a series of remarkable adventures.

1883

The term "eugenics" is coined by Sir Francis Galton of England to describe ways of "improving the stock" of humanity by removing those with imperfections and disabilities. In America, the eugenics movement is used as the basis to pass legislation to prevent people with disabilities from moving into the country, marrying, or having children. In many cases, it is used as the legal basis for institutionalization and forced sterilization of people with disabilities.

1890

The Dependent Pension Act is passed, increasing the scope of eligibility and providing pensions to veterans incapable of manual labor.

In Germany Friederich Golz creates the idea of using surgery to improve mental health by conducting the first lobotomy by removing portions of his dogs' temporal lobes to make them less aggressive. Gottlieb Burkhardt, the head of a Swiss mental institution, soon attempts similar surgeries on six of his human schizophrenic patients. Two die from the procedure.

1898–1902

A total of 306,760 American service members fight in the Spanish–American War, out of which 385 are killed in battle, 1,662 are wounded in the fighting, and 2,061 die in nonbattle deaths not in theater.

The United Spanish War Veterans group is founded.

1908

Clifford Beers publishes *A Mind That Found Itself: An Autobiography*, exposing the conditions inside state and private mental institutions, illustrating what it is like to have a mental condition, and calling for the reform of mental health care in America. Within a year, he spearheads the founding of the National Committee for Mental Hygiene, an education and advocacy group, which later evolves into the National Mental Health Association.

1912

The Sherwood Act awards pensions to all veterans of the U.S.–Mexican War and Union veterans of the Civil War automatically at the age of sixty-two.

1913

The Veterans of Foreign Wars group is founded. Ex-military members voluntarily create groups to advocate for veterans in the states and to obtain federal services.

1917–1918

World War I sees 4,734,991 American service members fight, out of which 53,402 are killed in battle, 204,002 are wounded in the fighting, and 63,114 die in nontheater service.

1917

The War Risk Insurance Act is amended to establish courses of rehabilitation and vocational training for veterans with disabilities.

1918

The Smith-Sear Veterans Vocational Rehabilitation Act establishes a federal vocational rehabilitation program for disabled soldiers.

1920

The Fess-Smith Civilian Vocational Rehabilitation Act establishes a vocational rehabilitation program for disabled civilians.

1921

The U.S. Veterans' Bureau is created by Congress to consolidate the functions of the Bureau of War Risk Insurance and the Public Health Service. Also providing benefits are the Bureau of Pensions and the National Homes for Disabled Volunteer Soldiers.

1922

The War Risk Insurance Act of 1914 is amended again to provide hospital care to veterans with psychiatric diseases and tuberculosis. Two years later, it is amended again to provide hospital care for veterans without battle-caused injuries.

1924

Congress passes the World War Adjusted Act to provide bonuses to the veterans based on the number of days they were in service. But payments above $50 are not paid to the veterans for another twenty years. This delay leads to the "Bonus March" of 1932.

1927

In *Buck v. Bell*, the U.S. Supreme Court rules that the forced sterilization of people with disabilities is not a violation of their constitutional rights. More than 63,000 people are sterilized in the United States without their consent between 1921 and 1964.

1930

Consolidating three existing agencies into one basic administrative federal structure, the Veterans Administration is created. President Hoover signs the executive order establishing the agency on July 21.

1932

Approximately 15,000 to 40,000 veterans march across the country to Washington, DC in the "Bonus March" to protest the delay in distributing the bonuses promised to them in 1924. Responding to the march, Congress authorizes the payment of the bonuses in 1936.

The Disabled American Veterans group is chartered by Congress to represent veterans with disabilities in their interactions with the government.

1933

Franklin Delano Roosevelt is sworn in as the first American president with a serious physical disability but chooses a "splendid deception" not to inform the nation about his disability. The White House and other buildings in Washington are made wheelchair accessible for the new president.

During his first year in office, President Roosevelt persuades Congress to pass the Economy Act that radically reduces veterans' benefits. When the president's authority to establish benefits by executive order expires in 1935, Congress votes to put back in place most of the benefits awarded to the veterans.

1935

The League for the Physically Handicapped is formed in New York to protest discrimination in the federal government's New Deal Works Progress Administration (WPA). It also engages in sit-down strikes for the right to work and arranges meetings with officials of the Roosevelt administration to discuss these issues.

In France Dr. Alexis Carrel (a winner of the Nobel Prize) publishes *L'Homme, cet inconnu* (*Man the Unknown*) advocating the improvement of the human race through a regime of forced eugenics and the use of gas chambers to rid humanity of "inferior stock."

1936

The first prefrontal lobotomy is performed in America by psychiatrist Walter Freeman (who does not have any surgical training). He invents the "ice pick lobotomy" by literally ramming an ice pick through the patient's skull to cut apart the brain. From 1939 to 1951 over 18,000 lobotomies are performed in the United States and thousands more around the world. Over time, the effectiveness of the procedure is questioned and many states and countries ban the procedure.

1938

In an attempt to treat schizophrenia, doctors first use electroshock therapy to induce convulsions in patients.

1939

Adolph Hitler creates *Aktion T4*, the Nazi policy of "racial hygiene" and orders the government and the medical community to eliminate "life unworthy of life." Between 75,000 and 250,000 people with disabilities are killed from 1939 to 1941. Hitler officially suspends the policy in 1941, but the euthanasia program quietly continues through drugs rather than gas chambers.

1940

The American Federation of the Physically Handicapped is founded as the country's first disability-oriented national political organization. It calls for an end to job discrimination for people with disabilities as it lobbies for a number of initiatives including legislation for a "National Employ the Physically Handi-capped Week."

Congress passes the Selective Training and Service Act, creating the nation's first peacetime draft, and guarantees redeployment rights to any service member who leaves a job to join the military.

1941–1945

World War II has 16,112,566 American service members fight, out of which 291,557 are killed in battle, 671,846 are wounded in the fighting, and 113,842 die in nontheater service.

1942

Henry Viscardi begins working as an American Red Cross volunteer at Walter Reed Army Medical Center in Washington, DC, training disabled soldiers on how to use their prosthetic limbs. But the Red Cross and military terminate the pro-gram despite the protests of First Lady Eleanor Roosevelt and other supporters of the program.

1943

Congress passes the LaFollette-Barden Act (the Vocational Rehabilitation Amendments) to add physical rehabilitation to the goals of federally funded vo-cational rehabilitation programs.

1944

Howard Rusk is assigned to the U.S. Army Air Force Convalescent Center in Pawling, New York and begins a rehabilitation program for disabled airmen. Rehabilitation medicine becomes a new medical specialty.

The GI Bill (Servicemen's Readjustment Act, Public Law 78-346) is passed, under the leadership of Edith Nourse Rogers from Lowell, Massachusetts. The bill provides a way to fund the health, educational, and employment needs of veterans.

1945

The Blinded Veterans Association (BVA) is formed in Avon, Connecticut.

President Harry Truman signs Public Law 176, a joint congressional reso-lution calling for the creation of an annual National Employ the Handicapped Week.

1946

VA policy (Memorandum Number 2) creates affiliations with medical schools. In subsequent years, the VA will train (at least partially) nearly half of all American physicians (as well as physicians from other nations).

The National Mental Health Foundation is created by conscientious objectors who served as attendants at state mental institutions during World War II. They work to expose abusive conditions at these facilities. Their work becomes an early impetus in the push for deinstitutionalization of individuals with psychiatric illnesses.

The VA establishes (through Public Law 79-293) the Department of Medicine and Surgery, thus creating professional departments to provide medical care to veterans.

President Harry Truman signs the National Mental Health Act, calling for the creation of the National Institute of Mental Health to conduct research to reduce mental illness.

1946

General Omar Bradley, the Director of VA Medicine, reports that the VA is operating ninety-seven hospitals with a total bed capacity of 82,241 patients with facilities for another 13,594 beds under construction. But because of the conclusion of World War II, the nation now has over 15 million veterans on its rolls and hospitals filled to capacity with long waiting lists.

1947

The Department of Defense (DoD) is formed, combining into one agency the War Department (founded in 1789) and the Navy Department (founded in 1780). Some of the regulations instituted by the new agency include initial efforts to racially integrate the military forces.

Congress passes the Navy–Army Services Integration Act, bringing women into permanent staff positions in the regular Navy and Army as officers.

The Paralyzed Veterans of America (PVA) organization is created to represent and advocate the needs of veterans with disabilities.

The first meeting of the President's Committee on National Employ the Physically Handicapped Week is held in Washington, DC. Its publicity campaigns emphasize the competence of people with disabilities with the statement "It is good business to hire the handicapped."

1948

Congress passes the Women's Armed Services Integration Act. Women are now eligible to serve in regular active peacetime forces. The law specifies that up to 2 percent of the nation's total force should be made up of women.

1950–1953

There were a total of 5,720,000 American service members during the Korean War. Records were not kept on the number who actually served in Korea, but 33,741 are killed in battle with an additional 2,833 killed in theater from other causes, 103,284 are wounded in the fighting, and 17,672 die in nontheater service.

1950

The Vocational Rehabilitation Act is passed to provide vocational rehabilitation services to veterans of the Korean War While extending this benefit to other veterans as well.

1952

The President's Committee on National Employ the Physically Handicapped Week becomes the President's Committee on Employment of the Physically Handicapped, a permanent organization reporting to the president and Congress.

1953

Reacting to the overwhelming demand for benefits, the VA establishes the Department of Veterans Benefits as a separate agency apart from the VA Department of Medicine and Surgery to manage the disabilities, education, and training of veterans.

1954

Congress passes the Vocational Rehabilitation Amendments, authorizing federal grants to expand programs available to people with physical disabilities.

1956

Congress passes the Medical Care Act, allowing DoD to provide health care to dependents of military service members.

Congress also passes Social Security Amendments to create the Social Security Disability Insurance (SSDI) program for disabled workers between the ages of fifty and sixty-four.

1958

New legislation adds a research component to VA treatment services, beginning a process to provide methods for financing research into the effectiveness of prosthetic devices, pharmacotherapy, and psychosocial interventions for veterans.

Congress passes Social Security Amendments to extend Social Security Disability Insurance benefits to the dependents of disabled workers.

1960

Congress passes Social Security Amendments to eliminate the restriction that disabled workers receiving Social Security Disability Insurance benefits need to be fifty or older.

1961

The American National Standard Institute, Inc., publishes specifications for making buildings accessible to physically handicapped individuals.

Psychiatrist Thomas Szasz's book *The Myth of Mental Illness* and sociologist Erving Goffman's book *Asylums* are published. In the latter, Goffman suggests that psychotic symptoms are a direct result of the effects of hospitalization.

1962

The President's Committee on Employment of the Physically Handicapped is renamed the President's Committee on Employment of the Handicapped, reflecting its increased interest in employment issues affecting people with cognitive disabilities and mental illness.

Ken Kesey publishes his novel *One Flew Over the Cuckoo's Nest* based on his experiences working in the psychiatric ward of a VA hospital. Kesey suggests that rather than having mental illness, his patients behaved in ways that society could not accept and were institutionalized. In 1975, the book is made into an Oscar-winning movie starring Jack Nicholson and generates discussions about the treatment of mental illness across the country.

1963

President Kennedy, in an address to Congress, calls for a reduction, "over a number of years and by hundreds of thousands" of individuals with mental illness confined to residential institutions. He asks that methods be found "to retain in and return to the community the mentally ill and mentally retarded, and there to restore and revitalize their lives through better health programs and strengthened educational and rehabilitation services." The president has a personal connection to this issue—his sister, Rosemary, is diagnosed with mental illness and at the age of twenty-three and has a lobotomy that leaves her incapacitated for the rest of her life.

Congress passes the Mental Retardation Facilities and Community Mental Health Centers Construction Act to provide the first source of federal money to develop a network of community-based mental health services.

1964

Congress passes Civil Rights Acts, protecting all U.S. citizens against discrimination.

1964–1975

The number of American service members is 8,744,000 during the Vietnam War period (out of which 3,403,000 are deployed to Southeast Asia). A recorded 47,424 are killed in battle, 10,785 are killed in theater from other causes, 153,303 are wounded in the fighting, and 32,000 die in nontheater service.

1965

The Vocational Rehabilitation Amendments are passed, authorizing the federal government to construct rehabilitation centers, expanding existing vocational rehabilitation programs, and creating the National Commission on Architectural Barriers to Rehabilitation of the Handicapped.

1966

Christmas in Purgatory by Burton Blatt and Fred Kaplan is published, documenting the appalling conditions at state institutions for people with developmental disabilities.

Legislation adds education to VA's treatment services through the Veterans Hospitalization and Medical Service Modernization Act (Public Law 89-785). The VA becomes one of the largest educational providers among federal government agencies.

Congress passes the Veterans' Readjustment Benefits Act ("The Vietnam GI Bill") to restore educational benefits to veterans. About 76 percent of Vietnam veterans eligible for these benefits participate in the program, compared to 51 percent of WWII veterans and 43 percent of Korean War veterans.

Congress creates CHAMPUS (Civilian Health and Medical Program of the Uniformed Services), a federally funded health program to provide military retirees with medical care as part of their treatment and recovery.

1967

The Women's Armed Services Integration Act is revised, removing the 2 percent limit and the existing promotion caps for women in the armed forces.

1968

The Architectural Barriers Act is passed, mandating that buildings and facilities constructed with federal funds be made accessible to people with physical disabilities.

1970

Congress passes the Urban Mass Transportation Assistance Act, declaring it a "national policy that elderly and handicapped persons have the same right as other persons to utilize mass transportation facilities and services." Passage of the act has little impact, however, as the law contains no provision for enforcement.

1971

Congress passes the Javits-Wagner-O'Day Act (JWOD) to mandate that federal government agencies purchase services and supplies from nonprofits employing the blind and the disabled.

The VA holds a series of conferences to alert leaders of VA centers about the special needs of Vietnam veterans and to discuss ways to improve the care of these veterans.

The automatic discharge for pregnancy is removed from the military's legislation and the Air Force becomes the first military agency to recruit women with children.

Congress creates a program to provide mortgage life insurance for severely disabled veterans for specially adapted housing to accommodate their disabilities.

1972

The Supreme Court removes differences between men and women with regard to dependent's benefits in the military.

The Center for Independent Living (CIL) is founded in Berkeley, California, creating the worldwide independent living movement.

1973

The draft ends as the Selective Service Act expires.

Congress passes Rehabilitation Act Amendments and establishes laws to guarantee rights to people with disabilities. Section 504 of this law states that "no otherwise qualified individual with a disability in the United States . . . shall, solely by reason of her or his disability, be excluded from the participation in, be denied the benefits of, or be subjected to discrimination under any program or activity receiving Federal financial assistance or under any program or activity" conducted by the government. Litigation arising out of Section 504 generates such central disability rights concepts as "reasonable modification," "reasonable accommodation," and "undue burden."

The first handicap parking stickers are introduced in Washington, DC.

1974

Women aviators in the U.S. Army become eligible for flying noncombat aircraft.

1975

The U.S. Supreme Court, in *O'Connor v. Donaldson*, rules that people cannot be institutionalized against their will in a psychiatric hospital, unless it is determined that they are a threat to themselves or to others.

1976

All of the military academies now open to women.

The passage of the amendment to the Higher Education Act of 1972 provides services to physically disabled students entering college.

1977

President Jimmy Carter appoints Max Cleland to head the US Veterans Administration, making Cleland the first severely disabled person to head the agency.

The White House Conference on Handicapped Individuals brings together 3,000 people with disabilities, their advocates, and disability policy and rehabilitation specialists to discuss federal policy toward people with disabilities.

The post-Vietnam era Veterans' Educational Assistance Act (VEAP) is established to match the contributions that service members put aside for their education.

1978

Handicapping America by Frank Bowe is published. The book reviews the policies and attitudes denying equal citizenship to people with disabilities and becomes a standard text of the disability rights movement.

Congress and federal courts continue to remove all barriers to women in the military and allow them to fully serve in combat.

1979

Congress authorizes the establishment of the Readjustment Counseling Service and its Vietnam Veterans Readjustment Counseling Program (Public Law 96-22) to create treatment units outside of medical centers in neighborhoods and communities in cities and towns across the nation.

The Supreme Court upholds the constitutionality of excluding women in the draft and selective service registration. Such legislation opens up opportunities for women to volunteer for military service but does not extend the conscription process for military service to women.

The National Alliance for the Mentally Ill (a support and advocacy organization) is created to provide support, education, advocacy, and research services for people with mental illness.

1980

DoD issues directives for the rehabilitation of military personnel with alcohol and drug abuse issues. Congress also creates Geriatric Research, Education, and Clinical Centers (GRECC's) to provide better care for older veterans.

1983

Congress passes legislation establishing the Secretary of Veterans Affairs Advisory Committee on Women Veterans. The same year, women in the U.S. military participate in the invasion of Grenada.

The Emergency Veterans' Job Training Act creates a new way to help veterans obtain and maintain employment by reimbursing employers for training costs incurred by veterans.

1984

The Voting Accessibility for the Elderly and Handicapped Act is passed, mandating that polling places be accessible or ways be found to enable elderly and disabled people to exercise their right to vote. Advocates find the act difficult, if not impossible, to enforce.

The Veterans' Educational Assistance Act (The Montgomery GI Bill) is passed by Congress to provide educational benefits to veterans. The Montgomery GI Bill is a replacement for the original GI Bill passed in 1944.

1986

The Air Carrier Access Act is passed, prohibiting airlines from refusing to serve people simply because they are disabled and from charging them more airfare than nondisabled travelers.

The National Council on the Handicapped issues "Toward Independence," a report outlining the legal status of Americans with disabilities, documenting the existence of discrimination, and citing the need for federal civil rights legislation.

The Employment Opportunities for Disabled Americans Act is passed, allowing recipients of Supplemental Security Income and Social Security Disability Insurance to retain benefits—particularly medical coverage—even after obtaining employment. The act is intended to remove the disincentives that keep disabled people unemployed.

Congress makes a significant change to the way that health care eligibility is determined for veterans by establishing eligibility assessment procedures based on veterans' income. Congress also mandates VA health care for veterans with service-connected disabilities and veterans with low incomes (and other special categories).

The National Alliance for Research on Schizophrenia and Depression is created by advocates for people with mental illness to help in the research for treatments and cures for schizophrenia and depression.

1988

President Reagan responds to requests to elevate the VA to cabinet-level status as the Veterans Administration becomes the Department of Veterans Affairs. The VA is now the largest federal agency in budget (and the second largest to DoD in the number of employees). One-third of the nation's population is now eligible for veteran's benefits. As a cabinet-level agency, the VA director now has direct access to the president.

The Fair Housing Amendments Act is passed by Congress to amend the Fair Housing Act (Title VIII of the Civil Rights Act of 1968) to increase housing opportunities for people with disabilities.

1989

The VA is reorganized. The medical treatment section is renamed the Veterans Health Administration, and the benefits section is now called the Veterans Benefits Administration.

Responding to the large number of veterans reporting symptoms of PTSD, the VA creates the National Center for PTSD to study and make recommendations on the treatment of mental illness.

The President's Committee on Employment of the Handicapped is renamed the President's Committee on Employment of People with Disabilities.

1990

Congress passes and President George Bush signs the Americans with Disabilities Act to protect people with disabilities from discrimination in the areas covered by employment, public services and public transportation, public accommodations, commercial facilities, and telecommunications.

The Computer/Electronic Accommodations Program (CAP) is created by DoD to provide electronic and computer technology to DoD employees with disabilities. It is later extended to the employees of other federal agencies.

1990–1991

During the Desert Shield/Desert Storm war period, 2,322,000 Americans are service members (and 694,550 are deployed to the Gulf), out of which 147 are killed in battle, 235 are killed in theater from other causes, 467 are wounded in the fighting, and 1,590 die in nontheater service.

A total of 40,789 women participate in the military in the Gulf War (13% of the force). Thirteen women are killed in action, and two female service members are captured.

1991

The Persian Gulf Conflict Supplemental Authorization and Personnel Benefits Act extends pensions, medical treatment, educational benefits, and other programs to veterans of the Gulf War.

1992

Congress passes legislation to create DoD/VA affiliations to form Defense and Veterans Brain Injury Centers. This legislation increases clinical, research, and teaching services for veterans with Traumatic Brain Injury (TBI) in response to heightened numbers of military returning with symptoms of TBI.

The Veterans Home Loan Program Amendments authorizes the VA to improve its benefits to allow more veterans to own their own homes.

1993

Congress changes CHAMPUS to TRI-CARE, increasing the scope of medical services for service members and veterans and their families.

1993–1996

DoD removes obstacles, allowing women to enter more than 260,000 positions in the military that were previously closed to them.

1994

The VA opens the Center for Women Veterans as the number of women serving in the military is expanded. The VA also opens the Center for Minority Veterans.

In response to "Gulf War Syndrome", Congress authorizes compensation to veterans with chronic disabilities from undiagnosed illnesses if the symptoms began during the service member's time in the Gulf.

1996

Senator Robert Dole becomes the first person with a visible disability since Franklin Roosevelt to run for president of the United States. Unlike Roosevelt, he publicly acknowledges the extent of his disability.

Georgia voters elect disabled candidate (and former head of the VA) Max Cleland to the Senate.

1997

The VA creates three Mental Illness Research, Education, and Clinical Centers (MIRECCs) that become the first centers within VA medical centers to focus research on the diagnosis and treatment of mental health disorders beyond PTSD and geriatric disorders.

DoD writes directives to revise the requirements for mental health evaluations among the military, which include redevelopment of resources for such goals as military fitness-for-duty evaluations.

Congress adds Section 508 to extend the 1973 Rehabilitation Act to include airports, colleges and universities, public libraries, playgrounds, band programs, special programs and assemblies, field trips, clubs, afterschool programs, and summer programs to the list of programs that must provide accommodations for disabilities.

2000

DoD develops OSCAR (Operational Stress Control and Readiness) to improve the range of mental health services provided in the military by focusing on operations, keeping services within units, using peer counselors, and adding prevention services.

2001

The President's Committee on Employment of People with Disabilities is closed, and its resources are transferred to the new Office on Disability Employment Policy, an agency of the Department of Labor.

2005

Congress passes legislation to enable the VA to create four regional polytrauma centers to coordinate rehabilitative care for veterans of the War on Terrorism and their family members.

On July 21, the VA commemorates its seventy-fifth anniversary. The agency has grown from an initial operating budget of $786 million serving 4.6 million veterans to a current budget of $63.5 billion and 25 million veterans served.

2006

The VA hires a hundred recently returned veterans to inform other returning service members about the services available to help them cope with the stress of combat.

2007

The John Warner Defense Authorization Act removes governors as the sole commanders of National Guard units within each state. The legislation increases the possibility of National Guard and Reserve members being activated by Presidential Executive Orders and is likely to expand the amount of time and the locations to which Guard and Reserve can be called to serve.

Present

Operation Enduring Freedom/Operation Iraqi Freedom is underway. As of January 2008 approximately 1.7 million U.S. troops have been deployed, and nearly 4,000 American service members have been killed in these conflicts; almost 30,000 have been listed as wounded, and reports suggest that close to 20% of service members are returning with psychological and mental health issues, and around 20% have traumatic brain injuries. Estimates suggest that possibly only half of these returning service members and veterans will seek help for these conditions.

Women make up 11% of the total fighting force. More than 80% of the military's positions and 90% of career fields in the military are now open to women. As a result, more women are being exposed to more types of combat experiences and are being disabled in numbers never before seen in America's history

The Future

The trends illustrated in this chronology are likely to continue: not only will the DoD and VA need to treat a wider and more diverse group of professionals in the military and veterans with physical and psychological trauma-related disorders, but they will also need to focus their efforts to help the wounded who wish to continue service in the military, or those who leave military services, supporting the wounded veterans' efforts to contribute to their families and their communities.

Bibliography

In addition to the first two chapters of this book ("Benefits for Veteran: A Historical Context and Overview of the Current Situation" by Rodney R. Baker and "Current Veteran Demographics and Implications for Veterans' Health Care" by Ann M. Hendricks and Jomana H. Amara), the following materials were used to create this chronology:

Baker, R. R. & Pickren, W. E. (2007). *Psychology and the Department of Veteran Affairs: A Historical Analysis of Training, Research, Practice, and Advocacy*. Washington, DC.

Baker, R. R. (ed.) (2007). *Stories from VA Psychology*. Bloomington, IN: Authorhouse.

A Chronology of the Disability Rights Movements. Downloaded from the Disability Programs and Resource Center at San Francisco State University, http://www.sfsu.edu/~Ehrdpu/chron.htm (retrieved April 24, 2008).

The Disability History Timeline. Downloaded from the Disability Social History Project. Downoladed from http://www.disabilityhistory.org/timeline_new.html (retrieved April 24, 2008).

Penk, W. E., Drebing, C., & Schutt, R. (2002). PTSD in the workplace. In J. C. Thomas and M. Hersen (eds.), *Handbook of Mental Health in the Workplace*. Thousand Oaks, CA: Sage.

Ralph, J. A., M. T. Sammons (2006). Future Directions in Military Psychology. In C. H. Kennody and E. A. Zillmer (eds.), *Military Psychology: Clinical and Operational Applications*. New York: Guilford.

Tanielian, T. L. & Jaycox, L. H. (eds). (2008). Invisible wounds of war: Psychological and Cognitive Injuries, Their Consequences, and Services To Assist Recovery. Santa Monica, CA: RAND Corporation. Downloaded from http://rand.org/pubs/monographs/MG720/ (retrieved May 23, 2008).

Timeline: Treatments for Mental Illness. Downloaded from http://www.pbs.org/wgbh/amex/nash/timeline (retrieved April 24, 2008).

Veterans Administration. *Fact Sheet: America's Wars*. Downloaded from http://www1.va.gov/opa/fact/amwars.asp (retrieved April 24, 2008).

Veterans Administration. *VA History in Brief*, http://www1.va.gov/opa/feature/history/index.asp (retrieved April 24, 2008).

Index

About the Editors
and Contributors

NATHAN D. AINSPAN, Ph.D., is an industrial psychologist in the Washington, DC, area. He has researched and written on improving the situation of employment for people with disabilities and returning service members and veterans with disabilities for a number of years. He worked for the Office of Disability Employment Policy at the Department of Labor in Washington, DC, and has conducted research and presentations along with seminars and workshops in these areas. His research interests have focused on understanding the symptoms and treatment of PTSD, using employment as a form of positive psychology, and the impact and effect of disabilities on the friends, family members, and supporters of veterans and returning service members.

JOMANA H. AMARA, Ph.D., is an assistant professor of economics at the Defense Resources Management Institute and Naval Postgraduate School in Monterey, California. Her areas of expertise include international economics, time series econometrics, defense economics, health economics, and the economics of the public sector. Her current projects include the economics of IED (improvised explosive devices) networks and reducing the energy footprint: methods, costs, and benefits. Working with Dr. Ann Hendricks (her coauthor for her chapter in this book), she has written about the impact of the OEF/OIF conflicts on the VA health services and is continuing her research of differences related to deployment.

RODNEY R. BAKER, Ph.D., began his forty-year VA career as a trainee at the VA Medical Center in Tucson, Arizona, in 1964. He continued as an intern at the West Haven, Connecticut, VA Medical Center. His first psychology staff position was at the Houston VA Medical Center in 1968. He became chief of psychology at the VA Medical Center in San Antonio in 1977 and served in that role until his retirement from the VA in 2004, also serving the last four years as director of the mental health service line. After retirement he continued to serve in leadership training and consultation roles for the VA. He has written extensively on the history of the treatment of veterans and about the history of the VA, including the books *Psychology and the Department of Veterans Affairs* and *Stories from VA Psychology*.

MARK J. BATES, Ph.D., is a licensed clinical psychologist and an active duty lieutenant colonel in the United States Air Force. He is currently the training director at one of the three Air Force clinical psychology internship programs at Malcolm Grow Medical Center at Andrews Air Force Base outside Washington, DC. His past psychology positions include serving as the director of an Air Force mental health clinic, where he oversaw outpatient mental health, family advocacy, and substance abuse prevention and treatment services.

STEPHEN V. BOWLES, Ph.D., is a licensed clinical psychologist and active duty Lieutenant Colonel in the United States Army. He is currently an assistant professor and director at the Division of Military Psychology and Leadership at the Uniformed Services University Health Sciences F. Edward Hébert School of Medicine. He served as Joint Task Force Command psychologist in Iraq and as the interim chief and deputy chief of psychology interim chief at Walter Reed Army Medical Center. He has been awarded the Army surgeon general "A" proficiency designator for his contributions in service to the nation as a health care professional in the military.

JAINE DARWIN, Psy.D., is a psychologist and psychoanalyst and a founder and codirector of SOFAR (Strategic Outreach to Families of All Reservists), a pro bono mental health project that provides free psychological support, psychotherapy, and psychoeducation and prevention services to the extended families of National Guard and Reserve members. She is a also a clinical instructor in psychology with the department of psychiatry at the Harvard Medical School as well as a faculty member of the Massachusetts Institute for Psychoanalysis. In addition, she is a clinical supervisor at the Victims of Violence Program at the Cambridge Health Alliance and also maintains a private practice in Cambridge, Masachussetts.

SHIRLEY M. GLYNN, Ph.D., is a clinical research psychologist at the VA Greater Los Angeles Healthcare System in West Los Angeles. Through the VA's Office of Mental Heath Services she provides training and consultation to improve family services nationally throughout the VA nationwide. She is also an associate research psychologist at the NPI (Semel Institute for Neuroscience and Human Behavior) at the University of California, Los Angeles. She has been conducting clinical research in family interventions for persons with serious psychiatric illnesses and combat-related PTSD for over twenty years.

WAYNE GREGORY, Ph.D., is a native Texan and a clinical psychologist at the Central Texas Veterans Health Care System Waco, Texas. His interests over the years have included individual and family experience of residuals of combat and, more recently, his work has extended to providing opportunities to veterans with PTSD and other serious mental illnesses to live in their strengths and to offer to others those products of their own individual strengths. Providing assistance to veterans and family members to thrive in their local communities is a guiding principle of his life's work.

ANN M. HENDRICKS, Ph.D., directs Health Care Financing & Economics, a research center at the VA Boston Healthcare System. She is also an associate professor of health policy and management at Boston University's School of Public Health, where she developed and has taught a course on health care cost effectiveness. Her current research focuses on the demand for health care, long-term care utilization, utilization across health care systems by patients with conditions such as schizophrenia, PTSD related to sexual trauma, diabetes and Parkinson's disease, and the costs of care. She is currently the principal investigator for an investigation of the VA patient population also enrolled in Medicaid programs nationwide and a simulation project that forecasts the potential for veterans' enrollment in a VA-Medicare HMO. She has numerous publications to her credit and has been guest editor for special VA-focused issues of *Medical Care* and *Medical Care Research and Review*.

SENATOR DANIEL K. INOUYE, J.D. (D-Hawai'i), served with the legendary 442nd Regimental Combat Team during World War II and was discharged with the rank of captain. He earned the nation's highest award for military valor, the Medal of Honor, when he led an attack on an enemy-defended ridge that guarded a key junction near San Terenzo, Italy. After the war, he earned both his bachelor's and law degrees on the G.I. Bill. In 1959, he was elected as the first representative from the state of Hawai'i, becoming the first American of Japanese descent to be elected to either the House or Senate. Since 1963, he has represented the state of Hawai'i in the U.S. Senate and achieved prominence as one of the chamber's most effective members. In addition to playing a major role in shaping the defense policies of the United States, he has worked to strengthen the armed forces and enhance the quality of life for America's military personnel and their families.

JOCELYN A. KILGORE, M.D., is a board-certified psychiatrist and an active duty major in the United States Air Force. She is currently assigned to the department of psychiatry and the Center for the Study of Traumatic Stress at the Uniformed Services University of the Health Sciences F. Edward Hébert School of Medicine. Her past tours of duty have included Ramstein Airbase in Germany, the Malcolm Grow Medical Center, Andrews Air Force Base outside Washington, DC, and a deployment to Kandahar, Afghanistan, where she worked for the Army in a NATO-run hospital.

JOHN W. KLOCEK, Ph.D., has been a staff psychologist in the Central Texas Veterans Health Care System and assistant professor at Texas A&M College of Medicine since 2005. Prior to returning home to Texas, he was an associate professor of psychology at the University of Montana. His primary research and clinical interests are in pain management and integrated health care. He completed a two year postdoctoral fellowship in pain management at the University of Virginia Health Sciences Center.

WALTER E. PENK, Ph.D. ABPP, is a professor in psychiatry and behavioral sciences at Texas A&M College of Medicine and a consultant for the Central Texas VA Health Care System. He retired after a forty-year career in the VA, including positions as chief of psychology service at the Edith Nourse Rogers VA Medical Center in Bedford, Masachussetts, and as the associate director, Bedford Division, VA Connecticut/Massachusetts Mental Illness Research, Education, and Clinical Center (MIRECC). In addition, he has taught at the Harvard Medical School at Cambridge Hospital, Suffolk University, the University of Massachusetts in Boston, Boston University, the University of Massachusetts Medical School, and Tufts University.

RALPH ROBINOWITZ, Ph.D., J.D., ABPP, is both a board-certified clinical psychologist and bar-qualified attorney in the state of Texas. He also was a commissioned officer during the Korean War era, completed his military service in the Reserve, and retired as a major. He served as a clinical psychologist in the Veterans Health Administration at VA medical centers in Waco and Dallas. He ended his career with the VA as director of the Drug Dependence Treatment Center at the VA Medical Center in Dallas, where his clinical specialties were psychosocial rehabilitation services for veterans with addiction disorders. After retiring from the VA, he pursued his interest in the law by completing law school and sitting for (and passing) the bar. In addition to his work in the legal perspective of disabilities, he has published extensively in the area of the diagnosis and treatment of veterans with PTSD and addictions.

CHARLES J. SABATIER, JR., J.D., is a 100 percent service-connected disabled Vietnam veteran who was shot and paralyzed with a bullet from an AK-47 assault rifle during the 1968 Tet Offensive. During his tour in Vietnam from 1967 to 1968 he served as an infantryman with the U.S. Army's 25th Infantry Division. After being honorably discharged, Sabatier used his G.I. Bill benefits to obtain his undergraduate degree and then went on to use the VA's Vocational Rehabilitation program to attend law school. He is licensed to practice law in California, Texas, and Massachusetts and currently works in the U.S. Department of Labor's Office of Disability Employment Policy as a senior policy advisor. He is the lead policy person on the America's Heroes@Work initiative—a program that is studying how returning service members are affected by TBI and PTSD issues, particularly in their return to employment in the private sector.

COLLEEN SAFFRON is one of the founders and creators of the group Operation Life Transformed which works to fill the gaps in veteran care related to family economic recovery by providing training and job placement opportunities to family member caregivers of injured service members. In conjunction with the

Department of Defense, VA, and the Department of Labor, this group addresses the unique challenges facing spouses and other family members while coping with the economic devastation that results from the dislocation and disruption of caring for an ill or injured service member. Since her Army officer husband's injury in Iraq in 2004 she has managed to care for him and their three children in Harker Heights, Texas, while also returning to school to graduate with honors.

LIONEL P. SOLURSH, M.D., is a board-certified internist/psychiatrist and Distinguished Life Fellow of the American Psychiatric Association. He works with the PTSD Treatment Team at VA Medical Center in Augusta and is professor of psychiatry at the Medical College of Georgia, Augusta. He has authored forty-four papers in professional journals, twelve books and book chapters, over a hundred presentations all over the world, and numerous audio–visual materials and book reviews, most of them related to psychotraumatology, substance abuse, and human sexuality.